973 Han
Handbook to life in
America. Volume V, The
age of reform, 1890 to
1920

$50.00
ocn368199684
09/10/2009

D0492631

Handbook to
Life in America

Volume V
The Age of Reform
1890 to 1920

Handbook to
Life in America

Volume V
The Age of Reform
1890 to 1920

Rodney P. Carlisle
GENERAL EDITOR

Facts On File
An imprint of Infobase Publishing

Handbook to Life in America: The Age of Reform, 1890 to 1920
Copyright © 2009 Infobase Publishing

Facts On File, Inc.
An Imprint of Infobase Publishing
132 West 31st Street
New York, NY 10001

Library of Congress Cataloging-in-Publication Data
Handbooks to life in America / Rodney P. Carlisle, general editor.
    v. cm.
  Includes bibliographical references and index.
  Contents: v. 1. The colonial and revolutionary era, beginnings to 1783—v. 2. The early national period and expansion, 1783 to 1859—v. 3. The Civil War and Reconstruction, 1860 to 1876—v. 4. The Gilded Age, 1870 to 1900—v. 5. Age of reform, 1890 to 1920—v. 6. The roaring twenties, 1920 to 1929—v. 7. The Great Depression and World War II, 1929 to 1949—v. 8. Postwar America, 1950 to 1969—v. 9. Contemporary America, 1970 to present.
  ISBN 978-0-8160-7785-4 (set : hc : alk. paper)—ISBN 978-0-8160-7174-6 (v. 1 : hc : alk. paper)—ISBN 978-0-8160-7175-3 (v. 2 : hc : alk. paper)—ISBN 978-0-8160-7176-0 (v. 3 : hc : alk. paper)—ISBN 978-0-8160-7177-7 (v. 4 : hc : alk. paper)—ISBN 978-0-8160-7178-4 (v. 5 : hc : alk. paper)—ISBN 978-0-8160-7179-1 (v. 6 : hc : alk. paper)—ISBN 978-0-8160-7180-7 (v. 7 : hc : alk. paper)—ISBN 978-0-8160-7181-4 (v. 8 : hc : alk. paper)—ISBN 978-0-8160-7182-1 (v. 9 : hc : alk. paper) 1. United States—Civilization—Juvenile literature. 2. United States—History—Juvenile literature. 3. National characteristics, American—Juvenile literature. I. Carlisle, Rodney P.
  E169.1.H2644 2008
  973—dc22
                              2008012630

Printed in the United States of America

MP GB 10 9 8 7 6 5 4 3 2 1

This book is printed on acid-free paper.

Contents

Volume V
The Age of Reform
1890 to 1920

*"I would rather belong to a poor nation
that was free than to a rich nation
that had ceased to be in love with liberty."*
—Woodrow Wilson

THE FLAVOR OF daily life in previous eras is usually only vaguely conveyed by examining the documents of state and the politics of the era. What people ate, how they spent their time, what entertainment they enjoyed, and how they related to one another in family, church, and employment, constituted the actual life of people, rather than the distant affairs of state. While governance, diplomacy, war, and to an extent, the intellectual life of every era tends to be well-documented, the way people lived is sometimes difficult to tease out from the surviving paper records and literary productions of the past.

For this reason in recent decades, cultural and social historians have turned to other types of physical documentation, such as illustrations, surviving artifacts, tools, furnishings, utensils, and structures. Statistical information can shed light on other aspects of life. Through examination of these and other kinds of evidence, a wholly different set of questions can be asked and tentatively answered.

This series of handbooks looks at the questions of daily life from the perspective of social and cultural history, going well beyond the affairs of government to examine the fabric and texture of what people in the American past experienced in their homes and their families, in their workplaces and schools. Their places of worship, the ways they moved from place to place, the nature of law and order and military service all varied from period to period. As science and technology advanced, the American contributions to those fields became greater and contributed to a different feel of life. Some of this story may be familiar, as historians have for generations commented on the disparity between rural and city life, on the impact of technologies such as the cotton gin, the railroad and the steamboat, and on life on the advancing frontier. However in recent decades, historians have turned to different sources. In an approach called Nearby History, academic historians have increasingly worked with the hosts of professionals who operate local historical societies, keepers of historic homes, and custodians of local records to pull together a deeper understanding of local life. Housed in thousands of small and large museums and preserved homes across America, rich collections of furniture, utensils, farm implements, tools, and other artifacts tell a very different story than that found in the letters and journals of legislators, governors, presidents, and statesmen.

FRESH DISCOVERIES
Another approach to the fabric of daily life first flourished in Europe, through which historians plowed through local customs and tax records, birth and death records, marriage records, and other numerical data, learning a great deal about the actual fabric of daily life through a statistical approach. Aided by computer methods of storing and studying such data, historians have developed fresh discoveries about such basic questions as health, diet, life-expectancy, family patterns, and gender values in past eras. Combined with a fresh look at the relationship between men and women, and at the values of masculinity and femininity in past eras, recent social history has provided a whole new window on the past.

By dividing American history into nine periods, we have sought to provide views of this newly enriched understanding of the actual daily life of ordinary people. Some of the patterns developed in early eras persisted into later eras. And of course, many physical traces of the past remain, in the form of buildings, seaports, roads and canals, artifacts, divisions of real estate, and later structures such as railroads, airports, dams, and superhighways. For these reasons, our own physical environment is made up of overlapping layers inherited from the past, sometimes deeply buried, and at other times lightly papered over with the trappings of the present. Knowing more about the many layers from different periods of American history makes every trip through an American city or suburb or rural place a much richer experience, as the visitor sees not only the present, but the accumulated heritage of the past, silently providing echoes of history.

Thus in our modern era, as we move among the shadowy remnants of a distant past, we may be unconsciously receiving silent messages that tell us: this building is what a home should look like; this stone wall constitutes the definition of a piece of farmland; this street is where a town begins and ends. The sources of our present lie not only in the actions of politicians, generals, princes, and potentates, but also in the patterns of life, child-rearing, education, religion, work, and play lived out by ordinary people.

VOLUME V: THE AGE OF REFORM 1890–1920

The era from 1890 through 1920 in the United States was characterized by technological innovations, political developments, and alterations in lifestyle that would represent a transformation in American life. Political reforms coming out of the Populist movement of the 1890s and the variety of progressive movements in the first two decades of the 20th century represented attempts to come to grips with the rapid industrialization, the development of the national price and market system, and the rise of a consumer economy that continued through these years. Political reforms to bring professional standards to city and state governments and to replace the old spoils system and political bossism with graft-free local government were one part of the movement. Other reforms and agencies, such as the Interstate Commerce Commission, food and drug laws, anti-trust legislation, child labor laws, a graduated income tax, the federal reserve system, political primaries, workmen's compensation laws, and votes for women were advocated by overlapping groups of supporters. Many of the reforms of the 1900s and 1910s gained enthusiastic support from middle-class groups such as journalists, teachers, attorneys, and other salaried and self-employed professionals.

While many historians have focused on these and other reforms that characterized the decades around the turn of the 20th century, other profound social and institutional changes affecting daily life swept the nation. With changes in communications technology, a national consumer culture burgeoned. Nationwide chains of newspapers, including those owned by William Randolph Hearst, Joseph Pulitzer, and Roy Howard, coupled with national wire-services, helped reflect the emerging national culture. National circulation magazines contributed to the same process of leveling taste and creating nationwide demand for specific products and styles, dampening the regional variation in favor of an emerging American culture.

Other innovations contributed to this homogenizing trend, including the development of motion pictures, the distribution of phonograph recordings (at first on cylinders, then on disks), and the publication of sheet music. By 1920 Americans from California to Maine were reading the same short stories and articles in magazines, reading the same news stories, listening to and playing the same music, buying the same breakfast cereal, drinking the same brands of coffee, smoking the same cigarettes, wearing the same brand-name shirts, and using the same kitchen utensils. While the material culture of the 1870s had often reflected the handcrafts and manufactures of local artisans, by the early 20th century, the artifacts of daily life were increasingly produced and consumed on a national scale.

Other profound changes wrought by technology were just beginning to be felt by 1920. The automobile, first introduced in the 1890s as a novelty or richman's plaything, had revolutionized travel. With the development of highways and filling stations as the necessary infrastructure to support auto travel, gasoline-powered cars, trucks, and tractors rapidly drove out competing battery-powered and steam-powered models, and increasingly replaced horse-drawn vehicles, although elegant horse-drawn carriages continued to be produced in these years. Rail, auto, and steam-powered ship travel contributed to the process of homogenizing and leveling out American culture. In what would become a flourishing industry, tourism transformed whole regions into travel destinations, including southern California, Florida, Hawaii, national parks, and rural New England.

Ship-borne immigrants continued to flood into the United States in the first decade of the 20th century, with increasing proportions from southern and eastern Europe, including Italy, Serbia, and Poland. During the years of World War I, 1914–18, that immigration was suddenly interrupted, to be replaced by a mass migration of African Americans from the deep south northward to Chicago, St. Louis, New York, and other northern cities where industrial employment and the promise of reduced racial segregation beckoned. These movements were more than just the relocation of individuals and families of course, for the migrants brought with them their customs, music, cuisine, and mannerisms.

WORLD WAR AND SOCIAL CHANGE

American participation in World War I was limited, as the United States remained neutral from the outbreak of the war in August 1914 until April 1917, when American neutrality was abandoned due to the German decision to unleash submarine attacks on neutral ships carrying goods and supplies to England and France. The American Expeditionary Force helped contribute to the defeat of Germany by November 11, 1918. American "doughboys" returning from several months in Europe brought home the scars of war, either in physical wounds, or the "shell-shock" of war trauma. Others, more fortunate and less exposed to the horrors of the front lines and trenches, came back with a new awareness of European values and lifestyles. It was hard to "keep them down on the farm, once they had seen Paree."

The war experience, as well as the emergence of a consumer-oriented culture, brought intangible but very real changes to American culture. It seemed that the age of innocence was vanishing, with new styles in art, in popular culture, and in morality. While some reformers hoped to enforce moral standards through regulation and legislation, it seemed that the younger generation refused to be constrained. The most well-known of such efforts, of course, was the introduction of Prohibition—making the sale and consumption of alcohol illegal. Yet there were other aspects of the same impulse, also resisted, as colleges and schools sought to prevent unescorted dating by young couples or smoking by women. Legislation continued to define former "sporting" practices as illegal, including drug consumption, animal-fighting, boxing, and the operation of brothels. Many locales prohibited the conduct of business on Sundays.

But the conflict between the older values, increasingly called Puritan in this period, and the behavior of the younger generation, ran like a current through the decade of the 1910s. To many in the older generation, the agitation to grant votes to women, and the movement of women increasingly into higher education and into professions, all seemed part of the collapse of an established way of life. As middle-class young women began to cut their hair short, wear more revealing clothes, and smoke cigarettes and drink in public, elders appeared shocked and appalled. Coupled with the transformation brought about by automobile travel, the flood of new immigrants into the country, and the declining influence of small-town and rural values in an increasingly urbanized nation, it seemed to many that the nation was changing in very dangerous directions.

Seen in this light, Prohibition was only one effort to hold back the disturbing social changes. Other movements that arose from the same reaction against the apparent collapse of older morality included fundamental religious revivalism, agitation for immigration restriction, and a hectic attempt during and immediately after the war to suppress "anti-American" political movements such as socialism, radical unionism, and other political ideas of the left. Although the Red Scare was quite brief, the effort to define any Marxist ideas as a form of disloyalty had considerable lasting success.

By 1920 the political, cultural, and social landscape of America had been transformed, taking on newly divisive characteristics that would be present through the next decades. Modernity clashed with tradition; the urban and urbane clashed with the rural and the rustic; jazz music, alcohol, tobacco, and sexual liberation clashed with a restrictive morality. Radical ideas of reform became defined as un-American. At the same time that such divisions over style and behavior swept the nation, deeply rooted forces tended to erase regional and local divisions, with national brands and tastes, rapid and more comfortable travel, and communications media that brought the same content to Connecticut Yankees, Florida Crackers, Down-easterners and Wyoming cowboys.

The new divisions and the new homogeneity that emerged between 1890 and 1920 would continue to shape American life over the coming decades.

RODNEY CARLISLE
GENERAL EDITOR

Chapter 1

Introduction

"The faith of Americans in their own country is religious."
— Herbert Croly

CALLED THE PROGRESSIVE ERA even at the time, the period of American history between the end of Reconstruction and the end of World War I was an age of reform and self-awareness. Americans were well-aware that they lived in changing times and often debated the nature of those changes and the import of that history eloquently and at length. It was a time of political and social change, a time of intellectual and scientific development in the wake of the Industrial Revolution, and especially a time when the meanings of things shifted. The Civil War and Reconstruction had redefined the Union, and the conflicts over plural marriage and the statehood of Utah had in essence tied American character to a particular notion of family, even as massive waves of immigration diluted any previous ethnic model of "Americanness."

While no era can be summed up pithily except at the expense of truth, historian Robert H. Wiebe's organizational hypothesis provides the best framework from which to examine this period, and this chapter will refer to it several times. Wiebe's hypothesis describes the era as one in which the individual American sense of cultural identity shifted from the local and regional levels to the national. In other words, to an increasing extent, Virginians stopped thinking of themselves as Virginians first and Americans second, and began to think of themselves as Americans first and foremost. This is no cosmetic or rhetorical change, nor is it a simple matter of federalism. During this period the national media were born, both news and entertainment; national professional organizations became the norm; and more and more companies manufactured and distributed products on a national level, which was especially true for recent introductions like canned goods and automobiles. Indeed that the rise of consumer culture succeeded this shift of cultural identity does not simply characterize the period of American history, it defines it.

INDUSTRY AND EFFICIENCY

By the turn of the century the United States had become the leading industrial nation, its abundance of resources and room for expansion empowering a second industrial revolution that put production on an entirely new scale. The development of the telegraph, telephone, and transcontinental railroad decreased the perception of distance, making the nation's far points more accessible to each other, even as organizations like professional associations and labor unions formed at the national level.

In the aftermath of the Industrial Revolution, as bureaucracy and the middle class grew, the so-called Efficiency Movement took hold in the United States and remained a powerful thread in American thought throughout the period, and ever since in one form or another. The Efficiency Movement advocated the expert identification and eradication of problems of inefficiency, which adherents believed plagued every aspect and institution of society. Louis Brandeis, influenced by engineer Frederick Winslow Taylor and the Taylorism that bears his name, coined the term "scientific management" to refer to this new efficiency-minded approach to industry, which called for working methods derived from scientific study of the work situation.

The last president of the era, Herbert Hoover, was one prominent advocate of efficiency, though the Depression that began during his presidency did much to discredit him. Inefficiency was often ascribed to corruption, incompetence, or laziness. In the mind of reformers, it was linked with sloppiness, messiness, and therefore the same unsafe practices about which muckrakers and labor unions complained. While politicians and progressive businessmen were able to focus on matters of procedure, muckrakers—generally reporters and writers, sometimes politicians—exposed problems that were clear-cut and vivid, problems that didn't need the deep

Model Ts coming off a Ford assembly line in Detroit, Michigan, in 1917.

Frederick Jackson Turner's Frontier Thesis

In 1887 the Dawes Act empowered the president to divide Native-American lands into large lots for assignment to heads of families or to sell the land to white settlers, an act designed to force Native Americans to integrate into the mainstream. Three years later the Census Bureau declared that the frontier was "closed": the country was densely populated enough that there was no longer any significantly sized area of settlement sparse enough to be called "frontier." Between the two events, the federal government seemed to be closing the book on the early history of the country: no longer was it a nation with a ragged edge, as territories coalesced into states and reservations into starter homes.

Three years afterward in 1893, Wisconsin professor Frederick Jackson Turner presented a paper resulting from the train of thought the Census declaration began, at the annual meeting of the American Historical Association. "The Significance of the Frontier in American History" remains the single most formative piece of writing about American history, with generations of historiography written in response.

Turner used the close of the frontier as an opportunity to examine its role in the development of the nation's history, and his conclusions shaped the course of the study of American history to come. Little research into the history of this country has been conducted in the century since Turner without being influenced by him, his followers, and his opponents. As a young intellectual at the end of the 19th century, Turner was part of that early generation that was familiar with Darwin and principles of evolution, and he saw history in much the same way: as a process in which an entity responded to changing conditions and adapted accordingly.

While the dominant view of American history was the "germ theory" that proclaimed American ideas as simply European ones brought over the Atlantic, Turner believed the United States was a unique place that had adapted to the existence of enormous amounts of available, arable land—a "safety valve" for people dissatisfied with civilization. The nation inched west, abandoning more and more of its "Europeanness" as it accumulated more and more of the dust of America.

The frontier, Turner said, had been the most prominent force in American history, and its close would mean that the further course of history would be distinctly different in character and impulse. Many intellectuals were influenced by Turner's thoughts and by the implication that a new age was opening up—not least among them, future President Theodore Roosevelt.

examination that foreign policy or tariff laws required. Unsanitary meat processing, child labor, poor living conditions—these were issues the general public could immediately recognize were wrong, with minimal prompting. Muckraking coincided with the rise of national magazines and newspaper chains, making such issues nationally prominent rather than merely local, which helped to encourage Progressive-minded federal legislation, such as meat packing regulations and food safety laws.

Bridging the gap between industry-minded efficiency and politically-minded reform was the Wisconsin Idea, first articulated in 1904—the same year as the Square Deal—by Charles Van Hise, president of the University of Wisconsin at Madison. The Wisconsin Idea stated that the university should conduct problem-solving research to benefit all citizens of the state—performing the functions of a state-funded think tank. This led quickly to legislation adapted from the university's proposals, including tax reforms and utility regulation, and the term was borrowed to refer to reforms of that sort, even when applied outside of Wisconsin.

POLITICS AND REFORM

Though there was a Progressive Party, it didn't include all—or even most—progressives, and references to progressives should not be taken to mean members of that short-lived party. Rather, progressivism was a strain of political thought—of social and cultural thought, which included but was not limited to political philosophy—that was adopted by some members of all parties. Republican Theodore Roosevelt's presidency is considered by many to be the start of the Progressive Era (though the 1890 close of the frontier is a much more elegant endpoint), but there is no mistaking the progressivism of Democrats William Jennings Bryan and Woodrow Wilson. Progressive reforms ranged from the trivial to the deep, and included Prohibition, women's suffrage, income tax, and the direct election of senators. The economic panic of 1893 provided a motive for much of this, and in hindsight it's easy to see a nation struggling to find a new identity for itself as everything from the technological to the spiritual changed. Bryan is a particularly interesting individual to illustrate the tides of progressivism, and especially the way that its inherent modernity did not make it inherently radical across the board. Bryan was a progressive Democrat and the party's candidate for president in 1896, 1900, and 1908, remaining an important figure in the party—one widely expected to be elected President eventually—despite losing every time.

"CROSS OF GOLD"

Bryan was a famed orator, his "Cross of Gold" speech at the 1896 Democratic National Convention succeeded in winning the party's support over the incumbent Grover Cleveland, one of the few times an incumbent president sought and lost his party's nomination. In the speech, Bryan argued against

After a liquor raid at the height of Prohibition, agents dumped confiscated alcohol into the sewer in New York City. Prohibition laws exemplify the power of reformers in the Progressive Era.

the gold standard—which, by preventing inflation, would serve creditors more than the working class indebted to them—declaring, "you shall not crucify mankind upon a cross of gold." He not only won the Democratic nomination, he became the Populist Party's nominee as well. But the view made him unpopular with Democratic newspapers, and he had to tour the country in order to drum up support from voters through public appearances and speeches. In the end he lost to Republican William McKinley, who appealed to the prosperous and middle class.

Around the turn of the century, Bryan became an anti-imperialist deeply opposed to the country's increasing involvement in foreign affairs. In the wake of his 1900 campaign loss he also became more deeply invested in his religious convictions. He was a strong supporter and public face of the Social Gospel movement, as well as the temperance movement and the resulting Prohibition, and was outspoken in his condemnation of all forms of Darwinism. In 1913 Wilson appointed him secretary of state, but Bryan resigned two years later when he believed Wilson exploited the *Lusitania* incident to manipulate the public.

The Allegory of Oz

L. Frank Baum, author of 1900's *The Wonderful Wizard of Oz* and its initial sequels, had always been a politically active writer, and had written extensively about political matters in his short-lived newspaper, *The Aberdeen Saturday Pioneer*. Since the 1960s, some scholars have suspected his first Oz book of being an intricate political allegory, and indeed the evidence is intriguing.

In the allegorical reading Dorothy—a middle-American whose name is also a phonemic anagram of "Theodore"—represents the average Everyman American, accompanied by Toto the Teetotaler. On her way down the Yellow Brick Road—representing the gold standard under which the United States operated—she meets the Scarecrow (farmers), the Tin Man (industry), and the Cowardly Lion (William Jennings Bryan, proponent of free silver). Many allegorical readers take the Wizard as representing the Republican Party, and the Wicked Witch of the West as William McKinley (who supported the gold standard). It is pointed out, though, that "Oz" is an abbreviation for ounce, the unit in which gold is weighed, and that Dorothy's salvation comes from her silver slippers. (Only in the movie are they ruby.)

Others point out the resemblance between William Denslow's illustrations, especially of Dorothy, the Tin Man, and the Scarecrow, and his political editorial cartoons, suggesting that the Oz characters are stand-ins for the figures in the cartoons. Monkeys, not usually flying, were also popular figures in political cartoons. The reading of the Wizard—the humbug exposed by the story—is a common puzzle for these readers, and may be seen as McKinley, or Teddy Roosevelt. The green of the Emerald City could refer to greenbacks, and the contrast between the "good" north and south and the "wicked" east and west may be a way to separate decent, hardworking Americans from the opportunistic robber barons of the west and industrialists of the northeast. In the end, it is compelling material that demonstrates not only the durability of Baum's work, but also the intricacy and fascination of the political and economic landscape of his time.

A 1903 poster featuring the Tin Man, who some believe represents industry.

Other reformers fought for the same sorts of rights that would consume later movements. The National Association for the Advancement of Colored People (NAACP) was founded in 1909, less than 50 years after the end of slavery, by a multiracial group that included suffragist Ida Wells-Barnett and W.E.B. DuBois. Because of the segregation policies in the United States, the NAACP's first meetings had to be held in Canada, where members could all convene in the same hotel room.

PROGRESSIVE AMENDMENTS

This 1896 cartoon attacks William Jennings Bryan for appropriating Christian symbols in his "Cross of Gold" speech.

Women's rights, and the right to vote, had been actively sought throughout the 19th century, and by its end had become a prominent topic. Temperance movements actually hurt suffrage somewhat, as liquor lobbies—perceiving women as the bulk of their political opposition—opposed it whenever possible. Suffrage tended to be adopted in western states rather than the eastern ones where the bureaucracy and status quo were more entrenched. The Utah Territory had granted women the right to vote in 1870, but the 1887 Edmunds-Tucker Act passed by the U.S. Congress revoked this while addressing the many other concerns the federal government had with the Church of Latter-Day Saints.

New Zealand, Australia, and several European countries had all granted women suffrage by the outbreak of World War I. In many cases, women had only recently been specifically excluded, as the right to vote had been tied to some other factor—usually land ownership—rather than explicitly being a gender issue.

In 1915 a bill was brought before Congress to amend the Constitution to guarantee the right for women to vote. It passed the House by one vote, and was twice voted down in the Senate. In order to pass the amendment in time for the 1920 elections, President Wilson called a special session of Congress; the bill again had trouble in the Senate, but eventually passed on June 4, 1919, and the 19th Amendment—prohibiting the denial of the right to vote on the basis of gender, by states or the federal government—was ratified by the requisite number of states by the following summer.

Four constitutional amendments were passed in the progressive era, two of which dealt in some way with the rights of the people (women's suffrage and the direct election of senators). The first of the remaining two seems an oddball at first: the 16th Amendment empowered Congress to tax income, a power previously limited by the requirement of Article I of geographical uniformity in excises. This meant that the taxes taken from citizens of a given state must be proportional to the population. For example, if 10 percent of the total taxes are collected from the citizens of a given state, that state would have to have 10 percent of the total population; the only way an income tax is possible with this restriction is in the unlikely scenario in which the average income is the same in every state. Income tax had been proposed and attempted before, and was always found suspect, as well as unconstitutional.

This tax was necessary to raise the money required not only for the sorts of reforms the Progressives wanted, but also to equip a modern military such as the one that a few short years later would prove a decisive factor in World War I. It did not directly provide more powers to the people, but it powered the government demanded by other reforms. Because of the immediacy of its financial ramifications, the 16th Amendment has been the subject of controversy since its ratification. Many have claimed that it was improperly ratified, for reasons ranging from petty concerns about the proper punctuation and phrasing used by some of the ratifying states, to the more serious claim that Ohio was not a state until long after its participation in the amendment's ratification. Of course, since enough other states ratified the amendment, Ohio's was not a "tie-breaking vote." It was not for decades after ratification that anyone acted on these arguments in such a way as to present them in court, though, and modern tax protests are more related to current political ideologies than to any anti-tax movements contemporary to the amendment.

The 17th Amendment changed the way that senators were elected. While they had previously been appointed by state legislatures, they would now be elected directly by the voters, just as representatives were. This had been proposed almost a century earlier, in the nation's early days, but when it was brought up again at the University of Wisconsin, it found more sympathetic ears. Again, this fits perfectly with the Wiebe model: as Americans began to think of themselves more and more as Americans, they wanted direct control over who they sent to represent them in Washington. Oregon and Nebraska had already adopted this change, and the amendment found little resistance.

The 18th Amendment was another story. This was the Prohibition amendment prohibiting the sale of alcohol. The Volstead Act, passed once the amendment was ratified, provided legal definitions for which forms of alcohol were prohibited, and empowered the federal government to enforce the amendment. Though the amendment was maligned, and an entire culture—not so far outside the mainstream—developed around speakeasies and illegal alcohol throughout the 1920s, perhaps no other federal law better demonstrates the power of reformers in the Progressive Era. Never before had an amendment passed that limited the rights of voters, but progressivism's emphasis on efficiency, purity, morality, and incorruptibility, among others, made it difficult for many people to take a stand in favor of alcohol.

THE PROGRESSIVE PRESIDENTS

When President McKinley was assassinated six months into his term, his Vice President Theodore "Teddy" Roosevelt became the youngest president in history, and an unusual president in every respect. He was the only president

Mishmash: Spelling Reform

One of the going concerns in the English language on both sides of the Atlantic had been, for some time, spelling reform. Due to its mishmash of heritage and influences, the English language has been subject to inconsistent spelling rules for centuries. There have been numerous attempts to reform it—notably with the introduction and popularization of dictionaries, which by nature required their editors to pick one or two spellings, and by their dissemination therefore advocated or proscribed spellings accordingly. During the Progressive Era this cause was taken up anew in response to the quickly modernizing times and the increasing popularity of English among non-native speakers as a result of American culture and British imperialism. There was also a sense, in some cases, that spelling reform would not have another chance—that the language was in danger of becoming static, once too many dictionaries saw print.

Andrew Carnegie, the philanthropist and industrialist, donated money to both British and American reform attempts. Mark Twain simultaneously supported and mocked reform—as much as he abhorred the ridiculous spellings the language had acquired, Twain recognized that there was no clear point at which to draw the line, and as alien as "lite" and "catalog" looked to some eyes, they would only be the start. "Catalog" in fact was Melvil Dewey's contribution: the inventor of the Dewey Decimal System was also a spelling reformer, and had changed his first name from Melville (and toyed with changing his surname to "Dui").

Theodore Roosevelt called for simplified spelling as well, and forced the public printer who issued presidential documents to use the system. Part of his Thanksgiving proclamation one year read:

When nerly three centuries ago, the first settlers kam to the kuntry which has bekom this great republik, tha confronted not only hardship and privashun, but terible risk of thar lives. . . . The kustum has now bekum nashnul and hallowed by immemorial usaj.

who did not swear on the Bible when he was sworn in, and one of the few who somehow managed to continue acting as an activist even while in office. A union supporter who loudly distrusted big business, Teddy "the trust buster" personally initiated lawsuits against 44 corporations when Congress failed to respond to his call to curb the power of monopolistic trusts. He believed strongly in federal regulations, and passed a great deal of legislation creating them, including those governing food safety and interstate commerce, two of the most important issues for early progressives.

His domestic policy was called the Square Deal—a fair agreement, phrased with the deceptive informality that so often downplayed his intelligence. He insisted on truth in labeling; on laws protecting consumers from dishonest, capricious, or opportunistic businesses; and believed that decisions involving trusts should be made by the executive branch, rather than being left to the federal courts. He could almost certainly have won reelection in 1908, but refused to run because he did not want to be the first president to serve more than two terms. He suggested William Howard Taft as his successor.

Taft was a lawyer with a bachelor's degree from Yale, where his father had co-founded The Order of Skull and Bones, the famous Yale secret society. His ambition had been to become a Supreme Court justice, but while he was a judge on the Sixth Circuit Court of Appeals, President McKinley appointed him to the chair of the commission to organize the government of the newly acquired Philippines in 1900, beginning his executive branch career. As governor-general of the Philippines, he bought lands owned by the Catholic Church and resold them to the Filipinos, and proved extremely popular and respected among his constituency. Taft went on to prosecute even more trusts than his predecessor had, and sponsored the 16th and 17th amendments.

Teddy had his Square Deal, and Taft had Dollar Diplomacy—the promise of loans and other economic incentives to further foreign policy objectives, which Taft and his Secretary of State Philander Knox, a former Carnegie Steel lawyer and attorney general, particularly applied in Latin America. One of the principles of Dollar Diplomacy was the belief that where an economic opportunity existed, if the United States—federally or privately—didn't take advantage of it, a foreign power would. Loans to Latin American countries and businesses meant preventing the creation of European economic ties as well as strengthening American ones.

It was Roosevelt who had explicitly said that if a Western Hemisphere nation—one to which the Monroe Doctrine was applicable—became destabilized enough to be vulnerable to foreign influence, the United States had a duty to intervene; the principle would guide not only Dollar Diplomacy, but also the Reagan doctrine at the other end of the century. Not long into Taft's presidency, American business interests became involved in the Chinese railways—breaking the philosophy of Dollar Diplomacy from the geographical constraints of the Monroe Doctrine.

Theodore Roosevelt posed with a globe and book in 1908. He worked for truth in labeling, promoted laws protecting consumers, fought business trusts, and even pushed for spelling reform.

Democratic candidate Woodrow Wilson defeated Taft's reelection bid in 1912. Roosevelt, meanwhile, ran and lost as a third-party candidate for the Progressive Party, despite his earlier support of Taft. The first true intellectual president—and to date, still the only one—Wilson was a lawyer with a Ph.D. in history and political science, a scholar who criticized the Constitution as archaic and in need of reform or abandonment, a professor at both Bryn Mawr College and Wesleyan University before assuming the presidency of Princeton, and a baseball fan—the first president to attend the World Series.

Though it should be kept in mind that many of the more down-to-earth reforms and issues had already been addressed by Roosevelt and Taft (and even McKinley to a lesser extent), it nevertheless seems unsurprising that the first term of this intellectual presidency was defined largely around economic policy, especially banking. The creation of the Federal Trade Commission enforced fair competition in interstate trade, another small movement in the shift from regional to national concerns. The Federal Reserve Act created the Federal Reserve System, a central banking system to replace the one allowed to lapse into dissolution by Andrew Jackson in the middle of the previous century. It also delegated Congress's power to coin money, and created Federal

The headline of the Cleveland Plain Dealer *announcing the end of World War I on November 11, 1918. Decades later, Armistice Day would be celebrated as Veterans' Day.*

Reserve notes (paper money), two actions that have had their constitutionality called into question ever since.

In Wilson's second term, he pushed for the United States to enter World War I despite widespread resistance. More hands off in the management of the military than most presidents, he delegated most command duties to General John Pershing while focusing on the need not simply to defeat the Germans, but to end the war, which Wilson believed represented a real threat to Western civilization because of the vast damage entailed. It was Wilson who called it "the war to end all wars," one that would "make the world safe for democracy." Wilson was the war's great orator and rhetorician.

In the years after the war, the United States was at the apex to date of its power and influence in the world. Despite being awarded the 1919 Nobel Peace Prize for his creation of the League of Nations (an organization like the later United Nations, intended to ensure peace and preserve national sovereignty), Wilson was unable to persuade the Senate to ratify his bill—and so his own country never joined the league. It was one of the biggest failures of any presidency up to that point, rivaled only by Lincoln's inability to prevent Civil War, and Johnson's failure to see Presidential Reconstruction through to the end.

An unconfirmed series of minor strokes seems to have affected Wilson in his last two years as president. He quickly alienated many of his former friends and political allies, and when he finally spoke in favor of giving women the right to vote, he did so only after repeated harangues from the suffrage movement, including protests in front of the White House. On October 2, 1919,

Jailed Suffragettes

As World War I progressed, the issue of women's suffrage raged throughout the United States. The suffragette tactic of parading and picketing gained special notoriety when pickets were established in front of the White House. Often the suffragettes were jailed as a public nuisance. Excerpted below is a letter to the commissioners of the District of Columbia protesting their treatment and asking to be treated as political prisoners.

As political prisoners, we, the undersigned, refuse to work while in prison. We have taken this stand as a matter of principle after careful consideration, and from it we shall not recede. This action is a necessary protest against an unjust sentence: In reminding President Wilson of his preelection promises toward woman suffrage, we were exercising the right of peaceful petition, guaranteed by the Constitution of the United States, which declares peaceful picketing is legal in the District of Columbia. That we are unjustly sentenced has been well recognized—when President Wilson pardoned the first group of suffragists who had been given sixty days in the workhouse, and again when Judge Mullowny suspended sentence for the last group of picketers...

Conscious, therefore, of having acted in accordance with the highest standards of citizenship, we ask the commissioners of the District to grant us the rights due political prisoners. We ask that we no longer be segregated and confined under locks and bars in small groups, but permitted to see each other, and that Miss Lucy Burns, who is in full sympathy with this letter, be released from solitary confinement in another building and given back to us.

We ask exemption from prison work, that our legal right to consult counsel be recognized, to have food sent to us from outside, to supply ourselves with writing material for as much correspondence as we may need, to receive books, letters, newspapers, our relatives and friends.

Our united demand for political treatment has been delayed, because, on entering the workhouse, we found conditions so very bad that, before we could ask that the suffragists be treated as political prisoners, it was necessary to make a stand for the ordinary rights of human beings for all the inmates. Although this has not been accomplished, we now wish to bring the important question of the status of political prisoners to the attention of the commissioners, who, we are informed, have full authority to make what regulations they please for the District prison and workhouse.

The commissioners' only answer to this was a hasty transfer of the signers and the leader, Miss Burns, to the District jail, where they were put in solitary confinement. The women were not only refused the privileges asked, but were also denied some of the usual privileges allowed to ordinary criminals.

President Woodrow Wilson enjoys the 1915 World Series before his failure with the League of Nations and series of strokes in later years.

he suffered a more serious stroke that left him partially paralyzed, blind, and requiring a wheelchair, walker, or cane for mobility. The travel and speaking appearance schedule of his tour to drum up support for his league may have been the main source of strain leading to this final stroke—certainly the stress of meeting such opposition was an exacerbating factor. The public remained unaware of Wilson's condition until his death, five years later and three years after he vacated the office, having failed to garner support for a third term.

REFORM AND RACE

The Progressive Era also saw the worst period of American race relations. Blacks were only a generation or two removed from slavery, immigration's record numbers provided an excuse for racial violence against Italians and others, and many southerners still openly spoke of the south rising again at some point in the future, seceding or retaliating for the harms of Reconstruction. In 1900 Senator Benjamin Tillman of South Carolina openly boasted that the men of his state had done everything possible to keep blacks from voting, including "stuffing ballot boxes and shooting them...we are not ashamed of it." Jim Crow laws had been and continued to be passed to enforce segregation and other special race-related codes, and two incarnations of the Ku Klux

Klan book-ended the era: the original, during Reconstruction, and a new version created in the midwest after D.W. Griffith's *Birth of a Nation* glorified the original. In the north racism was often a response to blacks migrating from the south, and nationwide, sundown warnings were posted: promises of arrest or execution for any blacks who stayed in town overnight.

Various forms of "scientific racism" were especially popular at the end of the 19th century, when it was not uncommon to find the skeletons of black men on display between those of apes and white men, portrayed as an in-between step of evolution. Darwin's advances in evolutionary science were borrowed to reshape racist scientific claims, which had previously focused on physical anthropology and the comparison of cranial capacity between different races in order to support claims of white supremacy.

This also led to the promotion of eugenics—the advocacy of human intervention in order to guide the development of the human race, through selective breeding. Eugenicists often called for the involuntary sterilization of undesirable individuals, to remove their genes from the pool. Inventor Alexander Graham Bell, for instance, recommended that deaf individuals be prohibited from marriage, in order to keep them from passing on any hereditary

D.W. Griffith, *director of the now notorious* Birth of a Nation, *working with costumed actors on location for a period film in the 1920s.*

deafness. Calls to sterilize patients of sufficiently severe conditions at mental hospitals were also common among eugenics proponents.

"Scientific racism" and eugenics capture some of the contradictions of the Progressive Era. Just as some progressive reform movements of the period were motivated by underlying anxieties over mass immigration and rapid social change, "scientific racism" used new methods to try to prove that racist attitudes rooted in the past had some basis in fact. It used the terminology of science, which was simultaneously bringing positive changes to people's lives, to try to cement an older social order in place.

BILL KTE'PI

Further Readings

Cooper, John Milton, Jr. *The Warrior and the Priest: Woodrow Wilson and Theodore Roosevelt.* Cambridge, MA: Belknap Press, 2007.

Diner, Steven J. *A Very Different Age: Americans of the Progressive Era.* New York: Hill and Wang, 1998.

Grossman, James R. *Land of Hope: Chicago, Black Southerners, and the Great Migration.* Chicago, IL: University of Chicago Press, 1991.

Hofstadter, Richard, ed. *The Progressive Movement: 1900–1915.* New York: Simon and Schuster, 1986.

Hofstadter, Richard. *The Progressive Historians: Turner, Beard, Parrington.* Chicago, IL: University of Chicago Press, 1979.

_____. *Social Darwinism in American Thought.* New York: Beacon Press, 1992.

Kazin, Michael. *The Populist Persuasion: An American History.* Ithaca, NY: Cornell University Press, 1998.

McGerr, Michael. *A Fierce Discontent: The Rise and Fall of the Progressive Movement in America, 1870–1920.* Oxford: Oxford University Press, 2005.

McMath, Robert C. *American Populism.* New York: Hill and Wang, 1990.

Painter, Nell Irvin. *Standing at Armageddon: The United States 1877–1919.* New York: W.W. Norton and Company, 1989.

Smith, Carl. *Urban Disorder and the Shape of Disbelief: The Great Chicago Fire, The Haymarket Bomb, and the Model Town of Pullman.* Chicago: University of Chicago Press, 1996.

Webb, Walter Prescott. *The Great Plains.* Lincoln, NE: University of Nebraska Press, 1981.

Wiebe, Robert. *The Search for Order.* New York: Hill and Wang, 1966.

Zunz, Oliver. *Making America Corporate, 1870–1920.* Chicago, IL: University of Chicago Press, 1992.

Chapter 2

Family and Daily Life

"A baby is God's opinion that life should go on."
— Carl Sandburg

THE FAMILY OF the Progressive Era was not remarkably different from that of the Gilded Age. The most dramatic transformations of the Industrial Revolution were already complete, with the shift from individual craft production to factory production. Already the movement of population from rural to urban areas was a pronounced trend that had substantially changed the makeup of American society. The family and daily life were by no means exempt from the spirit of reform that permeated the Progressive Era. Many of these threads had their roots in earlier decades, particularly the women's movement, which had its roots in the work of such leaders as Susan B. Anthony and Elizabeth Cady Stanton in the era immediately after the Civil War. Family arrangements that worked well enough in a small rural community in which everyone knew one another's business could easily become instruments of tyranny in the vast impersonal industrial cities, where people often had only the most passing acquaintance with their neighbors.

AT WORK IN THE PROGRESSIVE ERA
By the 1900s the industrial workplace was developing distinctive rhythms for blue-collar and white-collar employees. As a result of the spread of electrical lighting in American offices, many white-collar employees were beginning work as much as an hour later than their working-class counterparts.

In 1900 many middle-class families lived in austere, but comfortable conditions, reflected in this recreated bedroom of the era in Bradenton, Florida.

In the factories the major changes involved the push by reformers for a better workplace. Efficiency experts such as Frederick W. Taylor increased the pace of work through time-motion studies that streamlined processes. In doing so, they were forced to recognize the "design limitations" of the human body and work within them, creating the science of ergonomics. The Progressive Era saw the beginning of industrial hygiene as a science, with reformers such as Alice Hamilton identifying workplace hazards and pressing for changes that would prevent the deaths and crippling injuries of thousands of workers every year.

The office was not exempt from the changes of reformers, although efficiency experts tackled offices only after they had developed their reputations on the more easily quantifiable factory floor. New technologies such as the typewriter also changed the nature of office work, as did the movement of women into positions such as secretary, clerk, and stenographer. The development of these "lace collar" positions was noteworthy because they represented a movement of middle-class young women into the job market. While poor women had worked in the factories for their families' survival, women from middle-class families had generally regarded it as unseemly to work for pay. However the rise of the female telephone operator, with its demand for a classy deference, made it possible for young women of good reputation to leave the family home for the business world.

AT HOME IN THE PROGRESSIVE ERA

The Progressive Era saw important changes in the fundamental structure of the family, although they were not necessarily obvious except to the close observer. Because of the high level of mobility enjoyed by Americans, the extended family with several generations living under one roof was never as common as in many European countries. More common was the "stem" family in which younger siblings physically relocated to establish new family units, but could continue to rely on parental resources for assistance in times of need. This sort of family arrangement lent itself readily to the flexible work-force needed for industrialization.

American law throughout the 19th and early 20th centuries continued to enshrine the principle by which the family was effectively a *corporation sole* in the person of the male householder. When a woman married, her identity and legal personhood was subsumed into her husband's, a situation often referred to poetically as "the marital centaur." A woman not only took her husband's last name as her legal surname, but in public situations was referred to by placing "Mrs." in front of his first and last names, as though her own identity vanished entirely. She could not sign a contract, hold a bank account, or do any business independent of her husband. Even the pay she might earn legally belonged to her husband, and she could not hold it back even to prevent him from wasting household funds on drinking or other idle activities. A wife's status was not all that different from that of her children.

By the middle of the 19th century women had begun questioning this patri-archal family and the subordinate role it prescribed for women. But by the last decade of the 19th century, it was no longer just an *avant garde* of mavericks such as Lucy Stone, who refused to adopt her husband's surname, or Victoria Woodhull, whose run for the presidency was something of a joke. By 1890 the push for women's rights had become a mass movement, with respectable matrons agitating for such simple things as the right to have a savings account in one's own name.

The women's movement of the late 19th and early 20th century is gener-ally associated with the extension of the franchise to women, as shown by the term "suffragettes." However important the vote may have been, representing as it did the right to participate in civic life as a free citizen, women's suffrage was not the only issue with which this group of women reformers concerned themselves. If women were not able to dissolve the legal barriers that kept them subordinate and dependent upon their husbands, the vote would be merely a hollow, symbolic victory.

Many of the women reformers of the Progressive Era also championed a new model of marriage that fundamentally shifted the relationship between husband and wife. Instead of being hierarchical, with the husband effective-ly the sovereign of the domestic realm and the wife obliged to obey, this new "companionate marriage" made husband and wife co-equal partners and

The pioneering birth control activist Margaret Sanger in 1922. She broke down barriers to discussing contraception in the United States.

emphasized the sharing of life's burdens and joys. Although many proponents of this new model of marriage saw it in conjunction with more democratic ideas about child-rearing, some even went so far as to suggest a family that consisted of the man and woman alone, in which the absence of children was not a desolation, but a positive choice.

THE NEW CHILDBED

For those women who did give birth, the Progressive Era marked major changes that simultaneously reduced the risk to life and health, while making the process far more sterile and institutional. The development of the germ theory of disease largely eliminated "childbed fever," the infections that had previously carried away so many new mothers. These infections were largely iatrogenic, that is, the result of transmission from one patient to another through unsanitary medical practices. In earlier decades, neither midwives nor doctors followed any particular procedures regarding cleanliness. As a result, bacteria could easily be carried on hands or instruments and infect a large number of women. By washing hands and instruments in anti-bacterial agents such as carbolic acid or bleach, the risk could be greatly reduced.

Another factor that had been a constant of childbirth in earlier generations had been the pain suffered by the mother while delivering the child. The development of anesthetics made it possible to eliminate the pain. The earliest generation of anesthetics, including ether and chloroform, could be given only at the final stages of delivery, since they caused the relaxation of the muscles necessary for pushing the baby out, and could cross the placenta, resulting in a baby too drugged to take its first breaths.

However German physicians had developed an alternative known as "twilight sleep," which involved a relatively light dose of morphine combined with scopolamine, which blocked the transfer of short-term memories to long-term memory. As a result, women came out of the delivery room with no memories of the pain they had suffered, an effective equivalent to a painless childbirth.

Margaret Sanger and the Birth Control Movement

As a girl, Margaret Sanger watched her mother's health gradually decline due to a succession of difficult births. After her own marriage to William Sanger, she was told that she must not have any more children or it would destroy her own health. By this time Sanger had become a nurse and was working regularly with poor immigrant families, who had no access to the birth control information that wealthier women obtained in spite of laws against it. A woman named Sadie Sachs, who died in childbirth after the only suggestion her doctor could offer was to tell her husband to sleep on the roof, became a symbol of every woman whose life was destroyed because she could not control her own fertility.

Sanger began her work with a series of articles dealing with health and hygiene, entitled "What Every Girl Should Know." In 1912 it was barred from the mails as obscene by Anthony Comstock, and she ended up fleeing the country to avoid going to jail. In Europe she learned not only more reliable methods of preventing conception, but also tactics that would ensure that any legal action she might endure would help publicize her cause instead of silencing it.

In 1915 she returned to the United States to begin a speaking tour, informing women of their options. The police soon came to confiscate equipment and arrest Sanger for discussing contraception. In 1917 she was sent to jail, where she initiated a hunger strike in protest against the injustice of denying women the information that could save their lives and health. Attempts by the prison administration to force-feed her only made her into a hero, and she was released to the cheering of her supporters. By 1920 laws against the dissemination of information about reproductive health and contraception on the grounds of obscenity were falling all over the country.

By the end of the 20th century many abortion opponents had come to vilify Sanger as a harbinger of the "culture of death." Few of these critics recognized that it was only possible to teach the natural family planning techniques they championed because Sanger broke down the barriers that prevented discussion of the human reproductive system.

The American medical community refused to adopt this procedure through the first decade of the 1900s, largely as the result of opposition by religious leaders who considered it a contravention of the statement in the book of Genesis in which God told Eve that henceforth women would bear children in pain, which they understood prescriptively, rather than descriptively. Only when wealthy women traveled to Europe for the procedure, even braving the dangers of unrestricted submarine warfare in the early months of

World War I, did the barriers begin to fall. These women had not only wealth, but also influence with decision-makers, and were able to press for the availability of twilight sleep in U.S. hospitals.

Because twilight sleep could only be administered by a physician, and because the woman needed to be monitored more closely during the birthing process lest she injure herself, its adoption marked a movement away from home births to the institutional setting. Proponents argued that the modern hospital, with its emphasis on sterile procedure, was a primary line of defense against deadly infection for mother and child alike. Not only was it safer and cleaner, but it was also more efficient to have women come to a central location, rather than having the doctors travel to each individual home. However, by moving childbirth to the hospital, the familiar situation of home was replaced with that of an institution, where things were arranged for the convenience of doctors, rather than the woman.

THE SERVANTLESS HOUSEHOLD

Almost from the beginning of the nation's history, Americans felt uncomfortable about domestic service. Except in the south, where it was taken for granted that slaves and later freedwomen would work as domestics, the concept of the servant clashed with the egalitarian ideals set forth in the Declaration of Independence. However the sheer amount of work required to keep a household running led even the growing middle class to hire some form of assistance. Although some families hired servants, the employment relationship in the American city was never as simple and stable as in Europe. The breadth of opportunity afforded to a capable person meant servants were forever quitting for better jobs elsewhere. Letters and diaries written by women who employed domestics show a continual pattern of either being in search of help, or fearing the help will quit for other employment.

A child's wooden high chair with wheels from around 1900.

One solution that grew increasingly common in the industrial cities of the north in the later decades of the 19th century was the commercial service. Laundry in particular was frequently sent out, either to a laundress who did the work in her own home, or increasingly to a commercial laundry.

In 1900 few kitchens had running water, although some had an indoor pump, as in this recreated home in Tampa, Florida.

Sewing, baking, and other tasks previously performed at home by the woman of the house were increasingly done by commercial concerns. In some areas one could arrange to have pre-cooked meals delivered from a central kitchen each evening for supper. Hiring tasks out in this fashion was a business relationship, and thus not fraught with issues of personal subordination and social inequality. Furthermore, replacing multiple individual kitchens and other household facilities with a single centralized facility made the processes more efficient.

The culmination of this ideal was the apartment hotel. Unlike conventional hotels, which were primarily waystations for travelers, the apartment hotel was a residence for families. Each family would have its own private living quarters, but instead of being individually responsible for housekeeping tasks, those duties would be handled by a staff of paid employees. For instance residents had the option of going downstairs to a central dining room to eat, or having meals delivered to their apartments, often by a dumbwaiter system built right into the wall.

While housekeeping activities were increasingly commercialized and moved outside the home, another force was drawing them back into the home. The first decade of the 20th century saw the beginnings of the modern household appliance. With reliable domestic electricity, such devices as washing machines and vacuum cleaners became practical. As a result it

"Breaker boys" sorting through coal at a South Pittston, Pennsylvania, mine in January 1911.

The Problem of Children at Work

The Progressive Era also marked the beginning of concern about child labor. In pre-industrial times every pair of hands was essential to complete the necessary tasks of survival. In areas of colonial America populated by Puritans and Quakers, ideas of the moral value of effort only intensified the call that even small children be gainfully employed in useful activities. Children began helping their parents almost as soon as they began to walk. Many young people began apprenticeships that would train them for useful trades while not yet in their teens. The work children performed in earlier eras was at home or in the fields beside parents or other relatives. In the new industrial cities children worked for strangers in the company of large numbers of other children from outside the family circle. Furthermore these children often worked in ill-lit and ill-ventilated factories, with dangerous machinery, or on the streets. Boys in their early teens would sit on benches over a conveyor belt for 12 to 15 hours a day, seven days a week, picking slate from coal until their fingers bled. These "breaker boys" became the poster children of America's anti-child-labor movement, and the first actions of the National Child Labor Committee were to press for enforcement of minimum age regulations in the coal industry. Once the precedent of regulation was established, reformers could move on to other industries.

Not all the reformers were motivated purely by the high-minded ideals of protecting children from injury, and ensuring they could obtain some education. Many trade unions joined the campaign against child labor for the simple reason that child workers competed with adult workers for jobs, keeping wages low. In turn, low adult wages often drove children into the job market in an effort to supplement an inadequate family income, so the arguments of the labor unions were not entirely self-serving.

became increasingly easy for the woman of the house to do her own laundry and cleaning instead of hiring a commercial service to do it. Furthermore using an appliance to do such chores gave one greater control over the quality of the work. However the shift to the use of home appliances often meant that women actually ended up with more work. Jobs that were once done weekly or monthly could now be done daily.

A NEW ROLE FOR CHILDREN

The Progressive Era also saw major changes in the role of children. The shift from the traditional patriarchal family organized along authoritarian lines, to companionate marriage based upon shared lives, also led to new views of children. While the relationship of children to their parents had been previously based upon obedience, it increasingly became based upon mutual affection. Children were to be cherished rather than commanded, their characters molded by gentle reproof rather than harsh physical discipline.

This shift in attitudes about family and home life was intricately intertwined with the issues of child labor that were transforming the workplace. Even as late as 1896, a suit for the wrongful death of a two-year-old child was still phrased in terms of the child's economic value as a runner of errands, and rejected because the court could not believe that a child so young could do useful labor. But even a few years earlier, a father of a 14-year-old boy was less concerned about the lost earning power that his son's death represented, than the wrong that had been done the family by his loss.

Improvements in medicine and public works had drastically lowered the high infant mortality rate that had previously forced parents to hold themselves aloof emotionally from the very young, lest they be debilitated by a loss and the subsequent grief. As it became safe to invest emotionally in an infant, babies became an embodiment of innocence, and their loss from accident or disease became increasingly unacceptable.

The change of the role of the infant in the natal family was accompanied by a change in patterns of adoption. In previous eras older children were sought for their usefulness as laborers, and it was virtually impossible to find anyone willing to take an infant except for pay. By the beginning of the 20th century people increasingly sought infants because they would give love without reserve or guile.

Concern over a child's well-being and a sense of a child's death as a monstrous wrong was not confined to infants. Rather it extended well into the teen years, and was marked by a growing concern about children having safe places to play. Because most homes were quite small, particularly among working-class families, children typically played in the street, where they were vulnerable to being struck by vehicles. By the first decade of the 20th century, the driver of an automobile or trolley that struck and killed a child often had to be rescued from a mob of angry people.

Street justice was not the only means by which the safety of children was ensured. There was a considerable movement to create safe places for children to play, and to educate children about the dangers of playing in the streets. The result was a shift away from a relatively unsupervised childhood spent outdoors, to one increasingly confined by adult strictures.

DOWN ON THE FARM

Although much of the work of the reformers of the Progressive Era was directed toward the situation of working people in the city, life was changing for rural Americans as well. Much of this change was the result of increasing mechanization, which enabled each farmer to successfully work more land. The mechanization of the American farm had begun before the Civil War, with the introduction of the mechanical reaper by Cyrus McCormick. Because the reaper replaced 20 skilled scythe men with a driver and a person to bind the sheaves, thus freeing men to fight at the front, it was a significant factor in the Union victory in the Civil War. Further mechanical conveniences continued to be introduced in the Gilded Age, including the threshing machine.

By 1890 the earliest steam traction engines were becoming available to farmers. These machines were not tractors, and not particularly useful for work in small crop rows. Their sheer size (many were over 12 ft. tall and weighed up to 20 tons) and primitive steering systems made them too unwieldy for anything but the largest fields of the Great Plains. However they were very useful for providing mobile power sources for such applications as threshing.

Early threshing machines were powered by horses, usually on a treadmill or a carousel-like device known as a sweep. However horses tired, meaning teams had to be periodically switched out, and few teams could keep their pace as steady as necessary for optimal threshing. The steam engine provided just the sort of steady, tireless power a threshing machine needed, and by mounting that engine on wheels and arranging for it to drive those wheels, it was moved from one farm to another. Mobility was critical, because few farms were large enough to purchase and operate their own threshing machine. Instead a number of neighboring farmers would pitch in together to buy one and work together at threshing time, moving to each farm in turn.

Threshing day was one of the big events on the Progressive Era farm. The farmstead took on a festive air as the men gathered to operate the machinery and load in the bundles of wheat. Threshed grain was poured into sacks, while the separated straw was piled into a strawstack or loaded into the barn's haymow to be used as livestock bedding throughout the year. If it were being stored in the haymow, the boys were often recruited to do the stacking, and a friendly rivalry often developed between them and the men to see who could outwork the other.

The mass-produced Fordson tractor hauls a mobile advertisement for tractors and Ford cars as part of a parade in the 1920s.

In the farmhouse the woman of the farm and her daughters were hard at work in the kitchen preparing food for the men. These dinners were a source of considerable pride, even rivalry between neighboring women. A woman whose threshing-day meals proved inadequate in quantity or quality soon became an object of ridicule in those tight-knit communities.

Over the course of the Progressive Era, the steam traction engine gave way to the internal combustion tractor. The earliest tractors were as large and clumsy as their steam predecessors, and the first attempts to create small tractors produced machines so rickety as to be unusable. But Henry Ford, himself a farm boy by upbringing, applied his experience in automobiles to the problem of a durable small tractor that would substitute for the horse. Determined to make the best tractor he could, he kept refining his prototypes throughout the 1910s. Only the outbreak of World War I and the resultant need for men in uniform led him to finally put his Fordson into production. The Fordson tractor's ability to free farmhands to fight had an effect on the Allied war effort like what the reaper had done for the Union in the Civil War.

Not all gasoline engines on the farm were necessarily powering tractors. The farmers of the Progressive Era found innumerable uses for small one- and two-horsepower gas motors, from cracking corn for chicken feed, to churning butter and powering washing machines in the farmhouse. These little engines generally had a single cylinder and featured a large flywheel to keep them turning between power strokes, giving them a distinctive pop-pop-pop sound when in operation. However these "one-lungers" were invaluable in automating the countless small tasks that had made a typical day on the farm one of backbreaking labor.

Rubbernecking on the Party Line

The coordination of threshing days was made easier by the telephone. One of the enduring hardships of American farm life had been its isolation, since American farmers lived in individual farmsteads, rather than in central villages. Visiting one's neighbors might mean a half-hour brisk walk, or saddling a horse already tired from a full day's work.

Although the telephone companies seldom attempted to extend their networks into rural areas, citing the low population densities as unprofitable, the telephone was a simple enough technology that it could be assembled and operated by amateurs. Most farmers were inveterate tinkerers, so it was common for them to string their own telephone circuits between neighboring farms, attaching the wires to fence posts, or even trees. The central switchboard would be located in one of the farmhouses, and the women of that family would generally take turns in the role of operator, or Central.

Because of the way these early circuits were wired, in a manner known as a party line, anyone who took their phone off-hook while a conversation was in progress on other phones in the circuit would be able to hear it. As a result, a whole system of etiquette developed for the use of a party line. Deliberately listening in on another conversation was known as rubbernecking, and it soon became a way for farm women to visit socially. It was considered acceptable to chime in with an answer to a question if the original conversants did not know it, but to deliberately call attention to the presence of non-participating rubberneckers on the line was considered rude in the extreme.

Not only did the rural party line provide an important vehicle for social interaction between isolated farm families, it also provided life-saving links in an emergency. In the days before radios and National Weather Service tornado warnings, it was not uncommon for these lines to be used for storm alerts. The person who sighted the tornado would have Central ring everyone and pass the word. The telephone could also be used to call help in case of a fire or livestock escape, and if someone were ill or injured, Central could call a doctor in town, halving the time it took to summon help.

WAR AND THE END OF PROGRESSIVISM

Although America's participation in World War I was far briefer than its involvement in the one that followed, and the degree of economic mobilization far less, the Great War was still a major rupture in America's social fabric. The entire period of the Gilded Age and Progressive Era had been predicated upon an assumption of the perfectibility of human nature. In this view, if destructive influences could be removed from a person's environment, destructive impulses would abate and the person would behave in a civilized fashion. Thus the outbreak of war in August 1914 seemed like a horrific reversion to a barbaric past. America's official position for the first three years of the war was isolationist, distancing itself from the conflict and attempting to negotiate a peaceable settlement.

Continual provocation by the Germans, combined with some judicious British propaganda, finally led the United States to enter the war on the side of the Allies in 1917. Although the concept of the home front would not be formally articulated until World War II, there was no question in the minds of Americans that the war effort did not stop on the French and Belgian coasts, but extended all the way across the Atlantic. Almost immediately the war effort was brought home to every American family by programs to conserve food and other vital war supplies. Such sacrifices as meatless and heatless days became a way to bring the war home, although many of these formulaic measures were more symbolic and psychological than practical.

More substantial was the movement of women into various positions previously held by men. Throughout the Progressive Era there had been a strong ambivalence about women's work, with some progressives holding that reform meant creating a "family wage" for male breadwinners so women could stay at home, while others argued that a woman's right to earn and keep her own pay was a fundamental right.

American participation in the war meant that every civilian job that could be taken by a woman freed a man to fight. Some women even went to Europe to serve as military nurses, further giving evidence to the idea that a woman could be a strong and capable worker rather than a helpless damsel needing protection. The dislocation of the war helped finalize the breakdown of the traditional family, which had begun in the Progressive Era. As a result

This World War I poster used the "new woman" image to challenge men.

the decade that followed would witness a major transformation in family roles that would have previously been unthinkable.

LEIGH KIMMEL

Further Readings

Coontz, Stephanie. *Marriage: A History*. New York: Viking, 2005.

Dregni, Michael, ed. *This Old Farm: A Treasury of Family Farm Memories*. Stillwater, MN: Voyageur Press, 1999.

Ertel, P. W. *The American Tractor: A Century of Legendary Machines*. Osceola, WI: MBI Publishing, 2001.

Fetherston, David. *Farm Tractor Advertising in America, 1900–1960*. Osceola, WI: Motorbooks, 1996.

Gray, Madeline. *Margaret Sanger: A Biography of the Champion of Birth Control*. New York: Richard Marek Publishers, 1979.

Haber, Barbara. *From Hardtack to Home Fries: An Uncommon History of American Cooks and Meals*. New York: The Free Press, 2002.

Harriss, John. *The Family: A Social History of the Twentieth Century*. Oxford: Oxford University Press, 1991.

Hindman, Hugh D. *Child Labor in American History*. Armonk, NY: M.E. Sharpe, 2002.

Lasch, Christopher. *Women and the Common Life: Love, Marriage and Feminism*. New York: W. W. Norton, 1997.

Matthews, Glenna. *Just a Housewife: The Rise and Fall of Domesticity in America*. New York: Oxford University Press, 1987.

Root, Waverly and Richard de Rochemont. *Eating in America: A History*. New York: Ecco Press, 1997.

Schiff, Karenna Gore. *Lighting the Way: Nine Women Who Changed America*. New York: Hyperion, 2005.

Schneider, Dorothy and Carl J. Schneider. *American Women in the Progressive Era: 1900–1920*. New York: Facts on File, 1993.

Shepard, Sue. *Pickled, Potted and Canned: How the Art and Science of Food Preservation Changed the World*. New York: Simon & Schuster, 2000.

Tone, Andrea, ed. *Controlling Reproduction: An American History*. Wilmington, DE: S.R. Books, 1997.

Volti, Rudi. *Cars and Culture: The Life Story of a Technology*. Westport, CT: Greenwood Press, 2004.

Wilson, C. Anne, ed. *Waste Not, Want Not: Food and Society*. Edinburgh: Edinburgh University Press, 1991.

Yalom, Marilyn. *A History of the Wife*. New York: HarperCollins, 2001.

Zelizer, Viviana A. *Pricing the Priceless Child: The Changing Social Value of Children*. New York: Basic Books, 1985.

Chapter 3

Material Culture

*"The American talks about money because that is the symbol ...
for success, intelligence, and power."*
— George Santayana

AFTER THE CIVIL WAR ended in 1865, Americans turned their attention to the Industrial Revolution, which had been revolutionizing Britain for the past century. Advancing technologies paved the way for new discoveries in transportation, communication, entertainment, and homemaking that drastically changed daily life. The urbanization that was a byproduct of industrialization provided manufacturers with an eager market for the ready-made goods they were producing. These new and improved products made life easier and more enjoyable for those who could afford them. The result of these changes was what cultural critic Thorstein Veblen (1857–1929) called "conspicuous consumption."

Some of the most conspicuous consumers were individuals who squandered fortunes garnered from the California gold mines. East coast millionaires could also be ostentatious. For instance the dining room of William K. Vanderbilt's Newport "cottage" was embellished with bronze furniture and Algerian marble walls. When Thomas A. Mellon, a former Pittsburgh judge, became unable to manage his vast properties in 1890, he sold properties estimated at $2 million to his son Andrew for $1. The properties included more than 1,000 houses, and a large amount of underdeveloped property. Some millionaires responded to changing times by moving away from large cities. By the early 20th century, the city of Greenwich, Connecticut, was home to more than 200 millionaires. Ironically one of the richest American cities was the mining city of Butte, Montana.

The 700 mines located within a five-mile radius of the city had a monthly payroll of $900,000, and $125,000 in other expenses. Mine owners grew rich on the backs of the miners, who were often in debt to the company store. Although rents were exorbitantly high, some miners drew wages of only $3 a day. Homeowners could recoup one-half of construction costs in a single year.

Both industrialization and consumption reached new heights in the early 20th century. As a neutral country with strong ties to Western Europe, the United States was called on to provide warring nations with both military goods and necessities of life after World War I broke out in 1914. Three years later, President Woodrow Wilson (1856–1924) rescinded American neutrality, and the United States entered the war on the side of the Allies. Even though Wilson's failure to win the necessary support for American membership in the League of Nations led to the demise of progressivism in the political sense, progressive reforms continued to influence American politics and society. Economically, World War I was a boon for America, and the new prosperity meant that a larger percentage of the population could afford such luxuries as telephones, automobiles, washing machines, refrigerators, and radios.

CONSUMPTION IN DAILY LIFE

New technologies were essential in the consumer revolution that took place in American homes in the Progressive Era. Alexander Graham Bell (1847–1922) had invented the telephone in 1876, and advancing technology increased both the range and quality of transmissions. At the turn of the century 10 percent of all American households subscribed to telephone services. Prices

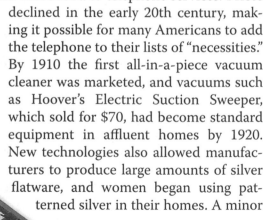

declined in the early 20th century, making it possible for many Americans to add the telephone to their lists of "necessities." By 1910 the first all-in-a-piece vacuum cleaner was marketed, and vacuums such as Hoover's Electric Suction Sweeper, which sold for $70, had become standard equipment in affluent homes by 1920. New technologies also allowed manufacturers to produce large amounts of silver flatware, and women began using patterned silver in their homes. A minor

Sets of silver flatware and many other consumer products became more affordable and available when manufacturing processes improved in the Progressive Era.

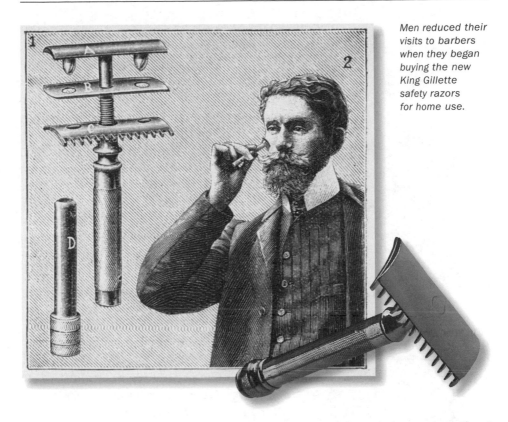

Men reduced their visits to barbers when they began buying the new King Gillette safety razors for home use.

scandal occurred in 1895 when President Cleveland's wife Frances ordered Dolley Madison's silver melted down to make new silverware for the White House. Mrs. Cleveland refused to cave in to criticism and refused all offers to purchase the silver. She demanded that the mint certify that only the original silver had been used in making the new flatware.

Throughout the Progressive/World War I era, Americans continued to spend large amounts on luxury items large and small, including new silver, china, and crystal that were designed to meet every purpose imaginable. American food budgets of the time were higher than those of any other nation in the world. Among the more affluent, a large part of the food allotment was spent on luxury foods. Between 1899 and 1919 the total amount spent on peanuts, for instance, which were usually served only on holidays, rose from $937,000 to $4.8 million. Hot-house strawberries sold for $1 a berry, or $14 a quart. One New York hostess paid $150 for 200 Florida strawberries, only to throw them out because she considered them inferior. The price of grapes, which were graded according to quality, ranged from $6 to $10 a pound. Strawberries and grapes were served at society luncheons in groups of four or five tied by ribbons that matched color schemes.

As Victorian barriers were broken down, women began buying cosmetics and perfumes. Between 1899 and 1919 the total spent on such items rose

A dress design from 1908, accompanied by a feathered hat.

from $3.9 million to $33.4 million. Large amounts were also spent on fashion. Men wore stiff collars, derbies, and top hats; women wore dimity dresses and shirtwaists with big shoulders, and carried parasols and fur muffs. Women responded to demands to discard unhealthy corsets with shortened hemlines. Visits to barbers were drastically reduced after men began shaving their mustaches. Visits were further curtailed by the introduction of the King Gillette Razor. Americans spent a good deal on cigarettes, and the number of cigarettes smoked rose from 40 per capita in 1890 to 454 in 1920. On the other hand, many Americans saved money by not purchasing prohibited alcohol.

MARKETING MATERIAL CULTURE

By the turn of the 20th century, large department stores were replacing small general stores. Mail-order companies were established to meet the growing demand for modern goods. After Rural Free Delivery was introduced in 1890, mail-order products became available to Americans in remote areas, expanding the targeted audience for advertisers. The most popular catalog was published by Sears, which had fine tuned the technique of marketing to mass audiences. Known as "The Thrift Book of a Nation," the catalog offered tens of thousands of bargains and guaranteed that 99 out of 100 would be shipped within 24 hours. The popularity of mail-order catalogs grew to such an extent that some local merchants offered $50 rewards to individuals who collected the largest number of catalogs to be burned.

Magazines that reached a large percentage of the population were ideal for spreading product information and promoting interest in new and improved products. Because mass production allowed goods to be manufactured at lower prices, what were considered luxury products in the past were placed within the means of average Americans. Those who could not stretch budgets to include high-priced items were sometimes able to afford cheaper knockoffs. By 1900 large numbers of Americans had become enamored with brand-name products, buying advertisers' messages that such products were necessary to attain the American dream.

New visual ads of the period were designed to be more exciting in order to lure in more customers, and advertisers were quick to identify target groups for specific products, appealing to consumer desires even as they shaped market demands to serve their own purposes. For instance ads for the 90 Degree Cadillac were designed to hammer in the point that the car was a symbol of wealth. Likewise ads for Ambassador's Packard cars proudly proclaimed that the Packard 6 model had appeared at London's Court of St. James and the Packard 8 at the gates of the Palais de l'Elysée in Paris.

Other advertisers targeted a more general audience. Ads for the Ideal Electric Cold refrigerator advised middle-class women that purchasing the product was necessary to winning a man's heart. Eastman Kodak created the market for its cameras through ads that encouraged Americans to document both their daily lives and special occasions. With prices ranging from $5 to $900, individuals from all walks of life could afford Kodak cameras. Between 1904 and 1910 the company began presenting a series of Christmas ads designed to tug the heart strings of American consumers at the same time they suggested gift ideas, including Kodak cameras.

An April 1904 advertisement for dress patterns featuring the latest dress styles with broad or draped shoulders, and still-corseted waistlines.

Critics of Crass Materialism

Of the many critics of materialistic culture, none was more vocal than economist Thorstein Veblen (1857–1929), who portrayed all capitalists as greedy barbarians living off the fruits of the labor of exploited workers. In *The Theory of the Leisure Class* (1899), Veblen insisted that the "leisure class" exhibited wastefulness in all aspects of their lives, resulting in the devaluation of hard work and resourcefulness. This demeaning wastefulness, he believed, had spread to architecture, entertainment, fashion, and leisure. Veblen believed that the decline had also negatively affected morals, religion, education, and society.

Writer John Dos Passos (1896–1970) was another harsh critic of the material culture of the Progressive/World War I era, although his works were not published until the following decade. In the *USA Trilogy*, which included *The 42nd Parallel* (1930), *1919* (1932), and *The Big Money* (1936), Dos Passos used newspaper headlines, popular songs, and biographies of cultural icons to paint a devastating portrait of materialism. Dos Passos was particularly critical of the waste of American lives and resources in World War I.

Among the "muckraking" critics of materialism, writer Upton Sinclair (1878–1968) holds a unique place in American history, because his writings directly affected political reforms of the early 20th century. In *The Jungle* (1906), Sinclair offered a pitiless examination of Chicago's meatpacking industry. Although his intention had been to highlight the plight of workers, public attention was aroused by the unsanitary habits in which meat was prepared for the American market. In response President Theodore Roosevelt (1858–1919) appointed an investigatory commission, and Congress enacted the Pure Food and Drug Act of 1906, giving the new Food and Drug Administration the authority to monitor the preparation and marketing of food and drugs.

Swiss immigrant and church historian Philip Schaff (1819–93) arrived in the United States in 1843 and enthusiastically endorsed his new country. He subsequently spent years lecturing on the United States in Europe. Schaff regaled his audiences with descriptions of the consumerism that allowed Americans to be comfortable in their own homes. These comforts, according to Schaff, included sofas, padded rocking chairs, pianos, illustrated books, and popular magazines. He contended that American homes were more inviting than those in Europe, and was particularly taken with the broad streets of small-town America. Schaff insisted that a love of luxury was much evidenced in large cities such as New York, Philadelphia, Boston, Baltimore, Washington, Cincinnati, and New Orleans, where faux nobility were living lives of tasteless ostentation. He observed that American prosperity was leading to a seemingly "bottomless materialism and worldliness."

Gimmicks were widely used to promote consumerism. Proctor and Gamble promised customers that brownies, fairies based on Scottish folklore, had produced Ivory soap with their mystical powers. Post Toasties cereal was allegedly prepared and packaged by elves. Jell-O used a Kewpie doll to hawk its products. The Campbell Kids were so successful at selling soup that they were made into dolls. The popular trading cards that were included with products such as coffee, tea, and soap became collector's items. Some of these full-color cards had movable parts. Soap ads, for instance, depicted nude bathers who were artfully covered by advertising material when they were maneuvered to stand up. Coca-Cola ads offered a cut-out coupon that could be exchanged for a free Coke. By 1910 trading stamps had become increasingly popular, allowing consumers to collect books of stamps to be traded for a variety of items.

In the past the copy and design of ads had remained in the hands of businesses. By the 1890s, however, advertising agencies were taking over these functions. In 1912 Proctor and Gamble launched the first multi-faceted advertising campaign that targeted middle-class Americans. Because advertisers understood that most purchasing decisions were made by women, they turned to women's magazines to hawk their products. This financial support allowed publishers to slash subscription rates, which in turn allowed them to reach a larger and more diverse audience. In this way, *Ladies Home Journal*

Two little girls promenading with their Campbell Kid doll in New York in 1912—the Campbell Kid was an early advertising success.

A shop window displaying vacuum cleaners at the J.C. Harding & Co. store. Vacuums such as Hoover's Electric Suction Sweeper became standard equipment in affluent homes by 1920.

had increased its circulation to more than a million by 1900. Two-thirds of the magazine's budget was generated from advertising by 1919. The *Saturday Evening Post*, which had been established in 1728 as a men's magazine, transformed itself into a family magazine in the early 20th century. A good deal of its fame came from its association with Norman Rockwell (1894–1978), who painted more than 300 depictions of American life for the magazine. Rockwell's paintings are still cherished by collectors of Americana.

In addition to offering a variety of items, large department stores created an ambiance for shoppers that encouraged them to spend a good deal of money. Stores advertised their establishments as "cathedrals" and "palaces." The period between 1890 and 1940 has been identified by historians as the "golden age" of department stores in the United States. Most stores, including Macy's, Marshall Fields, and Wanamaker's, were owned by families who built immense structures in elaborate and lavish detail to lure customers. In Philadelphia, Wanamaker's boasted 120 counters covering two-thirds of a mile. Inside a large model of the *Rue de la Paix* drew admiring crowds, as did a gallery of modern French paintings, an orchestra, and displays of fashions from around the world. A second, 12-story Wanamaker structure built in 1911 featured a grand court, and what was then the largest organ in the world. Shoppers at Macy's in New York were invited to spend time in elegant lounges and rest areas, loiter in reading and writing rooms, and visit the art gallery. Several restaurants offered a variety of luncheon choices. Other department stores enticed customers by providing child care facilities, beauty salons, meeting rooms, live music, post offices, and lecture halls.

AUTOMOBILES

By the early 20th century, the automobile had become an American symbol of success, partly because only the wealthy could afford the luxurious models available at the time. In 1908 Cadillac became the first automobile company to standardize parts. The following year the company was absorbed into General Motors. The Oldsmobile was easily the most popular American car in the early 20th century. By 1902 thousands of Oldsmobiles were being produced each year at a cost of $650 each, well beyond the means of the working class.

Henry Ford (1864–1947) produced the first vehicle accessible to average Americans. Ford had founded the Ford Motor Company in 1903 in Detroit, Michigan, with the intention of making the automobile an American necessity. The Model T, popularly known as the "Tin Lizzie," first reached consumers in 1908, available only in black. Because of Ford's innovative assembly-line method of production, the price of the Model T dropped from $850 in 1908 to $290 in 1924. Initially all automobiles were paid for in cash, but in 1919 the General Motors Acceptance Corporation began financing GM vehicles, and many customers began to purchase automobiles on credit. Dupont was the first to appeal to the female audience by offering autos in a variety of colors. By 1916 Ford was producing a million vehicles a year. His production methods, which became known as Fordism, spread to other industries, further increasing the availability of consumer products.

Many of the artifacts of the Progressive/World War I period are now on display at the Henry Ford Museum in Greenfield Village, Michigan. In addition to automobile-related relics, artifacts include the workshop in which the Wright Brothers built their first plane, a Victrola, phonograph records, and a Nickelodeon where visitors can watch silent movies and listen to music of the period. Popular exhibits include "Heroes of the Sky," which depicts aviation history; "Automobile in American Life," which follows the development of the automobile and its influence on American life and customs; and "Presidential Limousines," which displays automobiles driven by many presidents of the 20th century.

MATERIALISM AND ARCHITECTURE

One of the most renowned American architects, Frank Lloyd Wright (1856–1924) designed prairie-style homes that were viewed as embodying the first truly American style of architecture suited to changing suburban lifestyles.

The Sinking of the *Titanic*

Materialism reached new heights with the building of the giant passenger ship *Titanic*, which was marketed as the first unsinkable ship in the world. The luxurious ship, designed and built by the Irish firm Harland and Wolff, possessed a double-bottomed hull and 16 allegedly watertight compartments. The designers insisted that even if four compartments were flooded, the remaining 12 would keep the ship afloat. American financier J.P. Morgan who had purchased the *Titanic* for his White Star Line was scheduled to be a passenger on its first outing, but was forced to withdraw for business reasons. The passenger list on the *Titanic*'s maiden voyage in the spring of 1912 included the rich and famous of American and British society, all of whom were eager to experience the luxuries of the famous ship. One of the highlights of the *Titanic*'s interior was the hauntingly familiar grand staircase. Styles depicted in the staterooms included Louis Seize, Empire, Italian Renaissance, Georgian, Regency, Queen Anne, and Old Dutch. A lavish reading and writing room was exclusive to first-class passengers.

Regardless of its reputation as unsinkable, the *Titanic*, en route to New York from England, rapidly sank to the bottom of the North Atlantic off the coast of Newfoundland around 2 a.m. on April 15, 1912, after colliding with an iceberg. As the ship sank, the orchestra continued to play the hymn "Nearer My God to Thee." The death toll was recorded at 1,500. Most survivors were women and children from wealthy families who had been fortunate enough to make it into lifeboats. One of the most famous survivors was Denver socialite Molly Brown (1867–1932). A highly fictionalized account of her survival was depicted in the 1964 musical, *The Unsinkable Molly Brown,* in which actress Debbie Reynolds played the title role. A more realistic portrait of Brown was presented in 1997 in the blockbuster *Titanic* by actress Kathy Bates. It was almost an hour and a half after the ship was struck that the remaining survivors were rescued from the icy waters by the arrival of the *Carpathia*. On September 1, 1985, the *Titanic* was located in the North Atlantic at a depth of approximately 13,000 ft. The wreckage has since been studied by scientists, and scavengers have laid claim to a myriad of small artifacts.

Molly Brown, a Denver socialite and survivor of the Titanic *disaster.*

This two-story house with wrap around porches was built in 1912, and is now part of the Florida Heritage Village in Largo, Florida.

Buildings of this Prairie School were characterized by prominent overhanging roofs and horizontal window bands. Wright later turned his attention to building simple, low-cost homes for less affluent Americans. Wright's reputation also extended to public buildings. His projects include the cubist-styled Unity Temple erected in Oak Park, Illinois, in 1905, that has been designated a national monument. Wright's influence also extended to other countries. Built between 1914 and 1922, the Tokyo Imperial Hotel stood as a memorial to Wright's influence until it was demolished in 1967.

Many public buildings of the Progressive Age were modeled after the massive and often ostentatious edifices of the Gilded Age. Many architects of the Progressive/World War I era followed the Richardsonian Romanesque style made popular by Henry Hobson Richardson (1838–86), whose works included the Allegheny Country Court House and jail in Pittsburgh. Marshall Field's Department Store was also built during this period. The World's Columbian Expedition exercised a major influence on American architecture, leading to what became known as the American Renaissance. Projects completed during this period include the Boston Public Library, New York's Metropolitan Museum of Art, the Lincoln Memorial, and a number of state capital buildings. The

Children's Toys

Some of the most sought-after collectibles of the Progressive/World War I era are children's toys. The Smithsonian Institution has one of the original teddy bears that were created by the wife of a Brooklyn toy shop owner. The bears were named after President Theodore Roosevelt, who had spared the life of a bear on a hunting trip in 1902. The Smithsonian also has a five-story dollhouse that was built in 1900 and added to over five decades. Mass-produced mail-order toys were also popular during this period. Popular cast-iron items included a fire engine pulled by three horses, carriages with horses in a harness, and models of real-life figures. Beginning in 1890 cast-iron mechanical banks were the rage. Various ways were devised to drop coins into the banks. On a William Tell bank, for instance, the coin was shot from a crossbow over the head of Tell's son before it landed in a tree bank. More than 300 types of mechanical banks were manufactured during this period. Toys could be innovative, or reflective of the times, mirroring common racial and ethnic prejudices, and moral attitudes. For example in the Chinese-Must-Go cap gun, the cap was placed in the mouth of a Chinese man. Pulling the trigger activated a white male figure that kicked the Chinese male in the pants.

Dolls were often designed to promote traditional gender roles and morality, depicting highly idealized figures. Some doll designers, however, refused to comply with the dictates of the period. One of the most popular dolls of the era is still in great demand. In 1915 Indiana cartoonist Johnny Gruelle (1896–1979) gave his daughter, who was ill with leukemia, a rag doll that he had found in their attic. He named the doll Raggedy Ann and invented a series of adventures about her to entertain his daughter. After her death in 1916, Gruelle sold the Raggedy Ann books accompanied by a Raggedy Ann doll.

Another popular doll of the period became an American classic after magazine illustrator Rose O'Neill (1874–1944) began drawing a cartoon for the *Woman's Home Companion*. Her Kewpie, a child-like depiction of the mythological Cupid, caught on. The doll, which sold millions, is still considered a cultural icon.

A traditional style of doll manufactured in the 1910s.

The design of Whitehall, the massive home Henry Flagler built for his wife in Palm Beach, Florida, was influenced by architectural trends started by the 1893 Chicago World's Fair.

most outstanding example of notable railroad station entrances of the period is New York City's magnificent Grand Central Station (1903–13).

Construction during the Progressive/World War I era was made more affordable and comfortable for Americans, even those of modest means, with the introduction of mass-produced windows, doors, two-by-fours, and interior framing, and by central heating, electric lighting, and indoor plumbing. As throngs of workers crowded into large cities seeking work in factories and mills, many Americans moved to newly constructed single-dweller homes in the suburbs that were linked to cities by rail or roads. The small, efficient bungalow became a staple of small-town America. In 1908 Sears established a Modern Homes Department and began selling complete homes by mail order at prices ranging from a few hundred, to several thousand dollars. Mortgages were available for homeowners who resided east of the Mississippi and north of the Ohio River. Entire company towns were created with homes of this type.

Nowhere did wealthy Americans of this period practice more "conspicuous consumption" than in their choice of homes. In 1902 the *New York Herald* described Whitehall, the luxurious summer home that railroad developer Henry Flagler (1830–1930) had built as a wedding gift for his wife, Mary Lily Kenan Flagler, in Palm Beach, Florida, calling it more wonderful than any European palace and more magnificent than any other private home in the world. At

Actress Lillian Russell posing with a prop from the play The Grand Duchess *in the 1890s.*

66,000 sq. ft., Whitehall had 55 rooms and was designed according to the Beaux-Arts style that had become popular after the 1893 World's Columbian Exposition in Chicago. Outside, marble columns, a red barrel-tiled roof, and a decorated wrought-iron fence suggested the opulence within. Interior highlights of the architecture included a marble entrance hall, a grand double staircase, and a central courtyard. The first floor was given over to public rooms, a kitchen, an office, 12 guest rooms, and servants' rooms. The styles chosen to provide distinction to various rooms included Louis XIV, Louis XV, Louis XVI, Italian Renaissance, and Francis I. After the death of the Flaglers, a niece who inherited the property sold it to a hotel, which added a 300-room tower. The structure was rescued from demolition in 1959 by Flagler's granddaughter, Jean Flagler Matthews, and was turned into a museum where many artifacts from Henry Flagler's life remain on display.

MATERIALISM AND AMUSEMENTS

One of the most popular entertainments in the late 19th century was viewing moving pictures. For a nickel, viewers could watch brief films displayed on the Nickelodeon. By 1896 multi-viewer machines had replaced the single-viewer models of the past, and audiences flocked to see them at vaudeville performances, carnivals, fairs, lecture halls, and churches. Subjects ranged from travel scenes, newsreels, and comedy routines, to trick photography, such as running trains backward. In 1903 *The Great Train Robbery* was introduced, paving the way for the creation of the movie industry. By 1910 the emerging film industry forsook New York City for California. Hollywood became the film mecca of the country, and the studio system was established to create and promote movies to the American public. During the war, American films dominated the world market.

Charlie Chaplin, Theda Bara, Mary Pickford, and Lillian Gish emerged as leading stars of the era. In the post–World War I period, movies became the most popular form of American entertainment, in part because admission prices were low enough to appeal to even working-class Americans. At the same time they were entertaining viewers, movies served to shape the popular image of the "good life" and encouraged audience members to strive to emulate the stars by buying products associated with those lifestyles.

As always, music was an integral part of American life, encouraging consumers to spend both time and money in its pursuit. At the turn of the century, New Orleans was the center of musical life as Americans gathered to hear blues, ragtime, French dance music, Spanish rhythms that had been imported from the Caribbean, spirituals that had evolved from slave songs, and opera. In 1906 New Orleans pianist Jelly Roll Morton began traveling the country introducing "hot blues" ragtime to America. Over the next three years, the influence of New Orleans musicians became so strong that ragtime bands around the country began playing the New Orleans-style music that later became known as jazz. By 1917 musicians began migrating northward in large numbers, and the musical hub shifted from New Orleans to New York and Chicago.

During the 1880s the country club had emerged as a place in which more affluent Americans engaged in yachting, polo, tennis, archery, and golf. In the 1890s as leisure time expanded, membership in these exclusive establishments was extended to the middle class. Resort areas provided similar amusements to middle-class Americans, also offering archery, croquet, and track and field. Billiards, ping pong, and bowling were also popular activities. Consumption of equipment for these games rose from $919,000 in 1899 to $9.6 million by 1919. Spectator sports that often required expensive stadiums and fields also became popular, and crowds flocked to football, baseball, and basketball games, as well as to boxing and bicycle races. Automobile races were popular among the wealthy, ranging from dirt-track to cross-country contests. Offshore yachting contests began in 1904 with a race from New York to Marblehead. In 1906 American yachting enthusiasts first participated in two regattas that are still held in the 21st century: the Transpac Race from Los Angeles to Honolulu and the 600-mile Newport to Bermuda race.

Those who preferred quieter pastimes devoted themselves to such activities as reading, card games, music, listening to the radio, and gambling. Although the piano had been in American homes since 1700, it was not until the advent of the player piano in the 1890s that pianos became affordable to large segments of the population. By 1900 there was a plethora of perforated sheet music available for these pianos. Reformers insisted that children needed to be encouraged to engage in healthy entertainments, and cities began building public playgrounds and sand piles.

Before the 20th century vacations were generally restricted to more affluent Americans. In addition to frequent trips to Europe, wealthy Americans vacationed at popular summer resorts at Newport, Rhode Island, the Berkshires in Massachusetts, Long Branch and Cape May in New Jersey, White Sulphur

Well-dressed crowds on the boardwalk at Coney Island's Dreamland in 1904, the year it opened. Many buildings were painted white, much like the Chicago World's Fair.

Springs in West Virginia, and the Catskill, Great Smoky, and White Mountains. Hotels began springing up around major railroads and on the coasts. Travel agencies became increasingly important in planning trips, and the introduction of American Express traveler's checks in 1891 made travel much less threatening. Americans who could not afford wealthy resorts often settled for sojourns at new national parks that were opening around the country.

Held in 1893 in Chicago, the World's Columbian Exposition marked a turning point in American amusements, and amusement parks surfaced around the country, often at the end of trolley lines. One of the most popular attractions was the Ferris wheel designed by George Washington Gale Ferris at a cost of $35,000. The first Ferris wheel stood 264 ft. high, weighed 1,200 tons, and accommodated 2,160 riders. In addition to rides and food, most parks offered ring toss games, movies, penny arcades, and shooting galleries. The first modern-style amusement park was Water Chutes, constructed in Chicago by Paul Boynton. In 1895 Boynton opened Sea Lion Park on New York's Coney Island. Over the following eight years, three other parks were constructed at Coney Island: Steeplechase Park, Luna Park, and Dreamland. In 1914 a million people visited the Coney Island parks in a single day. During World War I their popularity declined, as did that of other parks around the country.

ENTERTAINING

Public entertainment in the Gay Nineties was often lavish, with hosts trying to outshine one another. One of the most lavish galas of the period took place in the spring of 1890 when New York's Shrine Theater was transformed into a Moorish Revival temple. Virtually all 525 members of the Shriners were in attendance, accompanied by female relatives or friends. The theme was chosen to compliment a production of *The Grand Duchess*, starring Lillian Russell. Each member of the audience, which was considered one of the most brilliant in New York history, was adorned with either a Turkish fez or tiger claw jewels. At the end of the second act, nobles Max Freeman and Harry Hallen were presented with jewels, and Lillian Russell was given a floral fez. All attendees were provided with souvenir programs.

The nation's capital was also the scene of extravagant entertainments. On January 8, 1890, at the traditional dinner for cabinet members, President and Mrs. Benjamin Harrison decorated the East Room with a border of palms and maidenhair fern. Cut flowers were scattered throughout the room, as were circular groupings of faux palms and foliage plants. Chandeliers were adorned with festoons of smilax, and a curtain of smilax and roses hung from

A typical upper-middle-class dining room table from the turn of the century with lace tablecloth, china, fine glassware, and silver.

the doorway. The mantles were embellished with potted plants banked by white hyacinths and scarlet gardenias and tulips. White palms with scarlet poinsettias were used in the Blue Room, and the Red and Green Rooms were adorned with palms and foliage.

In the state dining room, potted plants on the mantels were interspersed with white carnations and scarlet tulips with a drooping festoon of American Beauty roses. The centerpiece was composed of a floral arrangement of the ship of state floating on a mirrored lake flanked by coral reefs and yellow roses. Mounds of ferns with Pearl du Jardin roses were placed at either end of the table. Candles of silver and gold were decorated with yellow rose-shaped shades. Cut-glass dishes of *maron glace*, conserves, and nuts, were scattered along the length of the table. Each place setting contained five wine glasses and a water carafe. The First Lady wore white satin brocade accessorized with pearls and diamonds. The Second Lady shone in ruby velvet and diamonds.

Even children's entertainment was lavish during this period. On New Year's Eve 1889, the family of John Mclean of Washington, D.C., paid homage to 1890 by hosting a masked ball for their son Edward. Beginning at 3 P.M., the young host, wearing a white sailor suit, greeted guests decked out as queens, peasant maids, cowboys, cooks, sailors, courtiers, and characters from nursery rhymes. Flanked by eight Christmas trees and a room full of candles, Santa Claus distributed gifts. Guests included Vice President Morton, the secretary of state, the speaker of the house, several British nobles, and the Turkish and French ministers.

CONCLUSION

In the Progressive Era, new technology and mass production brought some of the previously unattainable luxuries of the Gilded Age to the masses. The growth of consumer culture and the development of national tastes through communication and marketing meant that families added many new products to their lists of wants and necessities. Telephones, electrical appliances, and automobiles all became widespread during this period. Glamorous department store "palaces" began catering to an increasingly sophisticated urban population and middle class that since then has never stopped desiring what the wealthy flaunt.

ELIZABETH R. PURDY

Further Readings

Adams, Judith. *The American Amusement Park Industry: A History of Technology and Thrills*. Boston, MA: Twayne, 1991.

Allen, Henry. *What It Felt Like: Living in the American Century*. New York: Pantheon, 2000.

Blake, Angela M. *How New York Became American, 1890–1924*. Baltimore, MD: Johns Hopkins University Press, 2006.

Braden, Donna R. *Leisure and Entertainment in America*. Dearborn, MI: Henry Ford Museum, 1988.

Dumenil, Lynn. *The Modern Temper: American Culture and Society in the 1920s*. New York: Hill and Wang, 1995.

Eyvig, David E. *Daily Life in the United States, 1920–1940: How Americans Lived through the "Roaring Twenties" and the Great Depression*. Chicago, IL: Ivan R. Dee, 2004.

Gowans, Alan. *Styles and Types of North American Architecture: Social Function and Cultural Expression*. New York: Icon, 1992.

Jacoby, Daniel. *Laboring for Freedom: A New Look at the History of Labor in America*. Armonk, NY: M.E. Sharpe, 1998.

Kronzberg, Melvin and Joseph Gies. *By the Sweat of Thy Brow: Work in the Western World*. New York: Putnam's, 1975.

Lebergott, Stanley. *Pursuing Happiness: American Consumerism in the Twentieth Century*. Princeton, NJ: Princeton University Press, 1993.

Marcus, Alan I. and Howard P. Segal. *Technology in America: A Brief History*. Fort Worth, TX: Harcourt Brace College Publications, 1999.

Scanlon, Jennifer. *The Gender and Consumer Culture Reader*. New York: New York University Press, 2000.

Schlereth, Thomas J. *Cultural History and Material Culture: Everyday Life, Landscapes, Museums*. Ann Arbor, MI: University of Michigan Press, 1990.

Schollander, Wendell and Wes Schollander. *Forgotten Elegance: The Art, Artifacts, and Peculiar History of Victorian and Edwardian Entertaining in America*. Westport, CT: Greenwood, 2002.

Sinclair, Upton. *The Jungle*. Urbana, IL: University of Illinois Press, 1988.

Skler, Robert. *Movie-Made America: A Cultural History of American Movies*. New York: Vintage, 1994.

Veblen, Thorstein. *The Theory of the Leisure Class: An Economic Study of Institutions*. New York: B.W. Huebsch, 1922.

Chapter 4

Social Attitudes

*"The supreme duty of the nation is the conservation
of human resources through ...
social and industrial justice."*
— Theodore Roosevelt

THE PERIOD FROM 1890 to 1920 was an exciting and often turbulent time for Americans. The country was in the process of moving from a rural, agricultural society to an urbanized, industrialized one. During this time millions of immigrants flocked to the United States, swelling the nation's cities, and introducing their various ethnic traditions and cultures. Since industrialization led to fewer required hands in farming, young native-born whites were moving from family farms to the cities, searching for new job opportunities and the excitement of urban life. African Americans were also on the move during this period. Many left the rural south to search for greater opportunities in northern cities and communities. The combination of population growth, movement of populations to the cities, industrialization, and scientific discoveries all contributed to an upheaval within American society that caused questioning and conflicts relating to issues such as immigration, labor, morality, religion, race, and gender.

Because these were new problems in American society, they required Americans to come up with new solutions. For this reason, the period from 1890 to 1920 is often referred to as the Progressive Era. The Progressive Era was a time of social awakening for Americans. They had to reexamine their institutions, their relationships with fellow Americans and, in some instances, American culture itself in their attempts to deal with the rapid changes occurring around them.

IMMIGRANTS

Between 1890 and 1920, the population grew by almost 70 percent, increasing from nearly 63 million to just over 106 million. This brought great change to the face of America, especially since more than a quarter of this growth was the direct result of immigration. Throughout the nation's history, much of the country's population growth had been due to immigration, but by 1890 immigration patterns had begun to change, causing consternation within mainstream society. For more than two centuries most immigrants to North America had been from northern and western Europe, but suddenly immigrants were arriving from southern and eastern European countries such as Italy, Greece, Poland, Austria-Hungary, and Russia. Some were escaping religious persecution, while others were looking forward to greater employment opportunities in the rapidly industrializing United States. The majority were poor and had received little education in their native lands, so they began their lives in America as unskilled laborers. Troubling to much of the native-born population was the fact that these "new" immigrants brought their native languages, traditions, and cultures with them to America. Most of these newcomers were of the Roman Catholic, Eastern Orthodox, or Jewish faiths, rather than sharing the Protestant faith of the majority of Americans. Mainstream Americans wondered if the newcomers could ever become assimilated into American society.

Some Americans reacted to the influx of the "new" immigrants by joining organizations like the Immigration Restriction League. Founded in 1894, the Immigration Restriction League lobbied for a literacy test for immigrants from southern and eastern Europe. Two years later Congress passed such a law, but President Grover Cleveland vetoed it. Many Americans agreed that such restrictions were not the answer to problems associated with immigration, feeling that a better response would be to educate the newcomers to become upstanding American citizens. Various groups, including large corporations and humanitarian reformers, began organizing "Americanization" classes. While most of the classes were educational, teaching the English language and American styles of dress and mores, some organizations attempted to convince immigrants to give up their entire culture.

While most immigrants welcomed the opportunity to become assimilated into American society, they also wanted to retain their traditional cultures. The various ethnic groups tended to reside in close-knit communities, to work together in the same industries, and to belong to immigrant associations. They preserved their heritage through newspapers in their native languages, churches and synagogues, parochial schools, and local organizations as they gradually learned to adapt to their new lives in America.

Nonwhite immigrants met with greater restrictions in their quest to live in America than did their white counterparts. In August 1882 Congress passed the Chinese Exclusion Act, prohibiting the entry of Chinese laborers, both

Moral Conflicts in America

The sense that the country's morals were rapidly declining was unsettling to many Americans at the turn of the century. Middle-class Americans in particular had placed high value upon the unwritten code of personal behavior that had become associated with Britain's Queen Victoria, often referred to as "Victorian morality." With its stress upon morals, manners, industriousness, and proper behavior, Victorian morality played an important role in creating distinctions among social groups and classes. The upper and middle classes adopted a self-righteous outlook, and used the Victorian code to judge and control a tumultuous, multi-ethnic, urban, industrial society.

Under the Victorian code women were given license to participate in purity crusades, prohibition campaigns, and other reform movements. Yet, at the same time, women were restricted to the "women's sphere," which was centered on the home. The 1890s saw challenges to Victorian ideas of the proper roles for women, as increasing numbers of young women were attending college, delaying marriage, and entering the professions. They were also adopting more practical clothing styles, in keeping with their participation in golf, tennis, and bicycling. For many Americans, such behavior brought concerns that these "new women" were undermining social stability. They were particularly troubled by the drop in the nation's birthrate, which fell from 33 per 1,000 in 1900, to 28 per 1,000 in 1920. Most of the trend toward smaller families came from the mainly Protestant middle and upper classes, not from the immigrant working class. While marriage was often delayed, divorce rates were on the rise, practically doubling between 1880 and 1900, and continuing to rise over the next two decades.

Largely due to Victorian morality, Americans avoided discussing sexual matters until the end of the 19th century. When progressive reformers began pushing for investigations and legislation to regulate prostitution and white slavery, and held public campaigns to fight venereal diseases, much of the general public was shocked. But soon Americans were freely discussing such issues as prostitution, age of consent, free love, and birth control. States passed age of consent laws, cities established vice commissions, and in 1910 the U.S. Congress passed the Mann Act, prohibiting the interstate transportation of white slaves.

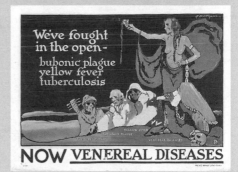

This circa 1918 poster was part of an attempt to begin to address venereal disease among World War I soldiers.

skilled and unskilled, for a period of 10 years. In 1892 this law was extended for another 10 years under the Geary Act, which also placed severe and unprecedented restrictions upon Chinese people already living in the United States, and presumed that unless a Chinese person could prove otherwise, he or she was in the country illegally. Anti-Chinese agitators were disappointed when few deportations occurred as a result of the act. Nevertheless the number of Chinese living and working in the United States decreased from approximately 125,000 in 1882 to just over 60,000 in 1920.

Between 1890 and 1910 the Japanese population in the United States swelled from about 2,000 to nearly 75,000. Most settled on the Pacific Coast, with approximately 40,000 Japanese in California in 1910. While there were smatterings of anti-Japanese activity in California during the 1890s, a much stronger anti-Japanese movement developed along the Pacific Coast beginning in 1900. That year the American Federation of Labor urged Congress to extend the existing prohibitions against Chinese laborers to include the Japanese. In 1905 the *San Francisco Chronicle* began a crusade against Japanese immigrants and the California state legislature sent a resolution to Congress

A blackboard and instructional sign in a Japanese school in Tacoma, Washington. Built in 1922, it was the second Japanese language school constructed by Japanese immigrants in the northwest.

asking that limitations be placed upon Japanese immigration. Japanese businesses were boycotted, and the San Francisco School Board ordered that Japanese children attend the same segregated schools as Chinese students. The country of Japan was much more powerful than China in 1905, and President Theodore Roosevelt did not want to cause a breakdown of Japanese-American diplomacy. Hearing of the School Board's decision, Roosevelt stepped in, and the school board backed down.

Between 1890 and 1920 Congress made several attempts to put greater restrictions upon immigration. Most failed, but in 1917 Congress overrode President Woodrow Wilson's veto to establish a literacy test for immigrants. Americans pushing to limit the influx of people from other cultures were now beginning to have their way. During World War I there was a surge in the movement for "100 percent Americanism," aimed especially at German immigrants and their descendants. Through violence and intimidation on the part of local vigilante groups, German-Americans were forced to swear allegiance to the United States and to give up their newspapers, clubs, and language.

HAWAII

The American annexation of Hawaii in 1898 caused some unforeseen problems for Americans once they realized that the majority of Hawaii's population was nonwhite. When Hawaii became a territory of the United States in 1900, all Hawaiian citizens became citizens of the United States. While they were not all citizens, three-quarters of Hawaii's population was of Japanese or Chinese ancestry, meaning that their children would all be U.S. citizens at birth. Despite fulfilling the qualifications for statehood, and numerous petitions beginning in 1903, Congress was reluctant to grant statehood to a territory with a nonwhite majority. Hawaii did not become a state until 1959.

NATIVE AMERICANS

The late 19th century found Native Americans struggling for existence. The Dawes Act of 1887 had provided for the division of their reservations. Some of the land was allotted to Native Americans for farming, but most of the land eventually ended up in the hands of whites. In 1890 many Native Americans began participating in the Ghost Dance religious ceremony, which they believed would bring back their lands and cause the whites to disappear. White Americans' misunderstanding of the Ghost Dance led to their belief that the Native Americans were planning an uprising, and to the massacre of about 200 Teton Sioux by the U.S. Calvary at Wounded Knee in South Dakota on December 29, 1890.

Over the next three decades circumstances remained dire for the Native American. Government policy and white reformers' beliefs of what was best for the Native American led to a push for their assimilation into mainstream culture. By 1895 there were 157 Indian boarding schools operating in the

Native American students in uniforms and nearly identical calico dresses in a choir at the Flandreau Indian School in South Dakota after the turn of the century.

United States, working to rid Native American children of their "barbaric" cultures and languages, and "Americanize" them. Just as they wanted for immigrants, both the government and reformers wanted Native Americans to become hard-working, patriotic American citizens. The result was a breakdown of Native-American culture without complete assimilation. Ironically, while whites were keen to eliminate Native-American traditions and culture, they paid money to be entertained by Native-Americans in their traditional dress in the traveling Wild West shows.

THE POOR

In 1890 the publication of journalist Jacob Riis's *How the Other Half Lives*, an illustrated and photographic tour of poverty-stricken New York neighborhoods, opened the eyes of middle-class readers to the conditions under which the urban poor were struggling to survive. Most of the book's readers had never seen anything like the grimy, airless tenements where the poor made their homes, and the suffocating sweatshops where they spent long hours trying to eke out a living. Other journalists had reported on the dirty, smelly, disease-infested tenements, but Riis, accompanied by a photographer using the recently invented flash photography, was able to capture pictures of dark basements and alleys.

"Scientific Racism"

The late 19th and early 20th centuries witnessed a growing interest in the sciences, including the budding social sciences. A significant number of intellectuals associated with the various scientific fields developed and promoted theories that supported racism. Without true scientific evidence, some Social Darwinists tried to apply Charles Darwin's theories of natural evolution to society. Sociologist Edward A. Ross of Johns Hopkins University, and John R. Commons of the University of Wisconsin, shared the belief that some human beings had further evolved than others and could better use their brains to establish laws and to govern. Physicians, physical anthropologists, and historians joined with other intellectuals by offering theories of white superiority. Likely the most influential among historians was William Archibald Dunning of Columbia University, who wrote books and taught young historians that blacks were an inferior and savage race, and thus needed to be controlled.

Psychologists of the early 20th century developed the IQ test, an "intelligence" test that supported many of their assumptions about race and ethnicity. Tests administered to native whites, immigrants, and blacks, resulted in much higher scores for native whites, and blacks in particular were graded "mentally inferior." While scientists have since found these tests to have been highly flawed, and therefore unreliable, the data was taken seriously at the time and for decades to follow.

The field of eugenics, the idea of improving the hereditary qualities of human stock, rose to prominence during the Progressive Era, particularly between 1910 and 1914, when numerous articles on the topic appeared in print. In a time when America saw a surge of dark-skinned immigrants, scientists helped set off fears that the Anglo-Saxons, with ever-shrinking families, were committing "race suicide." Seventeen states responded to the outcry 1907–17, with legislation that authorized the sterilization of people deemed inferior or dangerous.

There were some intellectuals who refused to accept the racist theories. One objector was cultural anthropologist Frank Boas of Columbia University, who believed that environment played a greater role than heredity in human development.

The growing awareness of the dark side of city life drew increasing numbers of middle-class Americans to take steps to improve conditions for the working poor. Some among the middle class believed that the first step to addressing the problems in the nation's slums was to take up residence there and open facilities within poor neighborhoods. They felt that only by personally experiencing the conditions that the poor faced every day could they truly

This 1883 magazine cover drawing entitled "Homes of the Poor" contributed to a growing consciousness of poor urban living conditions.

understand what needed to be done to help them.

Going into the urban slums to address the problems of the poor began in the 1880s with the Social Gospel movement and the establishment of settlement houses, but gained strength in the 1890s and early 1900s. Believing that Christians should follow the teachings of Jesus and engage in self sacrifice to help reduce poverty and improve living and working conditions for the less fortunate, Social Gospel leaders encouraged fellow Christians to join them in the movement. The first settlement house in the United States began operation in 1886. Five years later there were six settlements. From that point the movement experienced rapid growth, with settlement houses numbering approximately 400 in 1910. The settlement houses were largely staffed with young, energetic residents eager to participate in social reform by bridging the socioeconomic gap between rich and poor. Many residents were recent college graduates, often young women who had found that there were few other occupations open to college educated women. Although projects varied from one settlement house to another, the houses often served as meeting places for laborers, as safe places for children to play, and as centers for education in personal hygiene, child care, history, the arts, and "Americanization." Settlement house leaders campaigned on such issues as worker safety, local sanitation, and child labor laws.

LABOR

Laborers working long hours, often under dangerous conditions, and for little pay, received scant attention from the American middle class. It was not until the Depression of the mid-1890s affected people of all classes that some reformers realized that unemployment and poverty were not always due to individual failings. Wealth came to entrepreneurs who had the expertise to take advantage of the industrializing of America, and who were able to exploit

Boys in a woodcarving class at the King Philip Settlement House in Fall River, Massachusetts, in 1916. The boys worked in textile mills, iron works, stores, and a barber shop.

workers who were often recent immigrants. By the end of the 19th century, some workers had responded to their plight by unionizing, but the majority of workers did not organize. Most Americans, especially those of the middle and upper classes, did not trust unions, largely due to fears that they were associated with communists and anarchists.

By the early 20th century, reformers were paying an increasing amount of attention to the plight of workers, and in some instances came to their aid. This was particularly true in regard to helping working women. Founded in 1903, the Women's Trade Union League was comprised of working-class and upper- and middle-class women, who worked to eliminate sweatshop wages and conditions by political lobbying and by boycotting goods produced under conditions that did not meet with their approval. The National Consumers League, organized in 1899, was involved in similar campaigns.

With the onset of World War I, and the accompanying need to attract labor in industry, labor unions made significant gains for their workers in income and the reduction of working hours, and union membership almost doubled. However concerns about the rise of communism in America followed the Bolshevist victory over the moderates in Russia, and a Red Scare erupted in the United States in 1919. Fueled by corporate propaganda, the general public again came to fear that unions, especially those advocating strikes, were teeming with radicals.

WHITE COLLAR WORKERS

Those employed in white-collar occupations often felt they were superior to workers in blue-collar jobs. Overall, those hired as managers, clerks, and supervisors had achieved higher levels of education than those employed in blue-collar work. A good command of the English language was important, so most office workers were native-born Americans, though many were sons and daughters of immigrants on the path to upward mobility.

The United States saw a tremendous increase in clerical occupations in the late 19th and early 20th centuries, with numbers almost doubling with each passing decade. Much of the increase was made up of women, who were being hired for office work in rapidly increasing numbers. In 1890 women held 64 percent of typist and stenographic positions, but by 1920, they held 92 percent of those jobs. Men entered clerical work with the hope of advancing into management positions, but for women promotions were rare. Both employers and society expected that women would marry and leave their jobs within a few years of their hiring, and their wages were kept low compared with those of men. Some advantages of white-collar over blue-collar work included shorter hours, and usually an annual two-week paid vacation. Office workers also enjoyed the social prestige of their white-collar work.

JIM CROW

Devised by whites, Jim Crow was a system of laws and social conventions designed to discriminate against African Americans. Others, including Asians, Hispanics, Catholics, and Jews were affected to some extent as well. Although Jim Crow could be found throughout the United States, it was essentially a southern phenomenon. Once Reconstruction ended in 1877, southerners tried to restore as much of the old master/slave system as possible. By the 1890s the concept of white superiority dominated the social and political fabric of the entire region. While blacks who lived in the north were able to hold onto most of the gains that they had made during the era of Reconstruction, particularly in the area of education, southern blacks were denied almost every right and protection provided for American citizens under the U.S. Constitution. Poll taxes, literacy tests, "white-only" primaries, and intimidation kept blacks from voting in southern states. They were tried by solely white juries, confined to segregated sections of trains and trolleys, and sent to segregated schools (if a school was available). By 1890 large numbers of blacks had

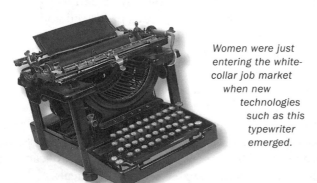

Women were just entering the white-collar job market when new technologies such as this typewriter emerged.

National Association for the Advancement of Colored People (NAACP)

Violent acts committed against African Americans, particularly during race riots at Springfield, Illinois during the summer of 1908, inspired the founding of the NAACP early in 1909. The founders, a multi-racial group of people, included Ida Wells-Barnett, W.E.B. DuBois, Henry Moscowitz, Mary White Ovington, Oswald Garrison Villiard, and William English Walling. In an era fraught with racism, the NAACP began its struggle to address social injustices that African Americans faced on an almost daily basis in early 20th-century America. During its first year the organization drew some prominent American reformers, including settlement house founder Jane Addams, feminist leader Harriet Stanton Blatch, Professor John Dewey, and Rabbi Stephen S. Wise, and by the end of 1910 membership numbered in the hundreds. That year, leaders of the five-year-old all-black organization known as the Niagara Movement decided that they too would join forces with the NAACP.

Despite the enthusiastic response of many reformers, progress was slow for the young organization during its early years. The NAACP lost its first case before the Supreme Court, a case that involved a black farm worker who had unwittingly killed a police officer who had broken into his home to arrest him on a civil charge in the middle of the night. Despite the loss before the Supreme Court, members of the NAACP became determined to continue their efforts to fight for justice for black Americans. The NAACP protested on a nationwide scale in 1915 when D.W. Griffith released his film about Reconstruction in the south, *The Birth of a Nation*, which portrayed Republicans and blacks as villains and celebrated the Ku Klux Klan.

The NAACP scored several victories in the late 1910s, with the Supreme Court's ruling in *Buchanan v. Warley*, in 1917, that cities could not officially segregate African Americans into specific areas, and, that same year, with the Army's decision to allow blacks to be commissioned as officers. The following year, President Wilson gave in to NAACP pressure and made a public statement in opposition to the practice of lynching. From the time of its founding, the NAACP never ceased its struggle for equality of justice, and continues its work to the present day.

moved to the north to escape discrimination and intimidation and to find better opportunities for employment, but it was not until World War I that blacks began to pour into the north in vast numbers.

Over the years, African Americans occasionally sued to defend their rights as American citizens, but rarely won. In one of the most famous Supreme

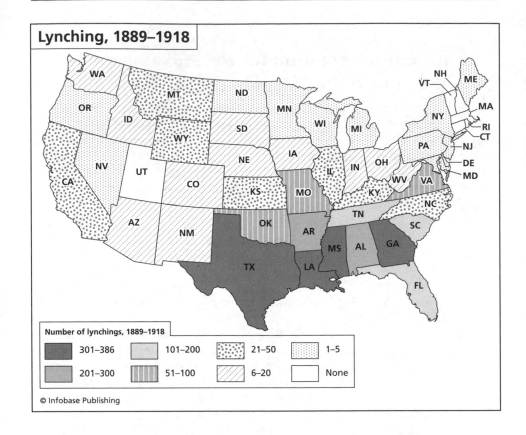

Lynching, 1889–1918

Number of lynchings, 1889–1918

- 301–386
- 201–300
- 101–200
- 51–100
- 21–50
- 6–20
- 1–5
- None

© Infobase Publishing

Court cases to deal with racism in America, *Plessy v. Ferguson*, in 1896, the court ruled that Homer Plessy had violated the Louisiana Separate Car Act by boarding a "whites only" railroad carriage. The court ruled that separation by race was legal so long as both whites and blacks were offered largely equal services and facilities. This landmark case legitimized Jim Crow in law, leaving southern racists free to discriminate against African Americans for decades to come. Southern states were given the go ahead to make decisions as to what qualified as "separate but equal," and southern blacks found themselves using facilities and receiving services that were vastly inferior to those accommodating whites. Black students often found themselves going to school in run-down shacks, with few textbooks. Workers were segregated in their places of employment, though blacks were usually placed in the dirtiest and least desirable jobs.

One hopeful sign for African Americans came in 1917 when the U.S. Supreme Court ruled in the *Buchanan v. Warley* case that it was unconstitutional for cities to legislate segregated-neighborhood ordinances. A number of large southern cities had passed laws restricting blacks' freedom to reside outside designated zones, and some smaller towns had been excluding blacks altogether. Although the 1917 decision was based upon property rights and did not render segregation unconstitutional, it did reveal that the nation's highest court was not adverse to establishing limits to Jim Crow.

After the outbreak of World War I in 1914, American industry in the north and west needed more workers. Hundreds of thousands of southern blacks answered the call. If the African Americans seeking opportunities in the north had believed they would escape racism by moving to the north, they were wrong. Although they did not have to endure the segregation found in the south and were given the opportunity to vote, they still faced discrimination. The newcomers were generally not as well educated as blacks born and raised in the north, and were often viewed by the working class as competition for the low-paying jobs. This would soon lead to racial tension that frequently developed into rioting, and sometimes murder. Blacks moving north usually found themselves in segregated ghettos, and white proprietors of restaurants and hotels could discriminate against African Americans if they wished. When the United States entered World War I, African Americans found themselves in a segregated military. President Woodrow Wilson shared the racist views of most southerners, and had no incentive to make adjustments to Jim Crow.

American society's acceptance of Jim Crow in relation to African Americans helped to justify discrimination against other groups considered "outsiders." These included Chinese, Japanese, and other Asians, as well as Hispanics, Jews, and Catholics. Discrimination ranged from segregation, as in the case of Chinese and Japanese on the west coast, to exclusion from jobs, colleges, and

In 1917 one teacher was in charge of 123 kindergarten and first grade children at this severely overcrowded school for African Americans in Muskogee, Oklahoma.

private facilities, as was frequently the experience of Jews and, to some extent, Catholics. In the west and southwest, registrars at the polls kept Hispanics from voting in much the same way that blacks were disfranchised in the south.

WOMEN

Society's attitudes regarding the place of women underwent considerable change during the period from 1890 to 1920. For instance, in 1890 only the state of Wyoming gave women the right to vote, and only three states, Utah, Colorado, and Idaho were added to the woman suffrage column by 1900. Yet in 1920 the Nineteenth Amendment was added to the U.S. Constitution, granting women full voting rights in all states and territories.

In addition to winning the vote, women made gains in education, the workplace, and in society as a whole. During the last quarter of the 19th century women had increasingly become involved in public activities, and by the 1890s they were heavily involved in charitable causes, social reform movements, and organizations aimed at beautifying their local communities. Groups such as the Women's Christian Temperance Union (WCTU), the Young Women's Christian Association (YWCA), and the General Federation of Women's Clubs drew women into their organizations nationwide. By 1900 the WCTU, the largest women's organization in the country, had 500,000 members. At the same time, the number of women graduating from the nation's colleges was on the increase, as was the number of women holding jobs outside of the home. Yet at the turn of the century opportunities for women, black or white, highly educated or not, were limited in comparison with those available for men. Jobs as clerks and domestic workers, and work in the textile industries were those most frequently occupied by young, single women. A woman with more education would be found in teaching, nursing, social work, or similar work because those jobs conformed to the idea of women as nurturers, and because parallels could be drawn between traditionally "female" jobs and women's role within the home. When World War I broke out, many women were drawn from their traditional jobs to go to work in industries and occupations that were normally considered to be positions that could only be handled by men. Although at war's end most women returned to their former type of

Back our girls over there Y.W.C.A. United War Work Campaign

This YWCA poster shows an American woman working as a telephone operator in Europe during World War I.

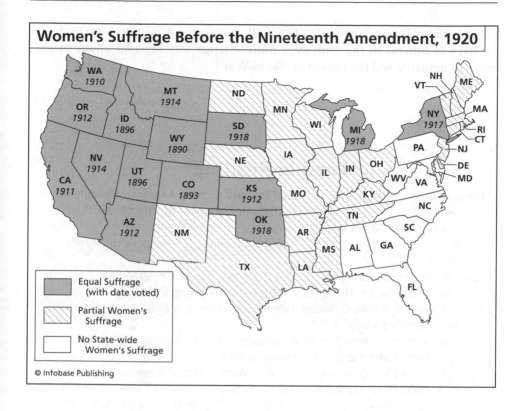

Women's Suffrage Before the Nineteenth Amendment, 1920

WA 1910
MT 1914
ND
OR 1912
ID 1896
MN
NH
VT
ME
MA
NY 1917
RI
CT
SD 1918
WI
MI 1918
PA
NJ
WY 1890
NE
IA
IL
IN
OH
DE
MD
NV 1914
UT 1896
WV
VA
CA 1911
CO 1893
KS 1912
MO
KY
NC
AZ 1912
NM
OK 1918
AR
TN
SC
MS
AL
GA
TX
LA
FL

Equal Suffrage (with date voted)

Partial Women's Suffrage

No State-wide Women's Suffrage

© Infobase Publishing

work, they did help to bring about an expanded view of women's capabilities. This influenced the outcome of the vote on the Nineteenth Amendment.

While middle-class white women fought for social reforms and for women's rights, they often excluded working-class women, and frequently excluded black women. Many of the middle and upper-class women campaigning for suffrage advocated an "educated suffrage," feeling that they were better qualified to vote than the normally less-educated immigrant males who were accepted at the polls. Campaigns to prohibit the sale of alcohol in the United States created conflicts between middle-class women, who pointed out the hardships faced by wives and children of heavy drinkers, and working-class males, who relied upon alcohol consumption as an escape from their overworked and often dreary lives. Women often found it difficult to accept the reality of needing the support of these male voters in their quest for women's right to vote. It was not until after the Eighteenth Amendment was added to the Constitution (1919), making Prohibition the law of the land, that women obtained the vote.

Rapid change in the Progressive Era had forced many people to reevaluate their thinking about those different from themselves, but with mixed results. Racism remained entrenched, with many African Americans finding no way out except to migrate north, and with some Asian migrants banned from the country entirely. On the other hand, some native-born Americans experienced a social awakening and made significant efforts—some misguided—to improve the lives of others. In the end, even more change was brought about by the needs of industry and the nation in World War I.

JUNE MELBY BENOWITZ

Further Readings

Carson, Mina. *Settlement Folk: Social Thought and the American Settlement Movement, 1885–1930*. Chicago, IL: University of Chicago Press, 1990.

Chambers, John Whiteclay, III. *The Tyranny of Change: America in the Progressive Era, 1890–1920*. New Brunswick, NJ: Rutgers University Press, 2000.

Daniels, Roger. *Guarding the Golden Door: American Immigration Policy and Immigrants Since 1882*. New York: Hill and Wang, 2004.

Diner, Steven J. *A Very Different Age: Americans of the Progressive Era*. New York: Hill and Wang, 1998.

Edwards, Rebecca. *New Spirits: Americans in the Gilded Age, 1865–1905*. New York: Oxford University Press, 2006.

Kennedy, David M.. *Over Here: The First World War and American Society*. New York: Oxford University Press, 1980.

Kessler-Harris, Alice. *Out to Work: A History of Wage-Earning Women in the United States*. New York: Oxford University Press, 2003.

McDonnell, Janet A. *The Dispossession of the American Indian, 1887–1934*. Bloomington, IN: Indiana University Press, 1991.

National Association for the Advancement of Colored People. "Timeline." Available online: http://www.naacp.org/about/history/timeline/. Accessed June 2007.

Ohio History Society. "Social Gospel Movement." Ohio History Central: An Online Encyclopedia of Ohio History, 2005. Available online: http://ohiohistorycentral.org/entry.php?rec=1527. Accessed May 2007.

O'Neil, William L. *The Progressive Years: America Comes of Age*. New York: Dodd, Mead and Company, 1975.

Packard, Jerrold W. *American Nightmare: The History of Jim Crow*. New York: St. Martins Griffin, 2002.

Pivar, David J. *Purity Crusade: Sexual Morality and Social Control, 1868–1900*. Westport, CT: Greenwood Press, Inc., 1973.

Prucha, Francis Paul, ed. *Americanizing the American Indians: Writings by the 'Friends of the Indian.'* Lincoln, NE: University of Nebraska Press, 1973.

Riis, Jacob A. *How the Other Half Lives: Studies Among the Tenements of New York*. New York: Charles Scribner's Sons, 1890.

Southern, David W. *The Progressive Era and Race: Reaction and Reform, 1900–1917*. Wheeling, IL: Harlan Davidson, Inc., 2005.

Chapter 5

Cities and Urban Life

*"The foundation for all good city government
must be laid in ... civil service reform."*
— Herbert Welsh

THE PERIOD BETWEEN 1880 and 1920 saw the transformation of urban America from a colorful bit-player in the background of the agrarian scene, to the engine of a modern industrial power. Between 1880 and 1900, the percentage of Americans living in cities grew from 28 to 40 percent. In 1880 only New York City had a population of more than one million. By 1920 New York City was home to 5.6 million people, followed by 2.7 million in Chicago, 1.8 million in Philadelphia, 993,000 in Detroit, and 800,000 in Cleveland. These new urban centers were often dirty, dusty, and disagreeable—but at the same time, they were lively, exciting and innovative. For all their faults, by the turn of the century they had become the nexus of American culture.

Not all this extraordinary growth came from native-born Americans moving from rural regions. A steady drip of immigration in the 1870s gave way to a deluge during the next four decades. Between 1881 and 1890, 5.2 million new citizens arrived from overseas, followed by 3.7 million between 1891 and 1900, and a staggering 8.8 million between 1901 and 1910. In 1905, 1906, and 1907, immigrants were arriving at a rate of more than a million a year, with the peak coming in 1907 at 1,285,349.

The face of late-19th and early-20th century immigration was much different from the pre-1880 picture. For generations the vast majority of immigrants had hailed from Ireland, England, and Germany, but now the average immigrant was more likely to come from Italy, Russia, or vast, crumbling Austria-Hungary. Croats, Slovaks, Slovenes, Poles, Lithuanians, and Greeks were as common as Irish or Germans. These new immigrant groups spoke unfamiliar languages, and were more likely to be Eastern Orthodox or Orthodox Jews than Protestants or Catholics.

While many had come to take advantage of the wide-open spaces of the west, millions ended up in the cities. By the 1890s there were more Germans in Chicago than there were in any German city except Berlin and Hamburg; there were more Swedes than there were in any Swedish city except Stockholm and Göteborg. Often downtrodden and discriminated against, these immigrants nevertheless enlivened urban life with their cultures, foods, celebrations, religious practices, and languages.

HABITAT

Crowded cities had to move upward as well as outward and skylines began to change. Prior to the 1880s most American buildings were under six stories tall. Masonry buildings could only go so high, and there was a decided lack of convenience in tall buildings without elevators. America's first skyscraper rose in Chicago in 1884–85: the Home Insurance Building on the corner of LaSalle and Adams streets. This nine-story structure was an innovative combination of old and new engineering. It was constructed on a granite foundation with a frame of steel, cast, and wrought iron. Steel-frame building was the technique that made it possible for buildings to soar, and the "Chicago frame" was soon duplicated in population centers around the country.

Chicago and New York City became locked in competition for the tallest buildings in the 1880s and early 1890s, but New York quickly took the lead with the New York World Building (1890) at 20 stories; the Park Row Building (1899) at 30 stories; the Singer Building (1908) at 47 stories; the Met Life Tower (1909) at 50 stories; the Woolworth Building (1913) at 57 stories; and culminating with the Chrysler Building (1930) at 77 stories and the Empire State Building (1931) at 102 stories. The Empire State Building remained the world's tallest for more than 40 years.

While these were the highest points on the American urban skyline, they were quickly joined by taller and larger "apartment" buildings, a type of dwelling space first called the "French flat" when they appeared in New York City in the 1870s. Apartment living was nothing new in Europe—the word "flat" is a corruption of the Scottish "flaet," meaning story or floor, and was used to describe single-family apartments in the crowded city of Edinburgh at least as early as the 16th century. But in America, the idea of the city flat had become tainted by the overcrowded tenements of the immigrant quarters, and "respectable" families generally lived with family or in boarding houses, where they had one or two private rooms, but shared communal meals and facilities. They were meant to be transitional housing, until a family could afford a private home of their own. As urban land grew more expensive, home-ownership became more difficult, and people were willing to accept the idea of the apartment as a permanent home, especially if it came with amenities like built-in closets, private bathrooms, central heating, and a well-equipped kitchen. By 1900, 75 percent of urban Americans lived in apartments. Even the rich and famous had taken to the lifestyle, and some apartment buildings had become

The Woolworth Building towered over surrounding buildings in New York City in 1913, but was quickly surpassed in height in the following years.

the most sought-after addresses in the country. The Dakota, one of a number of magnificent structures that had risen along the western face of New York City's Central Park in the 1880s, had its own wine cellar and tennis courts and offered its wealthy clientele suites of up to 20 rooms—a far cry from the slums of the Lower East Side, just a few miles away.

Modern tenements got their start in a design competition held in 1879. Architects tried to devise a way to allow landlords to maximize profits from the standard 100 x 25 ft. city lot, while meeting new city requirements that each room have at least one window. The new "dumbbell" tenements were characterized by an air shaft between the tightly-packed lots, making the buildings appear narrow in the middle and wider at the two ends. In reality, they were simply narrow, and remained dark and airless. Commonly, dumbbell tenements were six stories high, and each floor contained four apartments with three rooms, the largest of which was about 11 x 13 ft. Tenants had galley kitchens with a tub-sink and a wood-burning stove, but shared common bathrooms located either in the hallway landing on each floor, or in outdoor privies in the small back courtyards. The hallways usually had no windows, and one resident said that in navigating these halls, "one tumbles over human obstacles and other obstacles, especially little children."

The air shafts that were supposed to make the apartments feel less dark and claustrophobic were so narrow that it was often possible to reach out the window and shake hands with the neighbor in the next building. They became a dumping pit for kitchen refuse and garbage, creating a stink for the residents and a sanitation problem for the cities. The air shafts were also safety hazards, acting as funnels for fires, allowing whole blocks of buildings to go up in flames.

In 1901 the dumbbell design was outlawed for good, and New Law housing had to contain more spacious courtyards, a requirement that virtually outlawed building on single 100 x 25 ft. lots. New Law tenements, as they were sometimes called,

The exterior of a narrow New York City tenement house with laundry on the railings in 1912.

A few of the victims of the Triangle Shirtwaist Company fire being placed in coffins. With exits barred, hundreds of workers had no choice but to jump from the upper floors of the building.

had to have lighting in the hallways and private bathrooms connected to city sewer lines. Improved tenement design certainly did not solve all the problems of the urban poor, but it was a positive step forward.

WORK

While millions of American city dwellers went off to work each morning in pleasant shops, office buildings, and eateries, and were paid a decent, if not always munificent, wage for their labor, millions more labored in unsafe factories and industries for pennies a day. The plight of the working poor was a major focus of Progressive Era reformers, and as the idea of collective action became more popular, it fueled much of the labor unrest of the period.

The "sweatshop" was nothing new in labor history. A "sweater" was a term coined in 1840s England, at the very beginnings of the Industrial Revolution, to describe a worker who toiled hard for his or her pay. In 1890s America a sweatshop could be a run-down factory, or the bedroom of a crowded tenement house where a family worked 16 hours a day at piecework as subcontractors.

The problems and perils of sweatshop work was brought into tragic focus on Saturday, March 25, 1911, when a fire broke out at the Triangle Shirtwaist Company, located on the top three floors of the Asch Building at 32-29 Washington Place in Manhattan. Five hundred employees, mostly Eastern European and Italian, and some as young as 12, were nearing the end of their average 14-hour shift when fire broke out on the eighth floor. The workers tried to escape, only to find some doors locked and the stairwells and fire escapes choked with smoke and debris. Hundreds were forced to jump from the upper floors, attempting to reach safety nets held by firefighters below. One hundred and forty-one women died at the scene, and another seven died in the hospital—the single biggest loss of life in the workplace until the terrorist attacks of September 11, 2001.

FINANCIAL PANICS

The working poor were among the hardest hit from the financial panics, or depressions, that occurred between 1890 and 1920. The worst economic crisis came in January 1893. As with most depressions, the Panic of 1893 had many causes, including collapsing wheat prices that had touched off a wave of farm foreclosures, and a decline in railroad investments, which caused downturns in the steel industry. The final blow came with a severe drop in U.S. gold reserves, when frantic citizens raced to convert their silver currency to gold as silver prices plummeted. The Panic of 1893 lasted until 1896, with the effects felt in some quarters until the turn of the century.

The unemployment rate reached 20 to 25 percent in some industrial areas, and hovered at 12 to 14 percent overall. The ripple effect of so many out-of-work citizens was felt throughout society. Marriage and birth rates dropped slightly, as young people put off their weddings, and those who were already married avoided pregnancies. Evictions rose, with a single courtroom in New York City hearing 150 eviction cases in March 1894 alone. Arrests for vagrancy rose 40 percent in Baltimore, 29 percent in Manhattan, and 27 percent in

Settlement Houses

The settlement movement was a social movement that originated in England in the 1880s as a way for the middle-class Christian community to reach out to the urban poor, and it was quickly exported across the Atlantic as a way to help the burgeoning immigrant communities of America. Settlement houses offered immigrants a place to take a bath or have a hot meal, as well as learn English or a new trade, or participate in social clubs and excursions. Much of the outreach was directed toward young mothers, who were provided daycare, mothering classes, and even dispensaries for food and medicine should their children fall ill. The best-known American settlement houses were Hull House in Chicago and the Henry Street Settlement in New York City, but there were more than 500 settlement houses in operation all over the country by 1920.

Railroad tracks running by a row of old factories in York, Pennsylvania. During the financial panics of the late 19th century, manufacturing, railroads, and steel were all vulnerable.

Philadelphia between 1893 and 1894. In the comparatively small city of Buffalo, 11 percent of all arrests in 1894 were for vagrancy. Fears of anarchy were high. In 1894 populist leader Jacob Coxey led several hundred unemployed men on a march to Washington, D.C. to demand the government provide jobs through public works programs. Equally disquieting was the Pullman Strike of 1894, when a walkout by 125,000 strikers essentially shut down the American railroad system. The military was sent in to break the strike, and violence between the strikers and strikebreakers left 13 dead, 57 wounded, and did the equivalent of $6.8 million in damage.

Even the boom towns of the far west felt the impact of the panic. Seattle, which had been on track to become the most important city in the Pacific Northwest, saw the collapse of the region's timber and silver industries. Eleven banks failed in the first year of the panic, and local land values dropped by 80 percent. It was only the fortuitous discovery of gold in the late 1890s that got the city back on its economic track.

SANITATION
Overall the health of American city-dwellers improved dramatically between 1890 and 1920, largely due to improvements in city planning and sanitation. About one-half of all deaths in the late 19th century came from environmental causes, whether waterborne, airborne, or food-borne. These were the areas of

How the Other Half Lives

Jacob Riis in 1904. His 1890 book How the Other Half Lives *shed light on the lives of the urban poor for middle-class readers.*

Jacob Riis was one of the millions of Europeans who emigrated to America in the 19th century. The Danish-American carpenter arrived in New York City in 1870 at the age of 21, and spent his early years as just another faceless, poor immigrant in the city slums. By 1874 he was a police reporter for a city newspaper, and became a voice for the downtrodden of New York City.

Riis was one of the first photographers to use flash-powder, allowing him to take flash photos of immigrants living in dark apartments and working in dark sweatshops, and of orphan children sleeping in dark alleys. These photos brought the plight of the urban poor into sharp relief to middle-class Americans, who had not previously comprehended the depth of the problem.

most interest to an emerging generation of engineers, public health officials, landscape architects, and city planners.

In the early and mid-19th century, water sources were privately owned, either by property owners with backyard wells, or as the cities grew, businesses and corporations. By 1910 about 70 percent of cities with a population greater than 30,000 had moved to municipally-owned water systems. Construction of municipal sewer systems had begun in earnest in the 1870s, and picked up speed in the 1890s. By 1907 nearly every large city had a modern sewer system in place.

Municipal water and sewer added new levels of government bureaucracy, since once built, these systems required substantial workforces to keep them in good order. In the early years there were frequent squabbles between municipalities laying along the same water source. It was not uncommon for one city to have their sewer outflow directly upstream from another city's freshwater intake. While this was sometimes due to topography, often it was simply a matter of poor planning or thoughtlessness. By the 1910s, regional planning commissions were established to help settle conflicts and better allocate resources.

The cost and effort proved worthwhile: between 1910 and 1920 the American Medical Association estimated that the death rate from typhoid fever dropped from 19.6 deaths per 100,000 to 3.5 deaths per 100,000 in 57 of the largest American cities. In the very largest population centers, it fell even more sharply, dropping to 2.3 deaths per 100,000. Pittsburgh saw the biggest decrease, falling from 65 deaths per 100,000 in 1906 to 2.7 deaths per 100,000 in 1920.

Food safety also saw improvement during the Progressive Era. America had been an agrarian nation for the better part of 250 years, with most people relying on home-grown or local food sources. As the urban population became the majority, more and more people were relying on commercial food production. By the 1890s it was clear to many consumers that what they were purchasing was not always accurately reflected on the food label. Flour adulterated with ground rice and pulverized soapstone, sand mixed in with sugar, "olive oil" made from cotton seed oil, rat droppings in sausage—the list of adulterations and contaminants was endless, and often dangerous. Slaughterhouses and canneries were filthy beyond belief. Patent medicines were loaded with high levels of alcohol, opiates, or poisonous chemical compounds.

The "pure food" movement campaigned across the country for the enforcement of state and local laws and advocated for the passage of national food-safety standards. After almost 20 years of lobbying, they helped pushed through the Pure Food and Drug Act of 1906, signed into law by President Theodore Roosevelt the same day it was passed by Congress. The law created a federal inspection process for meat producers, forbade the manufacture, sale, or transport of adulterated foods, and enacted strict new standards for patent medicines. The government later used the law to create the Food and Drug Administration (FDA) to oversee compliance efforts.

Urban air quality was another target of reformers. Although germ theory was beginning to revolutionize the understanding of disease and infection, old ideas about "unhealthful air" remained. Underground sewers and storm drains contributed to

Improved sanitation, embodied by this New York City sanitation department employee sweeping a street around 1910, reduced urban health risks.

"Hog Butcher for the World"

In 1914 several of Carl Sandburg's poems, including "Chicago," were published in *Poetry: A Magazine of Verse*. In his poem, Sandburg offers a realistic portrayal of city life in early 20th century America.

Chicago

Hog Butcher for the World,
Tool Maker, Stacker of Wheat,
Player with Railroads and the Nation's Freight Handler;
Stormy, husky, brawling,
City of the Big Shoulders:

They tell me you are wicked and I believe them, for I
    have seen your painted women under the gas lamps luring the farms
boys.
And they tell me you are crooked and I answer; Yes, it
    is true I have seen the gunman kill and go free to kill again
And they tell me you are brutal and my reply is: On the
    faces of women and children I have seen the marks of wanton hunger.
And having answered so I turn once more to those who
    sneer at this my city, and I give them back the sneer and say to them:
Come and show me another city with lifted head singing
    so proud to be alive and coarse and strong and cunning.
Flinging magnetic curses amid the toil of piling job on job,
    here is a tall bold slugger set vivid against the little soft cities;
Fierce as a dog with tongue lapping for action, cunning
    as a savage pitted against the wilderness,
        Bareheaded,
        Shoveling,
        Wrecking,
        Planning,
        Building, breaking, rebuilding,
Under the smoke, dust all over his mouth, laughing with white teeth,
Under the terrible burden of destiny laughing as a young man laughs,
Laughing even as an ignorant fighter laughs who has never lost a battle,
Bragging and laughing that under his wrist is the pulse,
    and under his ribs the heart of the people,
                Laughing!
Laughing the stormy, husky, brawling laughter of
    Youth, half-naked, sweating, proud to be Hog Butcher,
    Tool Maker, Stacker of Wheat, Player with
    Railroads and Freight Handler to the Nation.

Horse-drawn streetcars, such as this one in New York City in 1895, left city streets sullied with manure. They were phased out in favor of "cleaner" electric and gas-powered transportation.

cleaner air, as did municipal garbage removal. Little could be done about factories belching toxins into the sky, however, or the waste produced by slaughterhouses and canneries.

TRANSPORTATION

One form of filth that proved particularly hard for cities to remove came from the legions of horses that were the engines of urban commerce well into the 1910s. In 1908 one commentator called New York City's 120,000 horses "an economic burden, an affront to cleanliness, and a terrible tax on human life." Each horse produced between 15 and 30 pounds of manure every day. It piled up on the streets, becoming a perfect breeding ground for disease-carrying flies, then drying and turning into a foul-smelling dust that traveled everywhere.

This created a big problem even in the smaller cities. In 1900 a public health official in Rochester, New York calculated that the city's 15,000 horses produced enough manure to cover one square acre of land to a depth of 175 ft. and breed 16 billion flies in a year.

Urban workhorses led nasty and short lives pulling heavy loads of goods to markets and factories, and were often maltreated by their owners and drivers. Paved streets increased the likelihood of stumbles and fatal leg injuries. Often the animals were left to die where they fell, becoming another form of waste to be hauled away. In 1900 Chicago sanitation workers collected 10,000 dead horses from city streets.

New forms of transportation seemed to offer the path to a cleaner future. Cable cars came into service in the 1870s, and the first electric streetcar debuted in Richmond, Virginia in 1887. By 1900 there were 850 electric streetcar systems running on 10,000 miles of new track in cities across the country. Inter-city rail lines also became popular, with 13,000 mi. of new routes established between 1900 and 1916.

The bicycle craze of the 1890s opened up new ways of getting out and about, at least for the middle class. Modern "safety" bicycles came onto the mass market around 1885 and quickly gained popularity among those who could afford the $20 to $30 price tag. Progressive health reformers tied bicycle riding to the "clean living" movement, touting it as the healthiest form of exercise for men and women.

From there it was a relatively small step to the greatest innovation of the age: the automobile. Once people had a taste of the freedom that came from personal transportation, they wanted to go further than their legs could carry them. Enthusiastic bike riders agitated for more paved city streets, helping put into place key infrastructure for the tender wheels of early cars. A generation of bicycle mechanics became the pioneers of automobile engineering, and bicycle companies became some of the first automobile factories. Electric automobiles were first produced in large numbers in the early 1890s, and New York City acquired its first fleet of cabs in January 1897. Over time the electric engine gave way to the internal combustion engine, and by 1905 changes in production had made cars more affordable for the average commuter. "It is all a question of dollars and cents," one writer explained, "this gasoline-or-oats proposition." Henry Ford's popular Model T had put more than one million cars on the road by 1920.

While there were those who lamented the quiet and the leisurely pace of the horse-drawn conveyance, most Americans eagerly embraced new ways. The automobile was cleaner, hardier, safer, and more impervious to weather than Old Dobbin. The streets were cleaner and the cities far less dusty. Along with streetcars, the personal automobile made it possible for families to move out of the apartments of the cities for the houses of the suburbs as bucolic small-town life once again asserted its hold on the American psyche.

HEATHER K. MICHON

Further Readings

Abbott, Edith, and Sophonisba Preston Breckinridge. *The Tenements of Chicago, 1908–1935*. Chicago, IL: The University of Chicago Press, 1936.

Addams, Jane. *Twenty Years at Hull-House: With Autobiographical Notes*. New York: Macmillan, 1910.

Barbuto, Domenica M. *American Settlement Houses and Progressive Social Reform: An Encyclopedia*. New York: Oryx Press, 1999.

Bender, Daniel E. *Sweated Work, Weak Bodies: Anti-Sweatshop Campaigns and Languages of Labor*. New Brunswick, NJ: Rutgers University Press, 2004.

Crane, Stephen, and Adrian Hunter. *Maggie: A Girl of the Streets*. Peterborough, ON: Broadview Press, 2006.

Cromley, Elizabeth C. *Alone Together: A History of New York's Early Apartments*. Ithaca, NY: Cornell University Press, 1990.

Dodd, Monroe. *A Splendid Ride: The Streetcars of Kansas City, 1870–1957*. Kansas City, MO: Kansas City Star Books, 2002.

Drehle, Dave Von. *Triangle: The Fire That Changed America*. New York: Atlantic Monthly Press, 2003.

Glazier, Jack. *Dispersing the Ghetto: The Relocation of Jewish Immigrants Across America*. Ithaca, NY: Cornell University Press, 1998.

Glowacki, Peggy, and Julia Hendry. *Hull-House*. Mount Pleasant, NC: Arcadia Publishing, 2004.

Hapke, Laura. *Sweatshop: The History of an American Idea*. New Brunswick, NJ: Rutgers University Press, 2004.

Kleeck, Mary Van. "Child Labor in New York City Tenements." *Charities and the Commons*. (v.19, 1908).

Lauck, William Jett. *The Causes of the Panic of 1893*. Boston, MA: Houghton, Mifflin and Company, 1907.

Lissak, Rivka Shpak. *Pluralism & Progressives: Hull House and the New Immigrants, 1890–1919*. Chicago, IL: University of Chicago Press, 1989.

Musselman, Morris McNeil. *Get a Horse!: The Story of the Automobile in America*. New York: Lippincott, 1950.

Novkov, Julie. *Constituting Workers, Protecting Women: Gender, Law, and Labor*. Ann Arbor, MI: University of Michigan Press, 2001.

Oney, Steve. *And the Dead Shall Rise: The Murder of Mary Phagan and the Lynching of Leo Frank*. New York: Vintage Books, 2004.

Recchiuti, John Louis. *Civic Engagement: Social Science and Progressive-era Reform in New York City*. Philadelphia, PA: University of Pennsylvania Press, 2006.

Riis, Jacob August. *How the Other Half Lives: Studies Among the Tenements of New York*. New York: Charles Scribner's Sons, 1890.

———. *Children of the Tenements*. New York: Macmillan, 1908.

Rockaway, Robert A. *Words of the Uprooted: Jewish Immigrants in Early Twentieth-Century America*. Ithaca, NY: Cornell University Press, 1998.

Ryan, Mary P. *Civic Wars: Democracy and Public Life in the American City*. Berkeley, CA: University of California Press, 1998.

Steeples, Douglas W., and David O. Whitten. *Democracy in Desperation: The Depression of 1893*. Westport, CT: Greenwood Press, 1998.

Thornton, Jeremy. *Religious Intolerance: Jewish Immigrants Come to America (1881–1914)*. New York: Rosen Publishing Group, 2004.

Todd, Anne M. *Italian Immigrants, 1880–1920*. Mankato, MN: Capstone Press, 2002.

Warner, Sam Bass. *Streetcar Suburbs: The Process of Growth in Boston, 1870–1900*. Cambridge, MA: Harvard University Press, 1978.

Willis, Carol. *Form Follows Finance: Skyscrapers and Skylines in New York and Chicago*. New York: Princeton Architectural Press, 1995.

Chapter 6

Rural Life

"Oh, the farmer is the man who feeds them all."
— Anonymous

AMERICAN RURAL LIFE during the Progressive Era and World War I marked a transitional period in the nation. The years that followed required the rebuilding and reestablishment of agricultural ways, while at the same time commercializing the farming industry. The start of the Progressive Era was marked in rural society by the decline of the Farmer's Alliance. Formed to combat the collapse of agriculture prices following the Panic of 1873, the Farmer's Alliance eventually developed into the reform-minded Populist Party. However the Populist Party was short-lived, and changes in the dynamics of American life threatened the existence of rural America. By the turn of the 20th century, many feared that rural America was all but doomed, unable to keep pace with a rapidly changing American landscape.

Millions of people migrated to cities from their rural dwellings, leaving behind abandoned homes, farmsteads, schools, churches, and markets. Consequently by 1910 less than one-third of the nation's population worked on farms. The shrinking role of rural society in food production, commerce, and economic security was deemed by pundits and reformers as "the rural problem." Historian James H. Madison noted that "industrialization, urbanization, and bureaucratization were fundamentally changing American life." Farmers could not be successful without incorporating a new, business-like approach to their work. This was no easy task, as Madison asserts, since "farm life and

81

This kitchen furnished in the style of the 1910s, complete with a cast-iron stove and a table set for a large family, is displayed at the Manatee Historical Village in Bradenton, Florida.

rural community institutions lagged far behind urban America, existing socially and culturally closer to the time of Thomas Jefferson than to that of Theodore Roosevelt." Thus the rural countryside attracted many Progressive Era reformers who hoped to update old-fashioned rural society. From technology to education, nearly every aspect of rural life was subject to scrutiny.

Perhaps the most important investigation of rural life came in 1908, when President Theodore Roosevelt established the Country Life Commission. The commission was charged with identifying the shortcomings of agricultural production and country life, and providing solutions. The impact of the commission has been debated by historians, but the report produced by the commission was one of the first attempts to provide a comprehensive solution to sustaining the agricultural economy of rural America.

FARMERS, AGRICULTURE, AND FOOD PRODUCTION

From 1890 to 1920 the role of the American farmer would be challenged as crops failed, the economy shifted, technology changed traditional work methods, and a world war demanded more resources than ever before. Farmers did their best to keep up with the times, while maintaining a symbolic status in American culture. A.M. Simons opens his 1902 book *American Farmers and the Rise of Agribusiness* by stating, "The American farmer is a distinct and peculiar social factor. No other age has anything comparable to him. No other nation has his counterpart. His problems, his history and his future evolution present complications and relations unknown elsewhere. At the same time he is more closely united to great world questions than any previous race of tillers of the soil. He is part of the great social development of his age to a greater extent than the farmers of any other nation, past or present." Simons's nationalistic description is an example of how the role of the American farmer has been romanticized.

At the turn of the 20th century, with industrial America booming, some farmers began to embrace the new technological resources available to them. Many city dwellers had regular access to household items such as automobiles and telephones, and farmers wanted to better commercialize their business by incorporating these new resources. However this increased their reliance on outside agencies to maintain their livelihood. Some farmers assimilated into the new age of farm machinery, while others continued more independent, traditional ventures. New machines and agricultural production methods were necessary to increase production and keep pace with a rapidly expanding industrial America. However the new technology eliminated the need for farmhands, which freed many workers to seek employment in the city.

With America's entry into World War I, the country relied on rural farmers to produce enough food to feed the nation. This was no easy task. The years preceding American involvement in the war had seen two devastatingly poor

Rocking chairs on the local country store porch represented a typical meeting place for residents of rural areas across America.

agricultural harvests in 1916 and 1917, as well as a boll weevil infestation of cotton crops in the south that damaged the region's sharecropping system. In response to the poor harvests, the Food Administration was created in 1917 as part of the war effort. Headed by future president Herbert Hoover, the Food Administration elevated prices for agricultural goods to encourage the production of agricultural products. It also encouraged food conservation with "wheatless Mondays," "meatless Tuesdays," and "porkless Saturdays."

From 1918 to 1919 an influenza pandemic spread across the world, claiming the lives of over 20 million people. In rural America, however, another microbial enemy emerged in the form of the 1918–1919 Stem Rust Epidemics, which caused the worst crop losses in U.S. history and devastated the American agricultural economy. This occurred just three years after a similar catastrophic epidemic in 1916 and poor harvests again in 1917. According to a report by the U.S. Department of Agriculture, over 50 percent of wheat crops were lost to the disease, which blackened crops with a chalky, sooty fungus. The wheat stem rust epidemic had a profound impact on U.S. agricultural policy, and in 1918 the government swiftly began a national program to eradicate all threats to wheat production in America.

HEALTH, CONNECTIVITY, AND THE FARM PRESS

In many ways, the care of the sick or mentally ill was inhibited by the lack of transportation and money. Consequently, traveling doctors visited rural

Progressive Era reformers examined nearly every aspect of rural life, including farm technology. These corn shellers were used to strip corn kernels from their cobs.

A class in progress at the Tuskegee Institute in Alabama in 1902, where George Washington Carver promoted agriculture and the education of African Americans.

The Tuskegee Institute and George Washington Carver

The Tuskegee Institute was established to give young black men and women an industrial education to promote self-sufficiency. At the institute George Washington Carver (1864–1943) became a beacon to students who were inspired by his ability to succeed despite many obstacles. At Tuskegee in the first decades of the new century, Carver continued the work he had begun in childhood, as he toiled to implement the ideas of crop rotation and crop diversification.

Carver understood that the soil was being depleted of its nutrients by "king cotton." To help replenish the land, Carver recommended planting legumes like peanuts and soybeans, also known as "nitrogen fixers." Farmers listened to Dr. Carver, which led to a new problem: too many peanuts. Carver set to work in his lab to find new ways to utilize the peanut. Discovering over 300 uses, he also experimented with the soybean, sweet potato, and other crops. Carver embraced a message of hope "to help the man farthest down," and produced a series of free agricultural bulletins aimed at providing the poor farmer with better farming techniques and recipes for nutritious meals.

Recognized as an expert on the peanut, he became the first African American to testify before a congressional committee, on behalf of a tariff on imported peanuts. He had a business friendship with Henry Ford, collaborating on soybean research. Carver was also a popular speaker at YMCA clubs and other organizations. Carver's rise as a symbol of interracial peace and harmony prompted Congress to authorize the purchase of the Moses Carver farm in 1943, establishing the George Washington Carver National Monument.

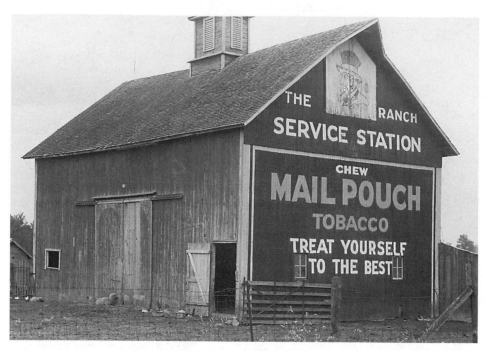

Twentieth-century barn advertising in central Ohio. Barn owners earned $1–$2 a year for the use of their barns for the "Chew Mail Pouch Tobacco" advertisements.

communities to prescribe medicines, and homeopathic medications became more frequent as well. Folk medicines and remedies made of local ingredients—spices, herbs, and the like—were more common in rural settings due to geographic and monetary restrictions. For most, poor roads and long distances isolated rural Americans from adequate medical treatment. Cities offered free clinics and district nursing, a greater knowledge of general healthcare, birthing centers, and regulated methods of maintaining medical standards. By contrast rural Americans were left to fend for themselves in times of medical necessity.

Rural populations had limited access to city resources; however, it was not uncommon for city doctors to travel the countryside in order to treat rural patients. Family members were often charged with the task of caring for the mentally ill on their own, without governmental support or institutionalization. However families with the financial means sometimes admitted relatives to city mental institutions, with the likelihood that the patients would never be able to leave.

The war overseas in 1917 created a greater need for proper care of the mentally ill. Soldiers from World War I returned "shell-shocked" from their traumatic experiences in battle. Physicians became interested in the specialized care of violent people through the use of moral treatment—practicing

Aesthetics and the American Barn

The American farmer's greatest tool, both in size and significance, has been the barn. In the infancy of the United States, the barn was a symbol of success and prosperity, serving as both an agricultural necessity to a nation of farmers, and an aesthetic architectural commodity. A barn's sheer size dominated its landscape. Decorative features such as paint first became common along the American frontier shortly after the Civil War. However by the dawn of the 20th century, barn painting was a relatively common practice.

While many early barns were not painted at all, farmers soon began to acknowledge the benefits of painting them, noting that they added both an aesthetic value to the structure while providing additional protection and longevity to the wood. By mixing animal blood, lime, and linseed oil, farmers and professional artists created a cheaply made red paint to adorn their barns. Similarly whitewash, occasionally mixed with oils, minerals, and lead, was mixed to create a white color for barns.

Progressive Era barns continued the practice of dating barns through unique shingle patterns or decorative paint markings on the barn's exterior. This tradition had been seen throughout the 18th century and earlier. However barns from the Progressive Era have been increasingly difficult for architectural historians to accurately date. Natural disasters sometimes damaged or destroyed portions of barns, and much of the decorative dating seen on historic barns today reflects the year in which particular roofing or new paint was affixed to the structure, rather than construction information about the barn itself. Barns could also feature shingle patterns that detailed the original barn owner's name.

The early 20th century also ushered in the heyday of barn advertising. Hundreds of companies featured their products on signs painted on the sides of barns in populated areas such as highways and thoroughfares. Perhaps the most enduring of these advertisements were the "Chew Mail Pouch Tobacco" advertisements placed by the Bloch Brothers Tobacco Company of West Virginia. Barn owners were paid between $1 and $2 a year for the use of their barns for advertisement purposes (a figure of approximately $20–$40 today). The upside for barn owners in allowing advertisement on their barns was that a fresh coat of paint would be applied to preserve the integrity of the wood. In the early 20th century, this was an important but expensive task. Mail Pouch painted their famous "Chew Mail Pouch" tobacco advertisements on one or two sides of the barn and painted the other sides of the barn in a color that the owner desired. The barns were often repainted every few years to maintain the paint colors. Painters often employed a technique call "ghost-lettering," which provided a secondary coat of paint that topped over the lettering, so when the sun faded the top layer, the bottom layer would display the advertisement text clearer for longer.

Farm tractor wheels before 1920 were often made of metal, with "lugs" or short metal projections for better traction in mud and deep soil.

positive interaction, humane treatment of patients, and occupational rehabilitation. By the early 20th century, the term "moral treatment" was no longer used to classify this practice of rehabilitation, yet the motifs of its discourse continued for several more decades. As part of their treatment plan, patients engaged in activities such as sewing their own clothes, growing their own food, and tilling the land around them. At the center of the moral treatment was a return to the rural lifestyle, which some physicians believed had a calming effect on soldiers.

As the 20th century progressed, transportation and communication between rural America and urban society were increasingly possible. The connectivity of information within rural society was important not only for rural-urban relations, but also for staying in touch with other members of rural society. Consequently a rural mail carrier system was introduced in the early 20th century. Some rural mail carriers used a horse-and-buggy system to deliver the mail, but by the end of World War I, automobiles became increasingly available and affordable to the rural population. The development of the farm press saw an increased connectivity between rural and urban populations through publications such as *Iowa Homestead* and *The Prairie Farmer*. These publications were produced weekly and featured up to 200 pages per

Warren H. Wilson:
Rural Sociology

Warren Hugh Wilson was a pioneer in rural sociology, and a major contributor to rural church reform in the early 20th century. Born near Tidioute, Pennsylvania, in 1867, Wilson spent his young adulthood in nearby Bradford, Pennsylvania. In 1890 he graduated from Oberlin College, and in 1891 he entered Union Theological Seminary in New York, while taking geology and criminology courses part-time at Columbia University.

After graduating from Union Theological Seminary in 1894, Wilson served as pastor of the Arlington Avenue Presbyterian Church in Brooklyn, New York. It was then that he enrolled at Columbia University in pursuit of a doctoral degree under the tutelage of distinguished sociologist Franklin H. Gidding. Wilson's dissertation, *Quaker Hill: A Sociological Study*, has been hailed as a landmark study in rural sociology. It helped propel to him into a combined role as both a rural sociologist and religious commentator. He used this role in his field surveys of rural churches as part of the rural church reform movement in an effort to further the cause of his denomination.

After receiving his Ph.D. in 1908, Warren Wilson joined the Board of Home Missions of the Presbyterian Church as a superintendent in their Department of Church & Labor, and eventually became the superintendent of the Department of Church and Country Life. In this role, Wilson helped other religious entities organize departments similar to the one at the mission; in doing so, Wilson influenced the development of a rural church policy, encouraging churches to partake in community building, in addition to their religious message.

While acting as superintendent of the Department of Church and Country Life, Wilson organized what historian James H. Madison called "one of the largest and most influential sociological surveys of the early twentieth century" from 1910 to 1912. The survey was thorough, particularly in Ohio and Indiana, and the survey committee concluded that there was severe dysfunction among small, interdenominational churches, creating the problem of too many churches competing for too few parishioners. Wilson sought to remedy the problem of "overchurching" and embarked on a campaign to educate and reform rural churches in a manner that would be more conducive to their longevity. World War I distracted rural reformers from the changes they wished to impose, but Wilson's landmark and broad surveying served as a model for future rural sociologists and greatly influenced the rural church reform movement.

Warren H. Wilson died in 1937, shortly before his 70th birthday. Warren Wilson College in Asheville, North Carolina, is named in his honor.

issue that catered to farmers. Subscription costs were low, approximately $1 a year, and articles covered topics such as crop farming and livestock care, housekeeping, food preparation, railroads, as well as family games and fiction. In effect, the publications showcased issues that were particularly important to people in rural America. According to a 1913 survey by the U.S. Department of Agriculture, roughly 75 percent of rural midwesterners surveyed received at least one farm newspaper.

RELIGION AND EDUCATION

For numerous people living in rural areas during the turn of the 20th century, religion was at the center of their daily lives. From 1890 to 1920 religion and education became increasing intertwined. Proponents of rural reform aimed to preserve rural lifestyles, while at the same time bringing rural culture in line with city-driven American industry. Like many of the reform movements of the Progressive Era, the major proponents of rural reform were overwhelmingly Protestant.

In the age before indoor plumbing, rural families would keep a washbasin by the hand-operated outdoor water pump.

In rural districts children's toys were often made from readily available cast-off materials, such as these dolls crafted from corn husks.

With technological advances being adopted by farmers across the country, young people who would have otherwise been working on the family farm were free to pursue an education. Progressive Era laws mandated that teenagers attend school, creating a need for high schools all over the country. This dramatically changed the face of rural areas, especially in the rural south, which had previously been dependent on family labor. In 1890 approximately 200,000 students attended high school nationwide, but by 1920 that number jumped to nearly two million students.

Along with meeting the demand for more schools, rural society faced another challenge: the role of religion in the classroom. In order to counterbalance ideas contained in the scientific theory of evolution, Bible reading was required in public schools by 1915, although discussion or interpretation of passages was not permitted in order to avoid a conflict of separation between church and state. Rural churches had their own share of problems to contend with during the Progressive Era and World War I. Plagued by interdenominational bickering and disorganization stemming from overchurching—an accumulation of unassociated small churches with meager membership rates—early reformers feared that rural churches had little effect on their surrounding locales, and were in jeopardy of collapsing.

The chaos of World War I diverted attention from the problems of rural America to the action overseas. Nevertheless the efforts of rural sociologist Warren H. Wilson influenced rural church reform, and ultimately gave way to the postwar Interchurch World Movement (IWM). The IWM attempted to remedy the problem of overchurching by condensing small churches into larger religious institutions and encouraging interdenominational worship. Like Wilson, the IWM collected a multitude of data through extensive surveying of rural communities and parishes.

Among rural populations where resources and community traditions varied, the task of burying the dead involved different rituals. From cremation to burial, the deceased were treated to an assortment of funeral rituals based on community resources and traditions. But in colder climates, especially in northern states like Minnesota and North Dakota, families had to preserve the dead in mortuaries because the ground was too frozen to dig a grave for their deceased loved one.

Religion certainly played a major role in the daily lives of rural citizens, but as author R. Douglas Hurt noted, "It has been said…that the South has never been

An elderly African-American couple having dinner by the fireplace in rural Virginia around 1900. Racism and poverty in rural areas led many African Americans to flee for northern cities.

more segregated than...at eleven o'clock on Sundays." Segregation, religious or otherwise, was the result of societal unrest regarding the issue of race.

WOMEN, AFRICAN AMERICANS, AND NATIVE AMERICANS
Rural America was a patriarchal society during the Progressive Era. Although the role of American women during this time marked social advances such as suffrage rights with the Nineteenth Amendment in 1920, the lives of rural women remained relatively unchanged. Rural women were expected to serve as mothers and wives above all, and to maintain the day-to-day functions of the family as homemakers. This is not to say that advances in women's rights did not reach rural society altogether. The Homestead Act of 1862 allowed single women, as heads of family, to acquire their own land. By the turn of the century, some single women did own land, but this was often due more to their business sense than any entitlement. In general, single women were not afforded any sense of long-term security as landowners.

Like other minorities of the time, rural women were routinely marginalized. Editorials, news, and literature from the early 20th century spoke of the ways that women eased the burdens of hard economic times for their husbands through their selfless acts as obedient wives and homemakers. When announcements of opportunities for land ownership along the plains appeared, rural men decided whether or not to move their family, and often without consulting their wives. Rural women were expected to maintain a submissive role. According to author Deborah Fink, family breakdown and violence were fundamental aspects of their existence.

During the Progressive Era, 90 percent of the African-American population lived in the south, and 83 percent resided in rural areas, especially on farms. The boll weevil infestation of cotton crops in the rural south damaged the sharecropping industry, freeing many African Americans from the superficial confines of white landowners. After years of continued oppression, intimidation, and discrimination in the Jim Crow south, the Great Migration of African Americans began in the early 1910s. According to author R. Douglas Hurt, African-American farms, including livestock, averaged a value of $799 in 1910 and $1,588 a decade later. White-owned farms, by contrast, were valued at an average of $2,140 and $3,911, respectively. This disparity left the remaining rural African-American population in enduring poverty. Those who fled to the north migrated to urban centers such as Detroit, Baltimore, New York City, St. Louis, and especially Chicago. Some found employment replacing white workers who had left to fight in World War I. Despite the "separate but equal" clause levied in the 1896 Supreme Court case *Plessy v. Ferguson*, African Americans found new freedoms from the destitute existence that they had endured in rural America.

During the first wave of the Great Migration from 1910 to 1930, over 1.5 million African Americans fled the south for the north. By the end of the migration in the 1970s, an estimated six million African Americans had left the south. This demographic shift completely altered the make-up of the rural population, and ultimately culminated in the assimilation of African-American culture into white urban life.

At the turn of the 20th century, Native Americans were synonymous with rural life. Some Americans misunderstood the complexity of this group, which had lost much of their land and cultural identity as a result of relocation programs by the U.S. government. Despite this, the Progressive Era and World War I was a time of assimilation in rural Native-American life. Native-American rural heritage was managed by government-mandated reservation facilities across the greater midwest, especially near Oklahoma, which was formed in 1907 out of the Indian Territory.

In 1887 The General Allotment Act (or Dawes Act) was passed, which divided Native-American reservation land into individual allotments that were to be held in trust by the government for a period of 25 years. The surplus land would then be bought by the government and sold after the land had been allotted to Native Americans on a reservation. In 1906 the Burke Act granted permission to "competent Indians" to acquire land allotments to sell or lease; a 1908 Supreme Court decision, *Winters v. United States*, found that Native Americans were entitled to water for agricultural needs on their reservations, and in 1919, the American Indian Citizenship Act granted citizenship to all honorably discharged Native Americans who served in World War I. This was a precursor to the 1924 mandate that made all Native Americans legal citizens of the United States. While Native Americans had been marginalized throughout the Progressive Era and World War I, the period afterward began a period of somewhat better understanding and care for their ways of life.

CONCLUSION

As a period of transition, change, and innovation, the Progressive Era and World War I had a major impact on American rural life. On the heels of the Industrial Revolution and an era that sought to reunite a people divided by the Civil War, 1890 to 1920 was a pivotal point in American history. Following the disintegration of the Farmer's Alliance and Populist Party and the pressure from urban America to change, rural America was forced to adapt to the world around it. No longer isolated from the rest of the country, rural America overhauled its school system and religious organizations, and established connections between rural societies.

In many ways, the changes implemented in rural society from 1890 to 1920 can be directly linked to the course of evolution that the farming industry has since followed—a greater commercialization, decreased autonomy, and assimilation into the flow of industrial society.

TREVOR J. BLANK

Further Readings

Birdwell, Michael E. and W. Calvin Dickinson, eds. *Rural Life and Culture in the Upper Cumberland*. Lexington, KY: The University Press of Kentucky, 2004.

Bowers, William L. *The Country Life Movement in America: 1900–1920*. Port Washington, NY: Kennikat Press, 1974.

Boyle, James E. *Rural Problems in the United States*. Chicago, IL: A.C. McClurg & Co., 1921.

Dittmer, John. *Black Georgia in the Progressive Era: 1900–1920*. Champaign, IL: University of Illinois Press, 1980.

Ensminger, Robert. *The Pennsylvania Barn: Its Origin, Evolution, and Distribution in North America*. Baltimore, MD: The Johns Hopkins University Press, 1992.

Fink, Deborah. *Agrarian Women: Wives and Mothers in Rural Nebraska, 1880–1940*. Chapel Hill, NC: University of North Carolina Press, 1992.

Fixico, Donald Lee. *Daily Life of Native Americans in the Twentieth Century*. Westport, CT: The Greenwood Press, 2006.

Fry, John J. "'Good Farming—Clear Thinking—Right Living': Midwestern Farm Newspapers, Social Reform, and Rural Readers in the Early Twentieth Century." *Agricultural History* (v.78/1, 2004).

———. *The Farm Press, Reform, and Rural Change, 1895–1920*. New York: Routledge, 2005.

Glass, Joseph W. *The Pennsylvania Culture Region: A View from the Barn*. Ann Arbor, MI: UMI Research Press, 1986.

Hester, Seth W. "The Life and Work of Warren H. Wilson and Their Significance in the Beginnings of the Rural Church Movement in America." M.A. Thesis. Madison, NJ: Drew University, 1946.

Hurt, R. Douglas, ed. *African American Life in the Rural South: 1900–1950*. Columbia, MI: University of Missouri Press, 2003.

Madison, James H. "Reformers and the Rural Church, 1900–1950." *Journal of American History* (v.73/3, 1986).

———. "John D. Rockefeller's General Education Board and the Rural School Problem in the Midwest, 1900–1930." *History of Education Quarterly* (v.24/2, 1984).

Montell, William Lynwood and Michael Lynn Morse. *Kentucky Folk Architecture*. Lexington, KY: University of Kentucky Press, 1976.

Noble, Allen B. and Hubert G.H. Wilhelm, eds. *Barns of the Midwest*. Athens, OH: Ohio University Press, 1995.

Peters, Scott J. and Paul A. Morgan. "The Country Life Commission: Reconsidering a Milestone in American Agricultural History." *Agricultural History* (v.78/3, 2004).

Sloane, Eric. *An Age of Barns: An Illustrated Review of Classic Barn Styles and Construction*. Vancouver, BC: Voyageur Press, Inc., 2001.

Stiles, Wardell. "The Rural Health Movement." *Annals of the American Academy of Political and Social Science* (v.37/2, 1911).

Swanson, Merwin. "The 'Country Life Movement' and the American Churches." *Church History* (v.46/3, 1977).

Tomes, Nancy. *The Gospel of Germs: Men, Women, and the Microbe in American Life*. Cambridge, MA: Harvard University Press, 1998.

van Ravenswaay, Charles. *German Settlements in Missouri: A Survey of Vanishing Culture*. Columbia, MI: University of Missouri, 1977.

Vlach, John Michael. *Barns*. New York: W.W. Norton & Company, 2003.

Yoder, Don and Thomas E. Graves. *Hex Signs: Pennsylvania Dutch Barn Symbols & Their Meanings*. Mechanicsburg, PA: Stackpole Books, 2000.

Chapter 7

Religion

"Every larger community is facing today
the problem of what to do for those
whom the church no longer attracts."
— Charles Sprague Smith

THE TURN OF the century brought changes in religion across America and across denominations. From the newer religions of Mormonism and Christian Science, to the end-of-the-world sects, to the continuing legacies of the Christian churches and the heritage of Judaism, the Progressive Era was not progressive in social and political life alone. In the Protestant environment, the Great Awakenings were a cycle of religious fervor particular to the United States, where a plethora of denominations thrived, many of them doing so nationwide and subject to regional variations in practice. The dominance of Protestantism throughout American history probably contributed to this cycle of religious revivals and revolutions, the third of which occurred from the 1850s to the 1900s. The Third Great Awakening was especially activist-oriented, meshing well with (and in a sense, sponsoring) the progressive movements. It was also generally postmillennial. Postmillennialism is a strain of Christian thought that declares the Second Coming of Christ can occur only after humanity has reformed and prepared the Earth for him—after the 1,000-year Golden Age mentioned in chapter 20 of the Book of Revelation.

THE SOCIAL GOSPEL
The most widespread postmillennial movement was the Social Gospel, a Protestant movement that applied Christian ideals to social problems such

Relief workers, protected by armed guards, unload food supplies from this wagon amid wrecked buildings and flooded streets after the devastating 1900 Galveston, Texas, hurricane.

as poverty, inequality, crime, and the consequences of those problems: poor living conditions, hunger, and drug and alcohol abuse. The combination of theology and social activism came from the idea that activism was a Christian duty and worldly evils had to be eliminated before the Second Coming could occur. In the south, the Social Gospel thrived among liberal Methodists in reaction to the prevailing Lost Cause sentiments of the day.

The refrain "what would Jesus do?" originated from turn of the century novels by Social Gospel Congregational Minister Charles Sheldon. Jesus was seen not simply as a savior, but also as someone who could be emulated and who had set forth an example others could follow. Though similar sentiments had been expressed through the whole of Christian history, their importance here cannot be stressed enough. In an increasingly secular world, the idea of Jesus as a role model was one that did not require (but certainly allowed for) supernatural beliefs.

In 1865 the Salvation Army was founded in England by former Methodist Minister William Booth as an evangelical organization to advance the cause of Christianity through charitable acts. It spread to the United States in the 1880s, where it focused on converting people at the margins of society—addicts, prostitutes, street criminals, and the homeless—and had particular success in fast-growing urban centers. The Salvation Army eschewed ritual, including baptism and communion, and believed that too much of modern Christianity had become devoted to the rote performance of ceremonies without mindful, conscious worship. So successfully did the Salvation Army rid itself of the trappings of Christianity that despite the name, many Americans are not aware that it is a religious organization.

At first the Salvation Army was not well-received. The Third Great Awakening had seen an explosion of religious denominations, and many of the newer ones, like the Restorationist groups and Christian Science, seemed far removed from the mainstream. While the Salvation Army's non-denominational, anti-ritual approach made it an adept converter for the mixture of immigrants in American cities, established churches still viewed it with some suspicion. However the organization's good reputation and respectability were sealed in the first decade of the 20th century, following the Galveston hurricane of 1900 and the San Francisco earthquake of 1906. The Salvation Army came to national attention with its hands-on relief efforts, alongside the American Red Cross, which had been founded around the same time in the 1880s.

According to theologian Walter Rauschenbusch, Christian "control of social forces" is not a new approach to Christianity, but rather the ultimate culmination of Christianity, the form toward which it had always been moving. In this underlying belief that the final phase of Christianity had arrived, Rauschenbusch and the Social Gospel were similar to many other Christian movements.

Although Christian sects have always been concerned to one degree or another with the end of the world, groups from the 19th and 20th centuries were especially focused on it. The idea of a pre-Tribulation rapture—the removal of Christians directly to Heaven in a single event—was popularized in the early 19th century, but was almost exclusively British. It was not until the turn of the century that it caught on in the United States. Dr. William Eugene Blackstone, a student of revivalist and scholar Dwight Moody, published *Jesus Is Coming* in 1881, proclaiming the imminent return of Jesus and the Rapture of all members of the "true Church." The true Church was not any one denomination, but rather all Christians who had been saved and were living the lives they should. This sort

William Booth, founder of the Salvation Army, in an 1894 engraving.

Altar and pews in a simple Methodist church dating from around 1900 in Florida. In the south the Social Gospel thrived among liberal Methodists in reaction to Lost Cause sentiments.

of theology perfectly fit in with the times, appealing both to the prevailing ecumenism of mainstream Protestantism (because the Rapture would not be specific to any one denomination) and the exclusionism of some movements (because only saved Christians would be subject to the Rapture, and mere church membership was not enough). It took some time for the theology of the pre-Tribulation Rapture to catch on, but by the 1920s, it had become a fixture in evangelical and revivalist theology—particularly in the south, which was more inclined toward premillennialism than the north.

REACTIONS TO REFORM

The 19th century had seen major developments in Judaism, beginning in Germany before being carried over to the United States a generation later. Reform Judaism, as it was called, was an organized effort to modernize—and to an extent, secularize and even Christianize—Judaism, by stripping away elements believed to be tied to historical circumstances that no longer existed, particularly those concerned with ritual purity and clothing. The movement explicitly based much of its vision of modern Judaism on Protestantism, and spoke at length about the importance of dismantling the model of Judaism as an ethnicity. Jewishness, for reformers, was a religious choice, not an ethnic identity. Emphasis shifted, at the same time, from the supernatural and spiritual to the ethical, with special disdain reserved for the Kabbalah and other supernatural trappings that had accumulated in Medieval Europe.

As often happens, there were many who agreed with some of the essence of the movement but felt that it went too far. In mid-19th century Germany,

The Millennium

The millennium is an important factor in Christian eschatology (the "study" of the end of the world). Chapter 20 of the Book of Revelation (verses 1 to 6 here) refers to a 1,000-year period:

And I saw an angel come down from heaven, having the key of the bottom- less pit and a great chain in his hand.

And he laid hold on the dragon, that old serpent, which is the Devil, and Satan, and bound him a thousand years,

And cast him into the bottomless pit, and shut him up, and set a seal upon him, that he should deceive the nations no more, till the thousand years should be fulfilled: and after that he must be loosed a little season.

And I saw thrones, and they sat upon them, and judgment was given unto them: and I saw the souls of them that were beheaded for the witness of Jesus, and for the word of God, and which had not worshipped the beast, neither his image, neither had received his mark upon their foreheads, or in their hands; and they lived and reigned with Christ a thousand years.

But the rest of the dead lived not again until the thousand years were fin- ished. This is the first resurrection.

Blessed and holy is he that hath part in the first resurrection: on such the second death hath no power, but they shall be priests of God and of Christ, and shall reign with him a thousand years.

The dominant view of the Catholic Church, as well as the Eastern Ortho- dox Church and the oldest Protestant denominations, is that the "thousand" years are figurative, symbolizing the spiritual reign of Christ on Earth through the body of the church. By this view, the binding of Satan that Revelation calls for has already been accomplished through the writing and spread of the Gos- pels. Some early church fathers were premillennialists, a view that enjoyed recurring popularity through history, and was revived among some Protestants in the mid-1800s. Premillennialism taught that the Second Coming would be followed by Christ's 1,000-year physical reign over the Earth. Premillennial- ism is generally popular in periods when its proponents feel that this Second Coming is imminent—rarely do you find premillennialist writings that assume the Second Coming is still centuries away. The imminence of this return is used as the stick to drive listeners to the folds of the faith, and the 1,000- year Golden Age serves as the carrot to reward them for doing so.

Postmillennialism views the Second Coming differently: the Second Com- ing is something for which the world must prove itself worthy. The Golden Age is not a reward; rather it is a task set forth for mankind. A small number of postmillennialists even believed that if the work of the Golden Age were done, no unsaved individuals or non-Christians would remain in the world. Others doubted this could be accomplished before the return of Christ.

In the 19th century Reform Judaism spread to the United States. The photo shows the interior of Temple Emanu-El in New York City in 1884.

Positive-Historical Judaism agreed with Reform Judaism's conclusions about the dynamic nature of Jewish law, but felt that Reform Judaism was too consciously innovative, too invested in "change for change's sake," without a thorough grounding in the vast body of the Jewish intellectual tradition. This intellectual German movement led to the Conservative Judaism movements in both Europe and the United States. American Conservative Judaism was specifically a reaction to the 1885 Pittsburgh Platform, in which a number of rabbis divorced themselves from ancient Jewish tradition and adopted the radical principles of Reform Judaism. Reform groups sometimes went out of their way to flout Jewish law, as in "trefa dinners," which ostentatiously served non-kosher foods such as the shellfish and pork that had been denied to Jews for thousands of years.

In 1886 the Jewish Theological Seminary was founded in New York City as a moderate alternative to the growing Reform Judaism movement. It grew slowly, providing an important intellectual and culture center for Conservative Judaism, but taking a couple decades before it really thrived. In time, though, Conservative Judaism became the nation's most popular form of Judaism.

At the other end of the spectrum, and developing at the same time, was neo-Orthodoxy, which disagreed with Reform Judaism about nearly everything except the core of Jewish ethics and the ability of Jews to continue interacting with the modern world. This was unlike cloistered Orthodox groups that sequestered themselves away from the world, preserving ancient and Medieval practices such as the Hasidim, some of whom had begun to settle in New

York City from Eastern Europe. Neo-Orthodoxy considered the Torah bind-ing. Proscribed practices did not become acceptable simply because the laws about them were old or the Jews to which they had originally applied lived in different circumstances. It was inappropriate to take such liberties with Mosaic Law and the rabbinical writings that surrounded it. Neo-Orthodoxy stressed the importance of Jewishness: "the Jew will not want to accomplish anything he cannot accomplish as a Jew," stated the German Rabbi Hirsch, whose writings helped to spur the movement along.

Various Orthodox groups formed, with varying degrees of conservatism. Conservative Judaism's slow start was due in part to its failure to appeal to the most conservative of American Jews, and the Jewish Theological Seminary (JTS) found itself somewhat in competition with Yeshiva University, founded in 1886 in Manhattan's Lower East Side. The movements in Judaism were still ill-defined—Reform Judaism found it easy to self-label because they wanted so many changes—and it was only with time that the JTS gradually became the center of Conservative Judaism, while Yeshiva became associated with Orthodoxy. Unlike Conservative Judaism, Orthodox groups never caught on in as great numbers outside of New York.

MORMON FUNDAMENTALISTS

In 1890 the president of the Church of Latter-Day Saints, Wilford Woodruff, issued a manifesto ending the practice of plural marriage. Not all Mormons agreed with this. Plural marriage had been an integral part of the faith as way of life, even a definition of family. Those who disagreed have become known as Mormon fundamentalists. Their specific rationale varies, but most claim that the 1890 manifesto was issued for political reasons, and that Woodruff never experienced a genuine divine revelation directing him to end plural marriage. It was the 1904 manifesto of Joseph F. Smith that really spurred the fundamentalist movement. In response to the controversy over the election of Latter Day Saint Reed Smoot to the Senate (and congressional hearings about whether a Mormon should hold federal office, given the recent issues with Utah prior to its induction into the Union), Smith declared that all polyga-mists would be excommunicated from the Church.

Banning plural marriage had been one thing; enforcing that ban in such a manner was another. Woodruff and others allowed plural marriage to continue in secret, and perhaps encouraged it. Certainly the practice still existed within the mainstream Church of Jesus Christ of Latter-Day Saints in 1904, if not as commonly as 20 years earlier. Groups began to separate from the church in order to continue the practice. Fundamentalist groups have remained largely unchanged in doctrine since the middle of the 19th century. Having been born in reaction to change, they have resisted it ever since. One effect of this, little noticed at the time of the schisms, is that it remained much more common among the fundamentalist groups for a man to marry considerably younger wives. Some were as young as 13 years old, although this would hardly be the norm. In a group with few new converts, in which men have multiple wives and marry younger women, there is a significant shortage of wives. In a few generations, this would become a serious issue among many fundamentalist groups, with younger men sometimes cast out in order to prevent them from competing for wives.

In other respects Mormon fundamentalist groups varied considerably. Some were small enough to exist within mainstream communities; others maintained their own small towns; a few were large enough to spread out around the world. From the beginning, and probably since before 1890, there were polygamous Mormon families that belonged to no denomination or sect. They simply observed their faith and their practices in private.

CHRISTIAN SCIENCE

In 1875 Mary Baker Eddy published *Science and Health with Key to the Scriptures*, a book about spiritual healing. Raised a Congregationalist in New Hampshire, the 54-year-old Eddy had spent the last few decades exploring alternative healing and pseudoscience before turning her time to Bible study. She found it more spiritually rewarding and medicinally effective than the quack devices she had been exposed to. Four years later she founded the Church of Christ, Scientist, first in Boston, before branches spread to the rest of the country and beyond. It was very much a product of its time, a thoroughly modern religion that issued a professional journal (the *Christian Science Journal*), a daily newspaper (the *Christian Science Monitor*) and two magazines (the *Christian Science Sentinel* and the *Herald of Christian Science*). Christian Science had no priests employed by a church. Instead Christian Science practitioners could charge a small fee for their services, primarily in healing or counseling, and were expected to make a living accordingly. The Christian Science Board of Directors governed the other branch

Mary Baker Eddy in a photo published after her death on December 3, 1910.

churches from the First Church of Christ, Scientist in Boston.

Though Eddy was more than open to praise in life, after her death the church did what it could to avoid any cult of personality surrounding her, including demolishing her home and a 100-ton pyramid built in her honor by the Freemasons. She established the fundamentals of Christian Science theology and its practice. Branch churches offered an hour-long worship service every Sunday with Scripture readings, hymns, and prayers, in accordance to a cycle of 26 "Lesson-Sermon" topics Eddy established.

Christian Science theology deviated from mainstream Christianity in its supernatural respects, though its ethics were largely similar. Jesus was revered as prophet more than as one with God. Though he was ac-

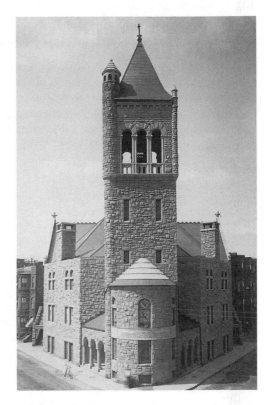

The Christian Scientist church in Boston in 1899, before large 20th-century additions.

knowledged as the son of God, his ministry and healing were seen as feats attainable by anyone. The Holy Spirit's place in the Trinity was taken by Divine Science. Since its inception, Christian Science has been the subject of controversy because of its stance on conventional medicine. According to Eddy, the perfection of God meant that imperfections such as illness and sin could not be real, but were lies told by the devil, lies Christians had to unmask and overcome. Medicine, then, was of no true use; only prayer could heal.

BILLY SUNDAY AND RELIGIOUS REVIVALS

The first commercial radio station did not begin broadcasting until 1920. In pre-radio America, popular forms of entertainment included traveling shows such as the circus, traveling carnivals, theater troupes, vaudeville, and the religious revival. While all the Great Awakenings had included revivals of religion, "revival" in this case refers to the revival meeting, held at a temporary camp set just outside town. These meetings had been a staple of religious life on the American frontier, where settlement was often too sparse to sustain a church, and revivalist preachers acted as the religious

Scofield Reference Bible

A former Confederate soldier and recovering alcoholic, Cyrus Scofield converted to evangelical Christianity at the age of 56, and was ordained as a Congregationalist minister four years later. He worked as a missionary and educator, and eventually succeeded Dwight Moody as pastor of Moody's parish and administrator of the Northfield Bible Training School. In 1909, he published his Scofield Reference Bible, with a revision following eight years later (at which point he had left the Congregationalist Church for the more conservative Southern Presbyterians).

The Scofield Reference Bible was a heavily annotated Bible intended in part as a study aid, usable in evangelical correspondence courses as well as for Bible study groups. Though Scofield did not intend it as a conversion device or a forum in which to pass along innovative theology, he nevertheless wound up introducing many Americans to evangelical theological notions. Scofield was a premillennialist, believing that the Second Coming was imminent and would be followed by a golden age, at a time when the most active Protestant movements, like the Social Gospel, were staunchly postmillennialist, believing that the world had to achieve this golden age to prove itself worthy of the Second Coming.

Scofield was very focused on eschatology and an essentially cynical view of the world, when most other Christians were concerned with social work and the attainable improvement of human society. When the Great War broke out a few years after his Bible was published, it seemed to validate Scofield's more pessimistic view of human nature. The war was certainly one of the factors that precipitated his revised second edition. Among the beliefs Scofield popularized was Archbishop Ussher's calculation of the date of Creation as 4004 B.C.E., which Scofield introduced as simple fact, as he did most of the interpretations in his notes. Little or no attention was paid to acknowledging disagreements among theologians or vague points in the text. Scofield selected a view and presented it as though it were self-evident, proven, or widely agreed-upon. His detailed notes on the books of Daniel and Revelation are the single most influential non-Scriptural text in the development of fundamentalist theology in the twentieth century—virtually no evangelical theologian does not owe Scofield an intellectual debt.

The Scofield Reference Bible appeared at a time when new readings of the Bible from Europe were also being introduced in American universities and seminaries.

Billy Sunday posed as if preaching. Interest in revivals and other live traveling shows eventually declined with the growth of radio and the movies.

equivalent of the traveling circuit court judge. Services held under the giant tents were often held all day, and even late into the night. Different speakers would take their turns, and at meetings featuring faith healers, townspeople could come to the front for healing, or to offer personal testimony about their religious salvation and experiences of miracles. Revivals were tied in with the spread of new denominations as well, especially those within the Restoration Movement.

Toward the end of the 19th century revivals became a more organized and profitable affair, thanks in no small part to Billy Sunday, the Elvis Presley of tent meetings. A well-known outfielder in baseball's National League (playing for the Chicago White Stockings, Pittsburgh Alleghenies, and Philadelphia Phillies) in the 1880s, Billy Sunday left baseball following his conversion to evangelical Christianity. He met his future wife, Nell Thompson, at a Presbyterian church around the time of his conversion, while both were in serious relationships. By all accounts they fell swiftly in love, and he ended his relationship with his previous girlfriend, and pursued Thompson diligently. They were married less than two years later.

His first job after professional baseball was at a YMCA, where he conducted most of his early ministerial work. From 1896 to 1908 he hit the road on the "Kerosene Circuit," so named because his revival tour took him through midwestern towns that had not yet been electrified. After 12 years the work took a toll on his marriage, and his children were left to the care of a nanny so that Nell could accompany her husband as his business manager. She changed Billy Sunday from an itinerant preacher to his era's equivalent of a rock star. By the 1910s, he was conducting revivals in major cities like Boston and Philadelphia, where he was still remembered as a baseball hero. By this time, he was earning more money per day than the average American made in a year. His social station rose accordingly, and his peers included industrialist John D. Rockefeller and President Woodrow Wilson.

A fundamentalist, Sunday preached the inerrancy and literal truth of the Bible. He was more popular with Catholics than most Protestant revivalists, in part because he originated no theology or interpretation of his own, and therefore had little to say that conflicted with what they heard in their own mass. Politically conservative, he nevertheless supported reforms that reduced suffering, especially those that ended child labor or improved the life of the poor. He was also a strong advocate of sex education in public schools. In the 1920s electric forms of entertainment began to take over—not only radio, but movie theaters and nickelodeons—and Sunday's star faded, as did the revivalist scene in general.

NEW PROTESTANT MOVEMENTS

Originating among Methodists in the 1830s, the Holiness Movement had emphasized the personal experience of Christian faith and the transformative power of the Holy Spirit, particularly as it cleansed one's sins. The Holiness Movement had spread in part through revival meetings, where speaking in tongues and—as witnesses wrote—"erratic movement" was common. The Pentecostal movement grew directly out of the Holiness Movement and this distinctly modern emphasis on personal faith and public ecstatic experience.

It began at the Shearer Schoolhouse Revival in 1896 in North Carolina, where many participants spoke in tongues, but it was the 1906 Azusa Street Revival in Los Angeles that really gave the movement its first boost. William J. Seymour, a black Methodist minister, had been expelled from his parish for preaching that speaking in tongues was evidence of "baptism in the Holy Spirit," as described in the Acts of the Apostles. The conventional view in most denominations, including Catholicism, had been that "spirit baptism" occurred in

The Azusa Street Mission in Los Angeles, California. Pentecostalism gained popularity after the 1906 revival at the mission.

the process of becoming a Christian. Seymour preached in an old dirt-floor building in downtown Los Angeles, appealing to all races and denominations and to the poor, and allowing women to lead services. He preached the need for immediate salvation because of the imminent return of Christ, and of speaking in tongues and faith healing. The Azusa Street Mission remains important to the Pentecostal faith, thanks to the impact Seymour had. The Pentecostals worried many; they seemed to be fanatic, wild, and chaotic. At first the movement was distinctly multiracial, with black and white members mingling together. With women leading services, there was something approaching gender equality as well. After the popularity of the Azusa Street Mission waned and the Pentecostal movement decentralized, this racial unity was no longer standard, although desegregated services did continue nationwide, where allowed by law.

When October 22, 1844, came and went without the return of Jesus that had been promised by the Millerite movement, many members were disillusioned. The Seventh-Day Adventists formed in 1863 around a core of Millerites, Baptists, and others. The group was centered around Ellen White, who claimed to be a prophet, and it grew quickly, picking up the pieces of other groups in the wake of failed prophecy. By 1903 it had relocated its headquarters to Washington, D.C. White died in 1915, and it was unclear what the church would do without a living prophet. The 1919 Bible Conference addressed the issue, but no consensus could be reached. While White's prophetic writings were clearly not inerrant and could not be held in the same esteem as the Bible, it seemed likely that parishioners would be devastated if any official declaration diminished their importance. In the end nothing was done, and the transcripts of the meetings were not published. Throughout the 1920s the Adventists adapted to their post-White world, adopting mainstream trinitarianism over their previous Arianism.

CONCLUSION
Reform and other modern movements appeared in several religions in the United States during the Progressive Era. Some were activist-oriented, and others centered around new interpretations of tradition, or more personal expressions of faith. Other changes, such as the rise and fall of tent revivals, were affected by the spread of radio and other new forms of entertainment brought by new technologies. However religion in America was at the cusp of even greater changes as millions of new immigrants, many of them not Protestants, as in the past, became more established in their communities in the decades to follow.

BILL KTE'PI

Further Readings

Curtis, Susan. *A Consuming Faith: Social Gospel and Modern American Culture*. Baltimore, MD: Johns Hopkins, 1992.

Dorsett, Lyle W. *Billy Sunday and the Redemption of Urban America*. New York: Eerdmans, 1991.

Hopkins, Charles Howard. *The Rise of the Social Gospel in American Protestantism*. New Haven, CT: Yale University Press, 1940.

McLoughlin, William G. *Revivals, Awakenings, Reform: An Essay on Religion and Social Change in America*. Chicago, IL: University of Chicago Press, 1978.

Nenneman, Richard A. *Persistent Pilgrim: The Life of Mary Baker Eddy*. Etna, NH: Nebbadoon Press, 1997.

Sizer, Sandra. *Gospel Hymns and Social Religion: The Rhetoric of Nineteenth-Century Revivalism*. Philadelphia, PA: Temple University Press, 1978.

Taiz, Lillian. *Hallelujah Lads and Lasses: Remaking the Salvation Army in America, 1880–1930*. Chapel Hill, NC: University of North Carolina Press, 1992.

Van Seters, John. *In Search of History: Historiography in the Ancient World and the Origins of Biblical History*. New Haven, CT: Yale University Press, 1983.

Ward, W.R. *The Protestant Evangelical Awakening*. Cambridge, UK: Cambridge University Press, 1992.

Winston, Diane. *Red-Hot and Righteous: the Urban Religion of the Salvation Army*. Cambridge, MA: Harvard University Press, 2000.

Chapter 8

Education

*"A man who has gone to school may steal from a freight car;
but if he has a university education,
he may steal the whole railroad."*
— Theodore Roosevelt

IN THE PROGRESSIVE ERA new discoveries in science and technology were changing the ways humans thought about themselves and their societies. Progressive educators believed that the purpose of public education was to create and shape students into thoughtful, productive citizens who could participate effectively in a democracy. While progressive educational reformers shared common goals, they used different approaches to achieve the changes they sought. Some, like John Dewey, sought to experiment with educational theories through practical applications in classrooms to see which methods worked the best. A second group of reformers, including Rudolf Steiner, emphasized the importance of artistic, emotional, and creative development. Still others sought to apply new knowledge to classrooms from fields such as psychology.

Between 1905 and 1908, French psychologist Alfred Binet worked to develop a series of tests that could aid in identifying and classifying students with mental disabilities. In 1916 Stanford psychologist Lewis Terman released a revised version of these tests called the "Stanford-Binet" tests. These tests were thought to provide a measure of a person's intelligence, and were soon adapted for use in determining children's giftedness as well as their potential disabilities. In general, such standardized tests were seen as part of a scientific approach to education at the turn of the century.

In 1913 Edward Lee Thorndike's three-volume *Educational Psychology: The Psychology of Learning* was published. It transformed the way educators understood childhood learning by proposing new theories of habit formation, suggesting that positive stimuli resulted in learning new behaviors, while negative stimuli did not. Thorndike suggested that rewards, properly administered, were a key to learning. He applied his observations from animal studies to hu-

Small communities often combined both the school and church in the same building, as in this preserved structure at Cracker Village at the State Fair Grounds in Tampa, Florida.

man classrooms, and many of his conclusions affected subsequent classroom practices. He also advocated the use of standardized tests in order to quantify educational achievement.

Progressive education, in addition to its focus on participatory democracy and scientific grounding, had several other characteristics. Progressive educators believed that children learned behaviors best through direct experience, and so the move toward hands-on experiential education began. Industrial education, manual education, and agricultural education programs also were part of this movement, as educators realized the importance of preparing students for career fields in which they took an interest. Critics of progressive education decried the lack of attention to traditional academic disciplines, and called for more systematic study than progressive approaches allowed. By the 1950s progressive education philosophies fell by the wayside in many public schools. As the United States entered the Cold War years, a new international competitiveness replaced the emphasis on student-centered learning with a move toward knowledge-based learning.

Although few public schools completely follow the progressive model today, several Progressive Era educational philosophies remain alive in today's public education system. For example science laboratory classes, vocational training, and after-school clubs often incorporate elements of the progressive approach to education.

TEACHERS AND TEACHING

During the last few decades of the 19th century tension increased between the advocates of practical-skills education and classic liberal-arts education. Some people believed that the goal of education should be to prepare students for work immediately upon graduation, while others believed that the focus of education should be to study the best of human achievement while preparing students for college. In 1892 the National Education Association was composed primarily of school principals, superintendents, and college administrators. That year the NEA formed the Committee of Ten. This committee was responsible for developing suggested curricular standards for each grade level, and its work formed the basis of the 12-grade-level educational system.

The Committee of Ten recommended eight years of primary education and four years of secondary education. It also advocated for specific curricular content at each grade level in the following subjects:

1. Latin
2. Greek
3. English
4. Other Modern Languages
5. Mathematics
6. Physics, Astronomy, and Chemistry

John Dewey and the Laboratory School

John Dewey (1859–1952) was a philosopher and psychologist whose writings contain valuable educational theories. After receiving his doctorate from Johns Hopkins University in 1884, he taught at the University of Michigan and the University of Minnesota before becoming head of the department of Philosophy, Psychology, and Pedagogy at the University of Chicago in 1894.

In 1896 Dewey founded the Laboratory School at the University of Chicago. His experiments in education there began with students aged six to nine, and eventually expanded to include children four to 13 years of age. In 1897 he wrote the essay "My Pedagogic Creed," which outlined his beliefs about the best possible educational system. Many of these beliefs were put into practice in the Laboratory School, and further questions were generated and tested by the teachers who worked with Dewey. Dewey detailed those years in several essays later collected into the book *The School and Society* (1907). His wife, Harriet Dewey, became principal of the Laboratory School (also known as the University Elementary School) in 1902.

At the Laboratory School, children's home and school activities were not separated. Children's activities in the Lab School included cooking, carpentry, and sewing, as they learned to care for themselves and their daily needs. As their needs for precise measurement grew out of their tasks, mathematics was taught. As their needs for communication grew, language and literacy skills became part of their daily lessons. Through this "learning by doing," children lived in the present as part of a cooperative community, instead of focusing solely on skills needed in an adult future. Rote memorization (then standard in public schools) was replaced by learning through students' natural curiosity; the goal was for students to solve problems by critical thinking and investigation in order to establish deeper knowledge. Interested children would be good students; no external motivators such as prizes or competitions were necessary. Teachers were asked to select challenging and stimulating experiences particular to each child, choosing problems based on their knowledge of a child's interests and abilities.

While his philosophy would later be classified as part of the school of pragmatism, Dewey called his philosophy "instrumentalism." Its central idea was that truth is an instrument that humans use to problem-solve; since problems change, truth changes, and thus no single truth can compose the whole subject of education. Instead humans must actively manipulate their environments as part of the learning process, solving problems and discovering truths. Dewey was a significant contributor to the progressive education movement. Although his theories were never fully put into practice outside his own schools, his ideas of "learning by doing" and careful study of the connections between culture and education have since contributed much to educational philosophy.

7. Natural History (Biology including Botany, Zoology, and Physiology)
8. History, Civil Government, and Political Economy
9. Geography (Physical Geography, Geology, and Meteorology)

The first committee-wide recommendation was for subjects to be introduced early in elementary education, then to be addressed in more detail in the secondary years. The second was that these subjects should be taught in the same fashion for students who planned to continue on to college as for those who did not. Then, individual "conferences" in each subject area also provided recommendations for specific content. The committee also strongly recommended putting off the tracking of students into classical, latin-scientific, and vocational classes until at least two years into secondary school. Their belief was that broad exposure to many subjects was desirable so that students could make educated choices as to their future courses of study and career path.

The Committee of Ten Report marked the first time that the idea of a "core curriculum" for all U.S. public schools was put forth by a national organization. While individual states and districts had organizations that determined what was appropriate to teach in public schools, there was no federal oversight of the curriculum. The school system was too fragmented prior to the turn of the century for there to be a unified approach to teaching subject matter. The Committee of Ten called for more highly-trained teachers at every level of education, but made few recommendations as to how to continue and improve training for those who were already teaching.

The gap between school administrators and teachers continued to grow over the first two decades of the 20th century, as a more centralized school system developed. Individual teachers lost much autonomy in their classrooms over that time period, and the pay gaps between male and female teachers continued to increase. In 1916 a new union, the American Federation of Teachers (AFT), formed to advocate for the economic and professional interests of teachers. The NEA resisted working with the teachers' union, and denounced teachers who joined the AFT as "unethical and unprofessional." While the NEA sought to be a professional organization that could unite teachers and administrators in working toward shared goals, the reality was that teachers' voices were often ignored by administrators, who formed a larger percentage of the NEA membership. It would take decades for the balance in the NEA to shift in teachers' favor.

A MODERN HIGH SCHOOL

While in many parts of the country the one-room schoolhouse was still the norm, in urban areas, new schools with rooms for each grade were being built to meet the demand of exponential U.S. population growth. In Minneapolis, Minnesota, 23 new schools were built between 1900 and 1915. These school buildings featured large windows, adequate ventilation and heating systems, indoor plumbing, and sometimes dedicated areas for manual training classrooms and

Rudolf Steiner, Founder of the Waldorf Schools

Rudolf Steiner (1861–1925) was an Austrian-born intellectual who contributed much to the fields of spiritual and educational philosophy. He received his doctorate in philosophy at the University of Rostock in Germany, and his first major project was the editing of Goethe's complete scientific works. He also collaborated on projects involving the works of Schopenhauer and Nietzsche, and met the latter philosopher shortly before his death. In 1899 Steiner became involved with the Theosophical Society, through which he became interested in a variety of approaches to exploring the spiritual world. Eventually he broke from the Theosophists and developed his own form of spiritual philosophy, known as Anthroposophy. Its goal was to bring the rigor of the natural sciences into the study of spiritual worlds and phenomena. Rather than advocating for a particular god or spiritual authority figure, Steiner's view centered on the individual human being. He posited that each human was composed of a temporal body, an eternal spirit, and a soul that evolved over the course of the human lifetime. He believed that people could develop a sort of supersensory consciousness to aid them in spiritual research, and that everyone had the capacity to become morally good and creative individuals.

This spiritual philosophy was put into practice, in part, with the founding of the first Steiner school in 1919. His belief in the importance of the imagination and of holistic thinking formed the basis for what is now known as the Waldorf school philosophy. The name comes from the Waldorf factory in Stuttgart, Germany, which funded Steiner's first school. The Waldorf idea incorporated early childhood education into a comprehensive educational philosophy that divided childhood into three seven-year stages. Steiner believed that children under seven years of age needed sensory-based, experiential learning. From age seven to 12, his middle-school curriculum focused on artistic and creative learning through drama, music, and the visual arts; foreign language instruction also began at age seven. Older children ages 14 to 21 worked on specific academic subjects, grasping abstract concepts, and developing moral judgment.

Today, there are over 150 Waldorf schools across the United States. The environment of Waldorf schools is non-competitive. Textbooks are rarely used, and individual teachers cycle through the grade levels with a class so that there is consistency of instruction over several years of a child's education. In addition to these "loop" teachers who remain with the same group of children, specialist instructors lead an increasing number of classroom activities each year until the age of secondary education is reached. Adolescents are taught solely by specialists at that point, similar to many other high school models. Letter grades are not issued; instead teachers write learning reports describing the child's progress in detail. Standardized testing is also discouraged.

This small school room with furnishings from 1908 is preserved at the Manatee Historical Village in Bradenton, Florida.

libraries. Outdoor playgrounds and gymnasiums were also added to several school designs to encourage students' physical development, and to provide the public with community meeting spaces.

By 1909 Minnesota public school teachers were required to have a high school degree, plus at least two years of advanced training at a normal school. Mandatory education laws specified that children had to attend school from the ages of seven to 16, and non-mandatory kindergartens for younger children also increased in popularity. The number of students enrolling in high schools grew sharply due to the increase in the age of mandatory education. Existing facilities could not provide adequate space for student instruction, so public funding was raised to build new school buildings.

In 1913 Central High School in Minneapolis opened with an enrollment of 1,600 students. It was one of the most modern high schools in the country. It included a greenhouse, a physics laboratory, a 1,800-seat auditorium, a running track, two gymnasiums, and a large library. A typical student's experience at Central has numerous similarities to those of current public high school students, although several elective subjects have changed since those days. A day at high school was broken into several time periods. Students switched classrooms to work with different teachers, and studied subjects including English, Latin, math, history, science, and art. Depending upon which track a student enrolled in, manual training courses such as woodworking, shop, drawing, housekeeping, and sewing were available, as were liberal-arts courses including Greek, orchestra, chorus, creative writing, and drama. There was a weekly student newspaper, the *Central High News*. Numerous student clubs formed around academic, athletic, and intellectual activities such as chess, speech, and debate. Sports were popular, although most teams restricted participation to boys. The school fielded competitive teams in baseball, football, basketball, swimming, tennis, and track in the 1920s. The school held an annual homecoming celebration during football season, and a senior prom in the spring.

Many of the young male graduates of Central High were drafted into World War I. The students participated in the war effort by raising money through activities and clubs, by rolling bandages and sending packages to the troops, and by keeping in correspondence with troops in the field. Twenty-six Central High graduates died in combat. When the war came to an end, the students raised money and built a memorial to the graduates who had died in the field. The world outside the school system colored students' experiences during World War I, as war rationing, friends and family in military service, and home defense preparations occupied students in addition to their studies and recreational pursuits.

Around 1900, children washed up before their lessons using a washstand in the classroom.

CHILD LABOR LAWS AND REFORM

Child labor reached a peak in the early years of the 20th century. While various unions called for an end to full-time work for children under 14, the practice continued even in states where laws had been passed. At the turn of the century many states had laws that made education compulsory for children below a certain age; still, these laws were only sporadically enforced. In 1892 the Democratic Party platform contained a plank that would have banned children under 15 from factory employment. This ban did not come to pass, in 1892 or in the two following decades. It would take until 1938 before a federal law passed regulating children's

An extremely young child laborer, this three-year-old girl was photographed hulling berries at Johnson's Canning Camp in Seaford, Delaware, in May 1910.

labor and setting minimum ages and maximum hours of work. By then, however, the number of child laborers had decreased.

Many states had laws intended to prevent children from working at the expense of their health and education. However these laws were almost impossible to enforce since both manpower and time were required to investigate each violation. Businesses with powerful local influences were unlikely to respond to requests for information about child labor practices, and parents who needed their children's wages were unlikely to self-report.

Two trends emerged in the early 20th century that were more successful than legislation in putting an end to most child labor in the United States. As the industrial age progressed, machines became increasingly complex, and trained adult workers were needed to operate and maintain them. Thus, adult labor became preferable to child labor because adults had the literacy and mechanical skills to complete the necessary tasks. Also, the growing demands for educated workers in fields outside of manufacturing made educating children a prudent long-term investment. Young children who could become literate and complete manual education training could earn many times the wages of unskilled workers. Thus it made economic sense for families to take advantage of free public education during children's formative years in order that their children could become self-supporting, skilled workers upon completion of secondary school.

HIGHER EDUCATION

In 1900 the Association of American Universities (AAU) was formed. Its original members were 14 doctorate-granting public and private universities, many of which are referred to as "Ivy League" universities today. The goal of the association was to give administrators from member schools the opportunity to discuss and generate policy recommendations for issues that affected all of higher education, including both graduate and undergraduate education. The AAU still exists, and has over 60 member institutions.

Also emerging during this time period were the nation's first community colleges. Some of these began as manual training schools associated with high schools; others began as teachers' colleges or other offshoots of existing colleges. The schools shared several common traits. Most were small, with less than 150 students. All were opened to meet a particular need within their local communities that other post-secondary institutions were not meeting at the time. Their goal was to provide low-cost quality education.

These community colleges quickly took the place of the former "normal schools" in teacher training, particularly in states where a bachelor's degree was not required in order to teach. Community colleges were accessible to women at a time when many other higher education institutions were not.

In 1914 Congress passed the Smith-Lever Act. This law was tied to the earlier laws that funded land-grant colleges in 1868 and 1890. It enabled land-grant colleges and universities to create "cooperative extension offices" that provided education to adults in the subjects of agriculture, rural energy, and home economics. Cooperative extension offices were the first federally funded attempts at adult education in the United States. Cooperative extension offices were very successful at conveying the most recent research findings from universities to farmers, ranchers, and other adults who could benefit.

JOIN THE
UNITED-
STATES
SCHOOL
GARDEN
ARMY

ENLIST NOW

Write *to* The United States School Garden Army,
Bureau of Education, Department of Interior, Washington, D.C.

During World War I students raised victory gardens and sold war bonds.

Helen Keller

Born in 1880 in Tuscumbia, Alabama, a young girl named Helen Keller suffered a terrible fever at the age of 18 months as part of an unidentified illness that might have been meningitis or encephalitis. She eventually recovered, but by 19 months of age she was completely deaf and blind. Education for disabled children was almost impossible to find in most parts of the country, but Helen's parents persisted in the search. Helen's

Helen Keller sitting beside Anne Sullivan, reading her lips by touch in 1897.

mother, Kate, traveled to Baltimore, where she met with a specialist. He informed her that a local expert, Alexander Graham Bell, had begun working with deaf children. The Kellers met with Bell, and he suggested they contact the Perkins Institute for the Blind in Boston.

The Perkins Institute had opened in the late 1820s, and had a long history of assisting blind people to become functional in society. The director of the institute sent a young teacher, Anne Sullivan, to work with the Keller family in 1886. By that time young Helen had already made up a language of hand gestures in which she communicated with her family, but she was increasingly frustrated with the barriers to self-expression that she faced daily.

Anne Sullivan was visually impaired, and her time at Perkins had taught her the importance of approaching education for disabled children through their functional senses. Anne tried to teach Helen the alphabet by spelling letters into her hand, but the teacher had limited success at first. After she had lived with the Kellers for about a month, Anne took Helen into the garden one day and turned on the water pump. She put one of Helen's hands under the running water, and used tactile sign language to spell the letters W-A-T-E-R into her other hand. Helen immediately had a breakthrough as she realized the connection between the letters she had been struggling to learn and the world she fought to describe. Helen learned over 30 words that first day.

Through Anne's patient teaching, Helen learned the Braille alphabet, and learned to print English as well. After two years of working with Anne, the two women moved to Boston, where Helen attended the Perkins Institute. She became a star student, and was eventually admitted to Radcliffe College in 1900. While in college Helen wrote an autobiography, *The Story of My Life* (1903). In 1904 Helen Keller became the first deaf and blind person to earn a bachelor of arts degree. She went on to become a social and political advocate for the disabled. Over her long career, she met with 12 U.S. presidents, toured the country many times, and wrote 12 books and numerous articles.

Mary McLeod Bethune

Mary McLeod Bethune (1875–1955) was a pioneering African-American woman who believed in the power of education to transform society. One of 17 children, she received her education through the charity of local religious missions. She was awarded full tuition to the Moody Bible Institute, where she received formal teacher training. She applied to become a missionary in Africa, but was turned down.

In time she realized her life's work lay in working with African Americans in the United States. In a 1939 interview, when asked about how her family reacted to her education, she recalled: "They knew that whatever I had, they knew I would adapt to use of the people there. Those were great days when the masses needed the few who could read or write so badly."

After graduation she taught in several states, including Illinois, South Carolina, and Georgia. She worked to educate both children and adults, teaching in Chicago prisons and Florida Sunday schools. She met her husband, Albertus, in North Carolina in 1898. They had one son, Albertus Junior. In 1904 she founded the Daytona Normal and Industrial School for Negro Girls in Daytona Beach, Florida. Tuition at her school was $.50 a week, and she began with five young female students. In 1923 her school merged with nearby boys' school Cookman Institute to become a co-educational high school. In 1924 her school became affiliated with the United Methodist Church. By 1931 the school evolved into Bethune-Cookman College, which is still in existence today.

Bethune was an admirable fundraiser, and her work and religious faith inspired many of the people that she met to give to her school as a charitable cause. She met famous philanthropists, including Lady Astor and Eleanor Roosevelt, and became politically involved with numerous women's issues. She was president of the Florida Federation of Colored Women, and eventually became president of the National Federation of Colored Women in 1924. At that time, that was the highest public office that an African-American woman could hold.

She worked tirelessly for women's suffrage and for an end to racial discrimination in education and the workplace. In 1935 she founded the National Council of Negro Women. She served in various capacities under four U.S. presidents, including Calvin Coolidge, Herbert Hoover, Franklin Roosevelt, and Harry Truman. She was vice president of the National Association for the Advancement of Colored People (NAACP) from 1940 until her death.

A year before she died, the U.S. Supreme Court put an end to "separate but equal" education with *Brown v. Board of Education*, and Bethune was a step closer to her most cherished dream of "full equality for the Negro in our time."

World War I had numerous impacts on higher education during the latter part of this time period. The vast majority of college-age men left school to participate in the war effort, and many women did so as well. University enrollments declined, and many campuses housed military training programs such as the Student Army Training Corps (SATC). The U.S. War Department needed skilled men to serve as officers and engineers on the front, and they needed to train them quickly and efficiently. By taking over residence halls, dormitories, and other college facilities, they found the space to house military trainees, and often the equipment needed for their training.

Efforts to fundraise swept the homefront, as college students sold liberty bonds, raised victory gardens, and participated in supply drives to support alumni who had joined the troops abroad. Women who were not actively participating in the Red Cross or the War Relief Society might be part of women's leagues or other social committees that planned events for troop socialization and entertainment. Because so many men were called into active military service, women had access to new career paths out of national necessity. Increased numbers of college women entered the fields of nursing and civil service, while the fields of engineering and business supervision opened to women at several universities for the first time. After the war ended in 1919, women won another triumph. After decades of efforts to win women's suffrage, U.S. women received the right to vote in 1920 with the passage of the Nineteenth Amendment. Their patriotism and attempts to defend democracy during the war earned them the right to participate in the country's governance when the war was won.

CONCLUSION

Trends in education during the Progressive Era were even more tied to trends in employment than usual. Educational reformers were at odds over practical approaches that emphasized work skills and more open-ended types of educational environments that encouraged creativity and moral judgment. While these debates intensified, child labor in the United States was also reaching its peak. In the end, it was technology that brought faster, more complicated manufacturing processes that meant adults were needed, not children. Better-educated workers were then more in demand. Another lasting trend that arose from more developed vocational training was the spread of community colleges, which have long brought educational opportunities to women and other underserved groups.

HEATHER A. BEASLEY

Further Readings

American Association of Community Colleges. *America's Community Colleges: A Century of Innovation.* Washington, D.C.: Community College Press, 2001.

Anderson, James D. *The Education of Blacks in the South, 1860–1935.* Chapel Hill, NC: University of North Carolina Press, 1988.

Dolan, Eric F. *America in World War I.* Brookfield, CT: Millbrook Press, 1996.

Gavin, Lettie. *American Women in World War I: They Also Served.* Boulder, CO: University Press of Colorado, 1997.

Gibson, William. *The Miracle Worker.* New York: Pocket, 2002.

Gitlin, Andrew. "Gender and Professionalization: An Institutional Analysis of Teacher Education and Unionism at the Turn of the Twentieth Century," *Teachers College Record* (v.97/4, 1996).

Guthrie, James W. *Encyclopedia of Education.* New York: Macmillan Reference USA, 2002.

"Helen Keller: The Story." Perkins School for the Blind. Available online: http://www.perkins.org/culture/helenkeller. Accessed May 2007.

Keller, Helen. *The Story of My Life.* New York: Pocket, 2005.

Minneapolis Public Schools Historic Context Study. "Early 20th-Century Public Schools: 1900–1915." Minneapolis Heritage Preservation Commission, 2005.

McCluskey, Audrey Thomas. *Mary McLeod Bethune: Building a Better World, Essays and Selected Documents.* Bloomington, IN: Indiana University Press, 2002.

Norris, William Dale. *The Promise and Failure of Progressive Education.* Lanham, MD: Scarecrow/Rowman & Littlefield Press, 2004.

"Oregon at War! World War I and the Oregon Experience." Oregon State Archives, 2007. Available online: http://arcweb.sos.state.or.us/exhibits/war/index.html. Accessed April 2007.

Schwartz, John A., ed. "1914 Smith-Lever Act," *History and Archival Resources in Higher Education.* Available online: http://www.higher-ed.org/resources/smith.htm. Accessed May 2007.

Steiner, Rudolf. "An Introduction to Waldorf Education." *The Rudolph Steiner Web.* Available online: http://www.rudolfsteinerweb.com. Accessed May 2007.

"Tribute to Triumph: Central High School 1860–1982." Minneapolis, MN: Central High School, 1982.

Chapter 9

Science and Technology

*"Automatism has been applied in all cases
where it would save time and secure accuracy."*
— John Vaughn

THE PROGRESSIVE ERA flows from the Gilded Age in such a way that it is often difficult to tell where one period ends and the other begins. This is particularly true in the fields of science and technology, in which the chief characteristic of the Progressive Era, the drive to social reform, is less prominent. In the 1870s and 1880s—decades that belong firmly within the Gilded Age—many scientists and inventors saw their work as having the power to improve the lot of humanity, as well as enriching themselves and their sponsors. Even Thomas Alva Edison, who frequently claimed that he never undertook a project without having a practical application firmly in mind, couched his public arguments for the electric light in terms of human benefits.

However the fields of science and technology were not immune from muckraking journalism and resultant political pressures for reform that characterized the Progressive Era. Whole industries came under fire for having a casual attitude toward the health and well-being of their workers in the name of profit. Disciplines such as industrial hygiene were developed with the express purpose of protecting workers from dangerous industrial practices. Industrial hygiene as a scientific discipline was largely a response to the growing inadequacy of existing social systems to deal with the dangers of the industrial workplace. Other industries developed during the first decades of the 20th century improved work conditions for many people.

THE UNSAFE WORKPLACE

In the traditional workplace of hand-powered tools, dangers were by no means absent, but they were generally understood by workers and reasonably easy to guard against. However the industrial workplace often had dangers that were not immediately obvious to workers. Fast-moving machines could catch the loose clothing of a worker who merely brushed against them. The ever-increasing drive to speed up production combined with the assembly-line methods of mass production led to workers having to repeat the same motions over and over, all day long. Chemicals introduced even more subtle dangers that could ruin a worker's health long after exposure had ceased.

Social factors only added to the dangers of the industrial workplace. Since many of the workers were immigrants who spoke limited English, it was often difficult to communicate safe procedures. The stereotyping of many workers as being lazy and shiftless went hand-in-hand with a lack of any real legal or social sanction against employers who fostered dangerous working conditions.

Ironically one of the first people to address issues of workplace safety was a man who had been vilified for ratcheting up the speed of production to a frantic pace. Frederick W. Taylor is generally remembered as an efficiency expert, but his time-and-motion studies also became the foundation of the science of ergonomics. Paradoxically Taylor's tendency to regard the human body as

These boys packing canned food worked around dangerous machinery in a cannery in Baltimore, Maryland, in July 1909.

a machine—which his critics deplored on moral grounds—enabled him to recognize the "design limitations" inherent to the body. Flexible as the body might be, it was not infinitely so, and one could not simply warp it at will to an arbitrarily designed workspace. By considering the most efficient way for the worker to move through a task, the possibility for injury was reduced.

However not every reformer had the advantage of the respect Taylor enjoyed with the industrialists. Many early pioneers in the field of industrial hygiene had to deal with suspicion and outright hostility from managers who regarded them as troublemakers. Even when they got results, it was not necessarily the ones they had wanted. The best-known example of this phenomenon was the response to Upton Sinclair's *The Jungle.* Although Sinclair had hoped to improve working conditions in the packing houses by describing the range of injuries to workers, readers responded to images of filthy conditions with demands for inspections primarily to ensure the cleanliness and safety of their own food, not the health of the workers.

Alice Hamilton, one of the first people to make scientific studies of workplace dangers and methods for ameliorating them, often used a carrot-and-stick approach to overcome management resistance. She would start by praising things a factory was doing well, then phrase her criticisms in terms of improvements to be made on problem areas. By starting with praise, she was able to establish a rapport with executives and get them to see her as a colleague, rather than an enemy.

Furthermore when Hamilton appealed to the public to gain legislative reforms of unsafe working conditions, she took pains to emphasize ways in which diligent workers were actually exposed to more dangers simply because they worked more quickly and handled more product. For example in her 1912 pamphlet "What Phosphorous Poisoning Really Means," she used as her example an attractive young widow who tried to provide for her family by taking a job with a match factory, and instead had her health destroyed by a malady known as Phossy Jaw. Not only were the pictures of the victim's slow degeneration appalling, but the fact that her exposure was the result of having wanted to avoid being a drain on the public treasury ensured readers' sympathy with her fate.

COOLING DOWN

In addition to measures deliberately taken to improve the work conditions for employees, other technological advances made things better for workers as well. For example air conditioning was developed because of a growing need to control the temperature and humidity at which certain industrial processes were carried out. However it often had the effect of making the workplace more healthful for the employees, since controlling heat and humidity not only reduced direct heat stress upon the workers' bodies, but also helped control molds and other environmental problems that proliferated in high humidity.

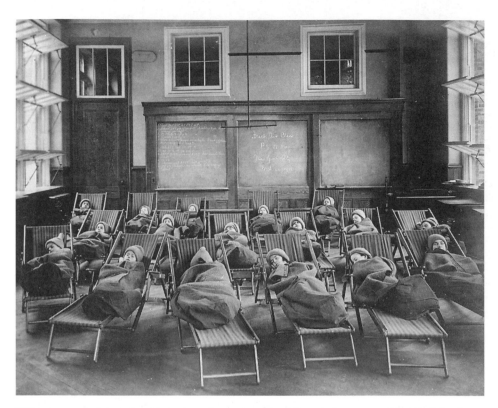

Children napping during rest hour in a classroom with all the windows open at Public School Number 51 in New York City during the early years of the fresh air movement.

Bakeries, for instance, had a great deal of trouble maintaining a consistent product in the summer. Because bread is a staple of the Western diet and could not be stored for long periods, it was simply not possible to suspend operations during periods of high heat and humidity. As a result many bakeries operated in basement rooms where the surrounding earth provided a modicum of coolness. However the resultant dampness often made basement bakeries an unpleasant place to work, and may well have created a less healthful product if mold spores infiltrated the bread even as it was removed from the oven.

By the latter part of the 19th century, efforts were made to control humidity in industries that worked with hygroscopic materials. Although one could add humidity to a heated room by boiling water or spraying a fine mist into the air, removing humidity proved more difficult.

In 1902 a paper company hired Willis Carrier to find a way to reduce the humidity in their factories so that newly produced paper would dry properly. He tackled the problem on the principle that cool air had less ability to hold moisture than warm air. If one could artificially reduce the temperature of the air, it

The Fresh Air Movement: "Crowd Poison"

It had long been noted that the air in a crowded room quickly became stuffy and unpleasant, even if there were no obvious sources of air contamination such as smoky fires or chemical processes. As science came to understand the composition of air and the products of respiration, it was theorized that carbon dioxide exhaled by the room's occupants was responsible for this "crowd poison" effect. As a result various standards were established calling for increased ventilation, even to the point of replacing all the air in the room on such a regular basis that heating systems could not keep up and remain economical.

In addition to the general malaise that a stuffy room could induce, bad indoor air was also blamed for the increase in cases of tuberculosis that was observed at the turn of the 20th century, particularly among children. Due to various conflicts between the engineering profession and the teachers and reformers—most of which boiled down to perceived intrusions upon one another's areas of expertise—the use of mechanical environmental controls to improve the air quality in schools was adamantly rejected. Instead reformers decided that what these children needed was to be taken out of the indoor environment altogether and given natural fresh air.

In 1909 the Chicago school system established an outdoor classroom consisting of a tent with one open side, erected on the roof of one of their schools. In spite of the city's famously icy winters, classes were held in this tent throughout the year for children with tuberculosis. In the absence of any artificial heat sources, the children were issued large insulated bags to wear in order to conserve their body heat.

The success of this experiment soon led to several classrooms for healthy children to shut off the heat and open windows for year-round ventilation. It was claimed that the cool, moist outdoor air had benefits not only for physical health, but for mental health as well. Children were said to think and behave better in these unheated classrooms, and proponents claimed that discipline problems were rare when children breathed natural, fresh air throughout the day.

The battle for children's air quality would continue for over two decades, and was often driven as much by political as scientific factors. Many of the fresh-air advocates had a marked bias against technology in general, and regarded scientific evidence of the healthfulness of mechanical climate control as meaningless and self-serving. In the end the virtues of mechanical climate control for the indoor schoolroom environment won the argument.

would be possible to force excess humidity to condense out of it. Using existing refrigeration technology that had been developed by the food preservation industry, he was able to create the first central-station air conditioning system.

However Carrier did not coin the term "air conditioning" for the process he had created. That would come in 1906, when Stewart Cramer used it in an article in a professional engineering journal. Air conditioning established itself rapidly after that point, and by 1911 it was a recognized branch of engineering, dealing primarily with humidity control, but also other aspects of air quality such as ventilation, temperature, and purity. Air conditioning technology advanced rapidly with developments in centrifugal pumps and improved refrigerants.

Once it became possible to exert control over the indoor environment, it was only natural in a social climate of reform to ask what was the most healthful way to maintain that environment. The results were a series of tests intended to determine the answer scientifically, rather than on the basis of commonly-held beliefs. Carrier was heavily involved, particularly in tests demonstrating the importance of humidity control in human comfort. In one rather theatrical experiment, Carrier and Dr. Leonard Hill donned clothes that enabled them to simulate wet and dry bulb thermometers on the human form, thus showing that dampness rather than temperature was the key factor in perceptions of chilliness. These and other, more serious experiments helped to reassure the public that mechanical climate control was indeed safe and healthful.

A NATION ON WHEELS

From its inception, America had been a mobile nation. Lacking the holdovers of feudal entailments on land tenure that restricted Europeans, Americans pulled up stakes and relocated with astonishing ease whenever they became dissatisfied with their current location, or were enamored of a change of scenery. The sheer size of the country and the energy of its people bred a love for speed, whether in horses, locomotives, or riverboats.

By 1890 a new instrument of speed had come into American life in the form of the safety bicycle. Unlike the old penny-farthing bicycle of Victorian England, this new bicycle with its equal-sized wheels was easy to mount and ride, opening the sport of cycling to women as well as men. The popularity of cycling drove improvements in bicycle technology such as tubular steel frames and ball-bearing wheels, lightening the bicycle for ease of handling, and making it so inexpensive that it was more economical than a horse. Soon the bicycle moved beyond recreation to become a means of practical transportation. People commuted to work on them, and took trips into town for activities.

Alongside the development of the bicycle as means of practical transportation, there had been development in small, light mechanical power sources.

The railroad had been invented in the early decades of the 19th century because the steam engines of the time had been so massive that they would have bogged down a vehicle running on regular roads. But by the 1890s there were steam engines so light that they could be put on a four-wheeled cart built from bicycle parts.

However steam power was no longer the only game in town, although the Stanley brothers had some success with their steam car. Given the growing importance of electricity in the closing years of the Gilded Age, it was only natural that inventors would seek to create electric cars. However battery weight and life proved an intractable problem, in spite of the efforts of no lesser luminary than Thomas Alva Edison himself. It was the four-stroke internal combustion engine that would prove the real contender, giving the best range and power for its weight. Invented in 1876 by Nicolaus Otto in Germany, it was soon attached to wheeled conveyances by two of his associates, Gottlieb Daimler and Wilhelm Maybach. The earliest automobile development remained almost entirely in continental Europe, and only in 1893 did Charles and Frank Duryea build their first automobile in the United States.

For its first decade, the American automobile was almost entirely the province of the wealthy. Other than experimental one-offs built by tinkerers,

By 1920 powerful steam tractors like this had been gradually replaced on farms by gasoline-powered models.

Early hand-crafted automobiles were the playthings of the very wealthy. The tycoon John Jacob Astor posed for this photograph in an automobile in front of a mansion in 1903.

cars were built by skilled craftsmen. Even the least expensive of automobiles was well beyond the means of an ordinary factory worker, and many came to resent the automobile as yet another way by which the wealthy flaunted their money.

However in this area change would not come as a result of muckraking journalism or of legislation, but from a man with a new business model. Henry Ford had his start as a tinkerer, building his Quadracycle in his spare time while working for the Edison Illuminating Company in Detroit. Once he proved his abilities, he was able to put together a partnership to build cars commercially. While his business partners assumed they would be building expensive cars for the wealthy, Ford had decided their best bet lay instead in taking advantage of the economies of scale to sell large numbers of inexpensive but solid cars, making their profits on high volume rather than high markup.

The concept of mass production was not new to Ford; it went back to the beginnings of the Industrial Revolution. Standardization and interchangeable parts had their origins in Eli Whitney's jigs to make large numbers of muskets for a government contract. What Ford added was the assembly line. Instead of the workers coming to each car in the workshop, the workers would remain at their assigned stations while parts and cars under assembly came to them.

Using principles of efficiency elucidated by Frederick W. Taylor, Ford sought every possible point at which waste could be eliminated, in order to produce more cars more quickly for less money. As a result Ford was able to reduce the selling price of the Model T each year, thus bringing this simple but reliable car into the reach of more households. However the ratcheting upward of the pace of work had its price in high turnover, to the point that some workers only stayed a matter of days before quitting. Deciding it was better to pay the money in wages to steady employees than for training for workers who might not stay, Ford instituted the $5 a day wage, an unheard-of level of compensation for unskilled workers at the time. By doing so, he also ensured that Fordism would be associated not only with hyper-efficient production, but with a humane attitude toward one's employees. The high wages also increased his potential market, since it ensured that every Ford employee could realistically save up to buy a Model T.

WORLD WITHOUT WIRES

By the turn of the century, Americans had become accustomed to the idea of being able to send a message by electrical impulses at speeds near that of light. However all the techniques available at that time required a wireline connection. This limitation made it difficult to contact vehicles in transit. Various workarounds had been developed to enable trains to pick up telegraph signals

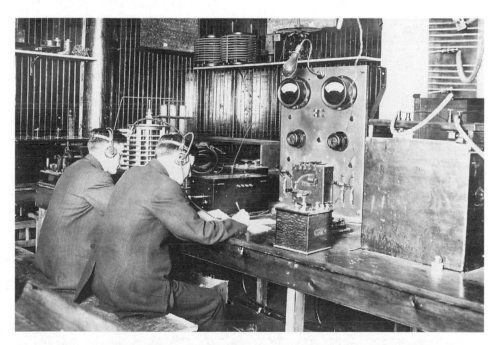

Early wireless transmissions required skilled operators. At the Marconi wireless school in New York, these operators in training copied messages transmitted from ships at sea in 1912.

Making the Airwaves Sing

Although Guglielmo Marconi was an inventor of a most entrepreneurial sort, he never thought beyond the wireless telegraph. However because his patents had been written in such a way as to cover only the narrowest applications of the technology, he inadvertently left the field wide open for rivals to develop alternate means of transmitting and detecting radio waves. Not all of them would necessarily depend on simply turning the transmitter on and off.

Among those rival inventors was Reginald Fessenden, a brilliant but often impractical inventor who realized that if one could generate a continuous radio wave, one could impose a far more complex signal upon it, even a human voice. No longer would the airwaves be the sole province of trained code operators. Just as the wires had become the home of everyone with a voice via Alexander Graham Bell's telephone, radio could as well.

However the alternator he designed would have to turn at such speeds that the engineers of the time were certain it would fly apart the moment it was turned on. The ordinary alternators at the power plant that produced household current turned at a leisurely 60 cycles per second. By contrast Fessenden's design would have to spin at an extraordinary 30,000 cycles per second.

Not discouraged, Fessenden fell back upon another solution to create an approximation of a carrier wave. He took an Edison foil phonograph cylinder and engraved it with thousands of tiny parallel grooves. With it he was able to generate thousands of sparks every second, a rather bad carrier wave, but one that would suffice. On December 23, 1900, he made his first transmission with it, a simple spoken request for his assistant to give him a weather report.

In 1906 Fessenden was finally able to find a man who could realize his design for an alternator that could generate a radio carrier wave. Ernst Alexanderson was the embodiment of the absent-minded professor, often greeting his friends and associates as though they were strangers, but he could work wonders with electricity and machines. However even he took the precaution of putting the newly-completed alternator in a pit and sandbagging it before turning it on for the first time.

On Christmas Eve 1906 Fessenden produced his first extensive test of voice transmission using the Alexanderson alternator. When the associates who were to speak and sing fell victim to stage fright, Fessenden took up his violin and played Christmas carols, proving that a radio could carry complex sounds. Although his test succeeded, he neglected to secure press coverage, and thus radio would remain a wireless telegraph until David Sarnoff saw its potential for public entertainment broadcasts in 1915. By that time World War I was a looming threat that America was desperately trying to stay out of, and thus broadcast radio would not come into its own until the 1920s.

from the wires they passed, but a ship at sea was effectively cut off from the rest of the world.

When James Clerk Maxwell published his unified theory of electricity and magnetism in 1873, he laid the groundwork for the development of a system of telecommunication not bound by wires. According to Maxwell's equations, if one were to send a current back and forth through a wire very rapidly, part of its energy would radiate outward in an electromagnetic wave. In the following decade Heinrich Hertz demonstrated that such waves actually existed, although he was only able to transmit them a few feet across his laboratory.

However it fell to a young Italian, Guglielmo Marconi, to make the first steps toward turning a scientific curiosity into a practical means of communication. As a result he has gone down in history as the inventor of radio, although he subsequently lost a patent infringement suit to Nikola Tesla, the eccentric Serbian-American inventor who had built a radio-controlled boat.

In 1895 Marconi began his investigations into the practical possibilities of radio waves, using a primitive spark-gap transmitter and a Branley coherer for a receiver. The spark-gap transmitter effectively created a miniature lightning bolt to spray energy into a section of the radio spectrum, not dissimilar from the way natural lightning bolts create static in the AM band. The Branley coherer was a tube of iron filings that would stick together or *cohere* when the air was energized with electromagnetic waves.

Because such a simple system could only be on or off, the only way to impose information upon the signal was to turn it on and off in patterns that represented the dots and dashes of Morse code. But such was the market for the ability to communicate without the constraints of a wireline connection that it would suffice, if it could be transmitted far enough. Understanding this necessity, Marconi set to transmitting a signal across the Atlantic Ocean.

On December 12, 1901, Marconi achieved the successful transmission of the letter *S* in Morse code, that is, three dots. Although detractors dismissed it as a hoax, largely because so simple a signal would not be easy to recognize amid the noise of natural static, Marconi soon used it as the basis of a thriving set of companies, including a U.S. subsidiary, American Marconi.

FLIGHT

The first decade of the 20th century also marked humanity's realization of its long dream of powered flight. Myth and legend throughout the world attest to the grip of that dream upon the imagination, but it remained stubbornly elusive. Cautionary tales such as that of Icarus suggested that flight was not for the likes of men.

Amid the intellectual ferment of the Enlightenment, which regarded all knowledge as properly the purview of humanity, the Montgolfier brothers of France made the first flight with a hot-air balloon. Once hydrogen was

Fighters and Aces

The use of the airplane as a scout in World War I was an obvious extension of the use of balloons, which dated back to the Civil War. Once both sides had airplanes up, it was almost natural for these hot-blooded young men to take potshots at the enemy's planes. However the pistols and rifles they took aloft proved grossly inadequate. To make aerial combat possible, it was necessary to throw far more lead at the target, a rate of fire attainable only with a machine gun.

Mounting a machine gun on the airplanes of the day was not easy. The earliest experimenters set them on the upper wing, just over the cockpit. However trying to aim upward while flying forward proved a less than satisfactory solution. The optimal solution would be to fire straight forward in the direction one was flying. However with a single-engine propeller plane, this would mean firing straight at the propeller. Inevitably one of those bullets would strike the propeller and destroy it. The first solution was hit upon by the French, who attached a piece of metal at an angle to deflect a bullet. However in time the stress of the bullets hitting the deflectors would fatally weaken the propeller blades. Dutch-born aeronautical engineer Anthony Fokker studied a captured French plane and realized a way around it in the ratio between the rotation rate of the propeller and the machine gun's rate of fire. It enabled him to devise the interrupter gear, a mechanism to prevent the machine gun from firing in the moment when the propeller passed in front of it. Fokker's invention, soon imitated by the Allies from captured German planes, enabled the invention of the fighter plane. Soon pilots particularly adept at this aerial hunt were distinguished by the informal title of "ace." Men such as the German Manfred von Richthofen, or "The Red Baron," soon became legends.

When the United States entered the war, its aircraft industry was not designed for mass production of military airplanes. As a result American pilots almost entirely used planes of French and British manufacture. Still several American pilots were able to win their place in history, most notably Eddie Rickenbacker.

Captain Eddie Rickenbacker holding an airplane model during a White House reception in September 1925.

Samuel Pierpont Langley, whose 1902 version of the aerodrome is shown above, was one of a number of aviation pioneers at work in several countries before the Wright brothers' success.

isolated, it too was used as a lifting gas. However, balloons had one notable drawback: they were completely at the mercy of the wind. Various sails and wings were attached to them in an effort to steer them, but such clumsy apparatus proved ineffective.

In 1901 the German Ferdinand Graf von Zeppelin devised a cigar-shaped rigid balloon with steering fins at its tail and fitted it with engines. Although the resulting airship could be steered at will, and could even carry substantial cargo, its sheer size and fragility made it vulnerable to wind. Furthermore the use of hydrogen as a lifting gas made even the tiniest spark dangerous, and several of the count's early airships went up in flames.

Meanwhile several different inventors were working on heavier-than-air powered flight. For decades brave men had taken to the air in gliders, using designs not dissimilar to those of Leonardo da Vinci's sketchbooks. Many died in the attempts, but their successors developed steadily improved designs. In the 1890s astronomer Samuel Pierpont Langley made a systematic study of the physics of objects in flight, which would become the basis of the science of aerodynamics. He developed a special ultra-light steam engine, and on May 6, 1896, his pilotless aircraft flew 3,000 ft., and by 1898 he was able to fly it as far as a mile. However even as late as 1903 he was still struggling to get his aircraft, which he styled the aerodrome, to be reliable enough to risk a manned flight.

Science of the Times

The late 19th and early 20th centuries were decades of progress in the sciences in America and around the world. This was especially true in the realm of physics, dominated by Albert Einstein, who was at his most productive in the early 1900s. A brief history of science during this time includes:

1890: The English geologist Arthur Holmes uses radioactivity to date the Earth from rocks. He concludes it is 4.6 billion years old.

1895: Previously thought only to exist in the sun, helium is discovered on Earth. In Germany, Wilhelm Conrad Röntgen discovers X-rays.

1896: Swedish chemist Svante Arrhenius studies the level of carbon dioxide in the atmosphere and global temperatures. He proposes that the ice ages were the result of lower carbon dioxide levels. In France, Antoine-Henri Becquerel discovers rays produced by uranium affect photographic plates: the first scientific observation of natural radioactivity.

1897: The Russian physicist Alexander Popov uses an antenna to transmit radio waves over a distance of five km. The electron is discovered by English physicist Joseph John Thomson.

1898: In France, Pierre and Marie Curie discover the radioactive elements polonium and radium. In Bombay, India, Paul-Louis Simond suggests that the fleas on rats transmit bubonic plague to humans.

1899: In Cambridge, England, Ernest Rutherford discovers that the radiation from uranium has at least two different forms, which he calls alpha and beta particles.

1905: Clarence McClung shows that female mammals have two X chromosomes and that males have an X and a Y. Albert Einstein provides a mathematical explanation of Brownian motion. Many see this as the first proof that atoms actually exist. Einstein also publishes his first and second papers on special relativity, including the famous equation $E = mc^2$.

1911: The first chromosome maps are developed. Ernest Rutherford presents his theory of the atom: a positively charged nucleus surrounded by negative electrons.

1912: Alfred Wegener, a German meteorologist, suggests the idea of continental drift, having studied how the coastlines of certain continents seem to fit together.

Orville and Wilbur Wright performing an aviation demonstration in September 1909 over New York harbor. The airplane had a canoe attachment for flight over water.

Thus the honor of being the first to attain powered heavier-than-air flight by a human being would fall to two brothers from Ohio. On December 17, 1903, Orville and Wilbur Wright briefly flew their airplane at Kill Devil Hills, not far from the village of Kitty Hawk, North Carolina. For the next decade, the development of the airplane was slow and incremental, largely because it was almost entirely the realm of hobbyists. All that changed in 1914, with the outbreak of World War I. As soon as the military potential of the airplane was realized, considerable efforts were put into the development of improved airplanes by both sides. By the end of the war specialized aircraft had been developed, ranging from nimble fighters to high-capacity bombers.

Although the beginning of the Progressive Era is in many ways an arbitrary mark on the timeline of history, there can be no question as to where it ended. It died on Flanders Field, in Argonne Forest, and in the mud and squalor of the trenches of World War I. So many of the wonderful inventions of the first decade of the 20th century saw horrific applications in the second decade that many people seriously questioned the Progressive Era ideas that reason and social reform could bring about the perfection of humanity. As a result it became that much easier for people to abandon themselves to self-indulgence in the decade following the war.

LEIGH KIMMEL

Further Readings

Baker, W.J. *A History of the Marconi Company*. New York: St. Martin's Press, 1971.

Bray, John. *The Communications Miracle: The Telecommunication Pioneers from Morse to the Information Superhighway*. New York: Plenum Press, 1995.

Brinkley, Douglas. *Wheels for the World: Henry Ford, His Company and a Century of Progress*. New York: Viking, 2003.

Cooper, Gail. *Air Conditioning America: Engineers and the Controlled Environment, 1900–1960*. Baltimore, MD: Johns Hopkins University Press, 1998.

Davies, L. J. *Fleet Fire: Thomas Edison and the Pioneers of the Electric Revolution*. New York: Arcade Publishing, 2003.

De Forest, Lee. *Father of Radio, the Autobiography of Lee de Forest*. Chicago, IL: Wilcox and Follet Co., 1950.

Hepler, Allison L. *Women in Labor: Mothers, Medicine and Occupational Health in the United States, 1890–1980*. Columbus, OH: Ohio State University Press, 2000.

Ingels, Margaret. *Willis Haviland Carrier: Father of Air Conditioning*. Garden City, NY: Country Life Press, 1952.

Kinney, Jeremy R. *Airplanes: The Life Story of a Technology*. Westport, CT: Greenwood Press, 2006.

Lebow, Irwin. *Information Highways & Byways: From the Telegraph to the 21st Century*. New York: IEEE Press, 1995.

Leinwoll, Stanley. *From Spark to Satellite: A History of Radio Communication*. New York: Charles Scribner's Sons, 1979.

Lewis, Tom. *Empire of the Air: The Men Who Made Radio*. New York: Edward Burlingame, 1991.

Oslin, George P. *The Story of Telecommunications*. Macon, GA: Mercer University Press, 1992.

Sellers, Christopher C. *Hazards of the Job: From Industrial Disease to Environmental Health Science*. Chapel Hill, NC: University of North Carolina Press, 1997.

Sinclair, Upton. *The Jungle*. New York: Modern Library, 2002.

Sobel, Robert *RCA*. New York: Stein and Day, 1986.

Traxel, David. *1898: The Birth of the American Century*. New York: Alfred A. Knopf, 1998.

Volti, Rudi. *Cars and Culture: The Life Story of a Technology*. Westport, CT: Greenwood Press, 2004.

White, Lawrence. *Human Debris: The Injured Worker in America*. New York: Seaview, 1983.

Will, Harry M., ed. *The First Century of Air Conditioning*. Atlanta, GA: American Society of Heating, Refrigerating & Air-Conditioning Engineers, 1999.

Chapter 10

Entertainment and Sports

"The moving picture drama furnishes entertainment
for the millions, literally reproducing
comic, tragic, and great events."
— George E. Walsh

ON OCTOBER 24, 1901, a 63-year old schoolteacher and dance instructor named Annie Edson Taylor climbed into an old oak pickle barrel and settled down with her "lucky" heart-shaped pillow. As newsmen looked on, her manager screwed down the lid and pressurized the barrel using a bicycle pump. He corked the small hole and pushed the barrel off the shore of Goat Island into the current of the Niagara River. For the next 18 minutes Taylor listened as the roar of Horseshoe Falls grew louder. Suddenly she plunged over the edge and disappeared into the mists at the bottom. To the shock of spectators lining the shores, she was pulled out of the barrel, bruised but alive, a few moments later, the first person to survive a trip over mighty Niagara Falls.

Annie Taylor was just one of hundreds, or perhaps thousands, of Americans who had yearned to make a name for themselves from some feat of daring. The Progressive Era was an age of spectacle, where new forms of entertainment and popular culture made it possible for the talented or the brave to rise to the top of public consciousness. Faced with unemployment and poverty in her elder years, Taylor hoped that she could make a living touring the country on the vaudeville circuit, recounting her tale of daring. This dream was crushed when her unscrupulous manager ran off with the barrel and left her all alone. She died in poverty in 1921.

THE BIG TOP AND WILD WEST SHOW

The traveling circus had been a popular player in American life since the 1820s or 1830s, but the period between 1870 and 1900 was its golden age. Between 30 and 100 circuses crisscrossed the country each year, some playing for audiences of up to 12,000 people a day. With their main street parades, exotic animals, games, "freaks," strong-men, trapeze artists, acrobats, and tent shows, the circus was a staple of small-town life for decades.

Beginning in 1872 P.T. Barnum's Museum, Menagerie and Circus began touring the country in its own train, an innovation that other large circus troupes would adopt. Unlike wagon travel, circus trains allowed owners to transport tons of equipment, performers, and animals across great distances at a minimal cost, and took them to hub towns where they were most likely to find large audiences. Train travel could be risky, as illustrated by the nearly 20 accidents involving circus trains between 1877 and 1906, including a collision with a Great Wallace Show train in 1903 near Durand, Michigan, that left 20 people and many animals dead. Circuses also benefited from larger tents, which allowed more seats and thus more profit. By 1881 tents were so large that Barnum's circus could have three exhibition rings rather than just one, and the three-ring circus soon became the industry standard.

The biggest circuses were Barnum & Bailey's out of New York, and the Ringling Brothers, who formed in Baraboo, Wisconsin, in 1894 and quickly became Barnum's great rival. Like Barnum & Bailey, the Ringling Brothers believed in running a "clean" show, tamping down the corruption and thievery that ran rampant in less savory outfits. In 1907 Ringling Brothers bought out Barnum & Bailey for $410,000 and rechristened itself the Ringling Brothers & Barnum & Bailey Circus. By 1916 it took 92 railroad cars to transport the circus's 1,000 staff and performers, not to mention its equipment, its 26 elephants, and its 16 camels.

Similar to the circus and yet unique, Buffalo Bill's Wild West show was another highlight of entertainment for Progressive Era Americans. Founded by showman William Cody in 1883 and touring almost continuously for the next 20 years, it was designed around the theme of the frontier west—a period already passing into history. The massive production began with a parade of horseback riders from America and abroad, often including Turks, Cossacks, Mongols, and Arabs. It ended with a reenactment of Custer's Last Stand, with Cody himself portraying Custer. Between these bookends, Cody presented a number of demonstrations and tableaux, including bronco-riding and roping exhibitions, mock bison hunts, staged raids on settlers by Native Americans, and other spectacles.

Trick shooter Annie Oakley joined the cast in 1885 and toured with the group until she was injured in a railroad accident in 1901. The five-ft. tall Oakley was billed as the ultimate frontier girl, but had never been west of the Mississippi before joining Cody. An excellent exhibition shooter (in various competition shoots, she hit 483 of 500 targets, 943 of 1,000 targets, and 4,772 of 5,000 targets) she was also a gifted trick shooter, able to split playing cards on their edge, snuffing candles, shooting corks off bottles and ashes off cigarettes. She employed this last trick while performing for Queen Victoria and her family during a European tour; the cigarette was held in the hand of a young man who would go on to be Kaiser Wilhelm of Germany. After the start of World War I the story was embellished to Annie shooting the cigarette out of his mouth, and if she had just shot the Kaiser rather than the cigarette, the carnage of the war might have been avoided.

Annie was a favorite of another Cody performer: Sitting Bull. The Sioux holy man joined the Wild West show in 1885 for a fee of $50 a week. He would ride around the main arena trailed by a group of 20 Native-American "braves." He stayed for about a year before embarking on the last act of his life, leading the Sioux uprising that led to his death in 1890. The presence of Native Americans was a problematical aspect of the Wild West show historians still debate today. On the one hand, Cody promoted the stereotype of savage Native Americans with mock attack scenes and the reenactment of Little Big Horn, while on the other hand treating his Native American performers with great respect and stating in his show literature that they were also Americans.

The trick shooter Annie Oakley in 1899 while she was in the cast of Buffalo Bill's Wild West Show.

THE GRAND EXPOSITIONS

While circuses and traveling shows brought entertainment to those Americans living in small towns and frontier outposts, tens of millions of citizens flocked to the giant expositions, or world's fairs, held between the 1890s and 1915. Usually pegged to the commemoration of some great historical event, world's fairs were a sign of America's growing importance on the global stage. Following the model set by Queen Victoria and Prince Albert in the 1851 London Great Exposition,

The entrance to the midway attraction "Dreamland" at the Pan-American exposition in 1901.

these events involved the construction of temporary cities dedicated to showcasing the newest technological innovations, celebrating the world's diverse cultures, and of course the selling of food, fun, and plenty of souvenirs.

The Columbian Exposition of 1893, also called the Chicago World's Fair, set the standard. Determined to show how brilliantly they had recovered from the fires of 1871, the city spared no expense, calling on the most prominent American architects and landscape designers to create 200 buildings on a 600-acre site. The White City, so-called because of the gleam of the new electric streetlights used to illuminate the white stucco exhibit halls at night, was visited by 27 million people in six months of operation, almost half the U.S. population at the time.

The White City introduced a slew of new consumer goods into American culture: Juicy Fruit gum, Cracker Jacks, Quaker Oats, Aunt Jemima Pancake Mix, and Shredded Wheat all debuted here, as did the Ferris wheel and the picture postcard. The term "midway" arose from the Midway Plaisance, a mile-long strip of park that was the center of the fair's amusements. Food historians still debate if the hamburger was introduced here or at the 1904 Louisiana Purchase Exposition in St Louis. Historians in general remember it as the place where Frederick Jackson Turner unveiled his frontier thesis of American history.

Another notable fair was the Pan-American Exposition at Buffalo, New York, in 1901. Some eight million people made their way to the city during the summer and fall. Among them was President William McKinley, who lauded expositions as "the timekeepers of progress. They record the world's advancements. They stimulate the energy, enterprise and intellect of the people and quicken human genius." The next day McKinley was shot by an anarchist named Leon Czolgosz as he attended a reception at the exposition's grand Temple of Music. He died eight days later, and Theodore Roosevelt was sworn in as the nation's 26th president.

By 1916 the Victrola with records on discs had replaced the earlier cylinders, bringing recorded music into more homes than ever.

THE VAUDEVILLE CIRCUIT

In October 1881 a Brooklyn-born comedic singer named Tony Pastor invited the public to see his "polite" vaudeville show at the Germania The-ater on 14th Street in New York City, and set into motion a form of enter-tainment that would dominate American popular theater for the next three decades. Vaudeville grew out of the minstrel and other traveling variety shows that had grown in popularity before the Civil War, but Pastor was offering his audience a show free from the vulgarity and risqué humor common in these older forms, not to mention a theater where alcohol was forbidden and smoking discouraged; in short, a place where a nice, mid-dle-class group of men and women would feel comfortable spending an evening. Though many performers derided it as the Sunday-School Circuit, Pastor's cleaned-up vaudeville style quickly gained public approval, and he and other budding impresarios began building nationwide chains of the-aters for their shows.

Vaudeville shows usually consisted of nine acts, each lasting between seven and 12 minutes. The entertainment varied wildly, featuring song and dance acts, acrobats, magic tricks, animal acts, dramatic readings, impersonators,

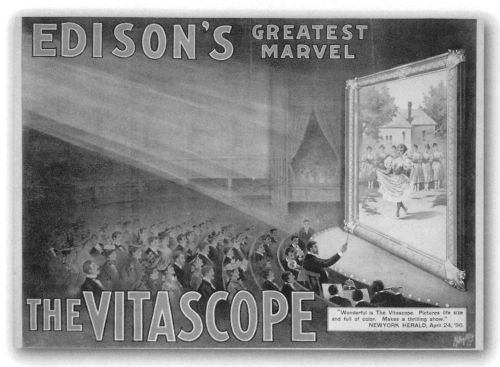

An 1896 poster advertising Edison's Vitascope motion picture device. Films began as short novelties showing scenes from everyday life, sporting events, or famous figures.

comedians, famous figures, and later, short motion pictures. Performers were independent contractors who signed on with a theater chain or circuit—dominated by the Keith-Albee Circuit in the east and the Orpheum Circuit in the west—and moved from city to city as theater owners tried to continually offer their audiences something fresh or new. It was a grueling lifestyle, and only a lucky few made it to a point where they could stay put and let the audiences come to them.

Vaudeville was often a family affair, with talented children going on stage at a very early age, either with their parents or as solo acts. Particularly in New York, this put them at risk from the New York Society for the Prevention of Cruelty of Children, commonly referred to as the Gerry Society after its founder, Elbridge T. Gerry. Founded in 1875 to protect child laborers in sweatshops and factories, the Gerry Society was much more interested in cracking down on child performers, who had little time for formal schooling, and spent most of their time in the morally corrupting atmosphere of the theater. Many of these youngsters were a family's sole means of support, and censure by the Gerry Society was a significant threat. Child performers were often taught to mimic adult behavior when suspected Gerry Society agents were nosing around, and many were passed off as little people.

Flourishing Burlesque

A rung down on the variety entertainment ladder was burlesque, which flourished during the same era. Burlesque had its historical roots in political and social satire. Similar to vaudeville in format, it was not family-friendly fare and did not cater to the genteel middle class.

It had no pretensions. Its core audience was the working-class man who wanted to enjoy some song and dance, and could handle a little naughty language or bawdy songs, or the occasional leggy chorus girl, while enjoying a nice cigar. By the end of World War I, they could be found all over the country, but were particularly popular in industrial and port cities.

Burlesque took a new turn around 1912 when the Minsky Brothers rented a small sixth-floor theater in New York City and found they had no money to book good vaudeville acts or decent motion pictures. Drawing on a visit to Paris and the burlesque shows at the Moulin Rouge and the Folies Bergere, they built a runway off the main stage into the heart of the audience.

Billy Minsky and his brothers didn't introduce the striptease to American audiences. That honor went to Lydia Thompson, a British chorus girl who came over for a tour in 1868, and "leg shows" had been popular barroom and dance-hall fare for years. However they made it the core of their business, with vaudeville acts filling in the time between the strip acts.

Burlesque made the Minskys wealthy and famous, and won them periodic police raids for indecency. By the 1930s the best strippers (or "ecdysiasts" as these women were called in more polite circles) were earning upward of $1,000 a week.

DeVere's High Rollers Burlesque Company promoted "Sylvia Starr: The American Venus" with this poster in 1898.

THE NEW INDUSTRY

After more than 20 years of dominating popular entertainment, vaudeville began to fall to the power of a medium that it had promoted: the motion picture. They began as a novelty act, with most early films less than a minute long and showing a scene from everyday life, a public event, a sporting event, or a famous figure. The first film to be copyrighted was a five-second film shot in January 1894 called *Fred Ott's Sneeze.* It was exactly that: one of Thomas Edison's assistants dipping a bit of snuff and sneezing for Edison's new Kinetoscope.

For the first decade or so, films were restricted to one fixed camera with little ability to shoot from multiple angles or splice together several shots. The public was fascinated by the moving pictures, and entrepreneurs were fascinated by the idea of giving an audience a show that did not involve managing (and paying) a large number of actors. The birth of the movies was pure profit for theater-managers; they could build bigger theaters and squeeze in more shows per day than they could with live performers. The first nickelodeon opened in Pittsburgh in June 1905, and proved to be such a lucrative business model that there were close to 5,000 such theaters around the country by 1907. Charging audiences $.05 per person for shows that ran 15–20 minutes, theaters could run 12 to 18 shows a day, seven days a week. Operating costs were about $200 a week. Outside the big cities, most nickelodeons were 199 seats or less to skirt the need for a theatrical license levied on establishments with 200 or more seats.

Between the technological advances in film and cameras and the market's clamor for new and interesting spectacles, the industry matured quickly. New film directors began developing a new narrative form, using multiple cameras, better lighting, cross-cutting, point-of-view shots, flashback shots, and animation. Storylines became more complex, and films became longer. Sound did not come along until the 1920s, but in 1908 directors began inserting lines of dialog as "intertitles" between shots.

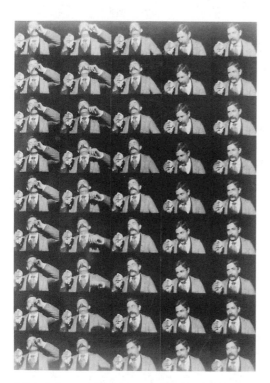

Edison's famous Kinetoscopic film Fred Ott's Sneeze *from January 1894.*

The American film industry came of age between 1914 and 1919 by filling the void left by the destruction of the European film establishment by World War I. Taking advantage of the good climate, sunny skies, and cheap cost of living in California, the Los Angeles neighborhood known as Hollywood became the home of American film. By the early 1920s Hollywood was releasing 800 feature-length films every year.

The rapid development of film pushed hundreds of hard-working vaudevillians out of work. Audiences and box office receipts shrunk, and old vaudeville theaters were converted to sumptuous new movie theaters. Performers were pushed into smaller venues, or into burlesque. However a few were able to make the switch to the new medium, with some going on to become Hollywood royalty: Buster Keaton, Charlie Chaplin, Mary Pickford, Lillian Gish, Mae West, Bob Hope, Fred Astaire, George Burns, Gracie Allen, Sammy Davis Jr., and Judy Garland were among those who got their start on the vaudeville circuit.

THE TEMPLE OF THE BODY

Theodore Roosevelt was one of the most vital, active presidents in American history, but he had not started out that way. Born in New York City in 1858, young "Teedie" was a scrawny boy who suffered from asthma as a child. When he was 14 years old, his father finally told him: "Sickness is always a shame, and often a sin." The only way Theodore could use his obvious intelligence and ambition was to first force his body to bend to his will. He spent countless hours at a local gymnasium, working with weights, primitive exercise machines, and horizontal bars. He took boxing lessons. He became a fearless horseback rider, a big-game hunter, an explorer, and a naturalist. Roosevelt never cured his asthma, he lost the sight in one eye to a boxing accident, and risked death on his expeditions and his headlong charge up San Juan Hill in Cuba in the 1890s, but he became one of the strongest proponents of what he termed "the strenuous life" as the only way to build the exceptional American male.

Roosevelt was not alone. Health and fitness took on new urgency in the middle and upper classes during the 1880s and 1890s, as fears that urbanization and the growth of the professional class was creating a generation of "soft" men and sickly women. Physical fitness became part of an overall conception of the ideal Christian gentleman as one who treated his body

Skiing, golf, and tennis grew in popularity along with the ideal of "the strenuous life" among the upper classes.

as a temple of God. While not as closely tied to spirituality, women were also encouraged to a more active life, although they often found themselves hampered by the rules of social propriety.

Outdoor activity was highly prized, both for the exposure to the health-giving benefits of fresh air and physical movement, and the communion with God and nature which, it was believed, was only possible outside the hustle and bustle of the city. Hiking, canoeing, rowing, hunting, fishing, horseback riding, swimming, diving, ice skating, sledding, and skiing were all popular for those who had the money and access. Golf and tennis became favored sports among the wealthy.

Within the cities there was an increase in the number of public gymnasiums and YMCA facilities where men could work out with dumbbells, Indian clubs, medicine balls, rowing machines, and spring-loaded resistance machines. Men could also join athletic clubs, most dedicated to track-and-field sports, gymnastics, boxing, and rowing. Even mid-sized cities were likely to have amateur baseball teams. Football grew in popularity in the nation's colleges, but despite regulations remained so violent that in 1905 alone 19 players were killed during games. President Roosevelt threatened to outlaw the game unless the sport figured out a way to regulate itself properly, and later that year, 62 colleges banded together to form what would become the National College Athletic Association, or NCAA.

This 1897 magazine cover captures the sense of freedom bicycling gave women.

Bicycles had been around for almost 30 years, but the introduction of the "safety bicycle" in 1885 catapulted it into a national craze. The new "Safties" had lightweight frames and equally-sized wheels driven by a chain, making for an easier, smoother ride. Pneumatic tires were easier to fill and repair. By 1896 150 bicycle manufacturers were producing over 1,000 different models, and selling about two million bikes a year. While the price tag of $30 to $100 was too steep for the working-class, the middle-class took to the sport with a passion, forming "wheelmen's clubs" for social events, and advocating the construction of bicycle paths and better paving on city streets.

Women seized on the bicycle as a sport and a form of liberation, so

President Theodore Roosevelt (center in white) showing his support for the U.S. Olympic team in September 1908.

The Olympics

Americans had a chance to introduce their athletic prowess to the world with the birth of the modern Olympic Games. The United States was one of the 14 nations that arrived in Athens in April 1896, and walked away with 11 gold medals, more than any other participating country. The American athletes dominated the track-and-field events, winning the 100-m. race, the 110-m. hurtle race, the high-jump, the pole-jump, the triple-jump, and discus-throwing. They also won the 25-m. and 30-m. shooting competitions.

They extended domination in track-and-field in the 1900 Games in Paris, taking 13 of the possible 21 medals in the sprint events. A Milwaukee-born dental student named Alvin Kraenzlein took the gold in the 60-m. race, the 200-m. hurdle, the 110-m. hurdle, and the long jump, the first (and so far only) Olympic athlete to win four gold medals in individual events in track and field. The Paris Games were also the first to include women athletes. Two women won first place in their events, including a 22-year old American golfer named Margaret Abbott. The games were horribly organized that year, and Abbott and her mother, who were living in Paris at the time, entered the contest just for fun. She knew she had won the match, but nobody ever informed her that she had made sports history as the first American female gold medalist, and one of the only medalists in golf, which was only included as a sport in the 1900 and 1904 games.

The 1904 games were held in St. Louis in conjunction with the Louisiana Purchase Exposition. Like the Paris event, the St. Louis Games suffered from disorganization and poor attendance, but the American competitors used the home-team advantage and walked away with 242 medals, 79 of them gold, dominating archery, track-and-field, boxing, tug-of-war, and other events.

much so that it became tied up in the greater women's suffrage movement. In an interview with pioneering journalist Nellie Bly in February 1896, Susan B. Anthony said: "Let me tell you what I think of bicycling. I think it has done more to emancipate women than anything else in the world. I stand and rejoice every time I see a woman ride by on a wheel. It gives woman a feeling of freedom and self-reliance. It makes her feel as if she were independent. The moment she takes her seat she knows she can't get into harm unless she gets off her bicycle, and away she goes, the picture of free, untrammeled womanhood." Despite the doctors who warned against the "excitement" women might experience by straddling a bicycle, or the moralists that claimed that the whole gender might be corrupted by a women's ability to ride out of the sight of a watchful community, women kept riding.

One rode all the way around the world. Annie Kopchovsky was a 23-year-old Jewish housewife and mother of three small children living near Boston. In June 1894 she set off with a Columbia bicycle, a change of clothing, and small revolver in a bid to win a bizarre wager by two local businessmen. She had to complete the trip in 15 months, bring proof in the form of signatures from American consuls along her trip, and bring home $5,000 above her expenses. If she completed this task, she would win $10,000. After accepting a $100 corporate sponsorship from the Londonderry Lithia Spring Water Company, and agreeing to change her name to Londonderry for the duration of the trip, she "sailed away like a kite" down Beacon Street in Boston. She returned home in September of the following year to claim her prize. She moved her family to New York City and became a columnist for the *New York World*. "I am a journalist and a 'New Woman,'" she told her readers, "if that term means that I believe I can do anything that a man can do."

HEATHER K. MICHON

Further Readings

"Annie Londonderry—The First Woman to Bicycle around the World." Available online: http://www.annielondonderry.com. Accessed January 2008.

Chindahl, George Leonard. *A History of the Circus in America*. Caldwell, ID: Caxton Printers, 1959.

"Circus Historical Society," Available online: http://www.circushistory.org. Accessed January 2008.

Cook, David A. *A History of Narrative Film*. New York: Norton, 1990.

Erdman, Andrew L. *Blue Vaudeville: Sex, Morals and the Mass Marketing of Amusement, 1895–1915*. Jefferson, NC: McFarland & Company, 2004.

Enss, Chris. *Buffalo Gals: Women of Buffalo Bill's Wild West Show*. Guilford, CT: Globe Pequot, 2005.

Fox, Charles Philip. *A Ticket to the Circus: A Pictorial History of the Incredible Ringlings*. Seattle, WA: Superior Pub. Co., 1959.

Gilbert, Douglas. *American Vaudeville, Its Life and Times*. New York: Whittlesey House, McGraw-Hill Book Company, Inc., 1940.

Matthews, George R. *America's First Olympics: The St. Louis Games of 1904*. Columbia, MO: University of Missouri Press, 2005.

Robinson, David. *From Peep Show to Palace: The Birth of American Film*. New York: Columbia University Press, 1996.

Rydell, Robert W., John E. Findling, and Kimberly D. Pelle. *Fair America: World's Fairs in the United States*. Washington, D.C.: Smithsonian Institution Press, 2000.

Sayers, Isabelle S. *Annie Oakley and Buffalo Bill's Wild West*. New York: Courier Dover Publications, 1981.

Thompson, Kristin and David Bordwell. *Film History: An Introduction*. New York: McGraw-Hill, 2003.

Warren, Louis S. *Buffalo Bill's America: William Cody and the Wild West Show*. New York: Knopf Publishing Group, 2006.

Chapter 11

Crime and Violence

*"The real significance of crime is in its being a breach
of faith with the community of mankind."*
— Joseph Conrad

LIKE MOST ERAS of American history, the decades between 1890 and 1920 had their share of shocking crime waves and violent incidents. During this era the frontier had disappeared as lands were settled and cities grew. The era also saw the professionalization of police work and the rise of organized crime. The forces of crime and violence in America in those decades were closely linked to social and labor unrest, both in cities and rural areas, as labor violence came to the Idaho Mountains and West Virginia valleys, usually as a result of bitter mining strikes.

THE WILD BUNCH

During the last decade of the 19th century there appeared one of the more legendary criminal figures of the Old West—the train robber—manifested by Robert Leroy Parker and Harry Longabaugh, better known as Butch Cassidy and the Sundance Kid. Cassidy formed the Wild Bunch in the 1890s and was based out of Hole-in-the-Wall, Utah. While Sundance would be remembered by his Hollywood portrayal, available evidence indicates that he was not Cassidy's close friend and confidante, that role falling to another lesser-known gang member, Elzy Lay.

The Wild Bunch's first robbery on August 13, 1896, consisted of a bank holdup in Montpelier, Idaho, during which the gang made off with $7,000 in notes and coins. On their way out of town the robbers clipped the telephone wires, a precaution previous western outlaws did not have to consider. After dividing the loot, Cassidy hid from the law in Michigan, but when he saw a deputy sheriff who had been pursuing him, Cassidy had to flee again. Short on cash, he rounded up the Wild Bunch for another job, robbing the payroll of the Pleasant Valley Coal Company in Utah on April 21, 1897. The gang stole $8,800 from the coal mine and then made their getaway.

The Wild Bunch did not surface again until June 2, 1899, when they robbed the Union Pacific's Overland Flyer near Wilcox, Wyoming, possibly their best-known robbery. Cassidy and the crew used dynamite to open the train's safe. The robbery resulted in a massive manhunt led by Pinkerton detective Charlie Siringo, but the Wild Bunch escaped. On July 11, 1899, Elzy Lay led the Wild Bunch in a train robbery in Folsom, New Mexico. The robbery led to Lay shooting and killing Sheriff Edward Farr and drawing imprisonment in New Mexico for the crime.

The imprisonment of Lay frightened Cassidy. He sought amnesty from Utah Governor Heber Wells, who advised him to seek it from his principal robbery victim—the Union Pacific Railroad. A parley was arranged, but bad weather prevented the railroad's negotiators from reaching the meeting. Cassidy resumed his life of crime, again aiming at the Union Pacific Railroad. The Wild Bunch struck the Union Pacific on August 29, 1900, blasting open a freight car's strongbox with dynamite.

Laura Bullion, a female member of the Wild Bunch, wearing a man's suit in a Pinkerton's Detective Agency mugshot.

The Wild Bunch robbed the First National Bank in Winnemucca, Nevada, on September 19, 1900, making off with $32,640. The gang celebrated the robbery in Fort Worth, posing for the famous photograph of the five robbers—Cassidy, Sundance, Bill Carver, Harvey Logan, and Ben Kilpatrick—in suits and derbies. The Pinkerton Detective Agency used the photograph in their "wanted" posters. Rejoined by Kid Curry, the gang again robbed the Union Pacific's Overland Flyer, this time on September 19, 1900. To everyone's astonishment and Hollywood's later amusement, the train guard who endured this robbery was the same one who faced the Wild Bunch in Wilcox.

This robbery was the final stand of the Wild Bunch. A pursuing posse killed Carver. Kilpatrick was captured the following December in Knoxville, Tennessee. Curry slew a police officer in the same city, then fled the authorities to Montana, where he killed a rancher who had shot his brother years before. Cassidy and Sundance also fled the law, making for New York City with Sundance's lover, Etta Place. The trio sailed for Argentina in 1901, and their fates became the stuff of mystery and legend. Accounts vary, but they may have commit-

This famous photograph of Butch Cassidy, the Sundance Kid, Bill Carver, Harvey Logan, and Ben Kilpatrick was taken after they robbed a bank in Winnemucca, Nevada.

ted bank robberies in Argentina, and they may have also set up a ranch. In November 1908 robbers struck the payroll office of a silver mine in San Vicente, Bolivia, and local police moved in on the lodging house where the two suspects were staying. A night gun battle ensued, punctuated by shots fired inside the house. The Bolivians waited until dawn, and hearing no further firing, moved in. They found two dead men, apparently suicides. The bodies were buried in unmarked graves, and were presumed by authorities to be those of Cassidy and Sundance. However these claims have been disputed ever since, with varying stories claiming that both robbers returned to America, living out their lives under assumed identities and in obscurity, the last of the great western robbers.

ORGANIZED CRIME

Butch Cassidy and his Wild Bunch were the last of a dying breed. Their type of lawless marauding began to disappear from the headlines as the 20th century opened. Technological developments like the telephone, the automobile, and radio were made available to law enforcement agencies, and gave them new power against freewheeling marauders like Cassidy and Sundance. While such robbers would continue to commit crimes and make headlines, crime and violence—and the response to it—was becoming more professionalized in the new century.

By 1890 the popular image of the city police officer was the nightstick-twirling Irish cop on his beat, wearing an English-style helmet, escorting kids across streets, pounding burglars and drunks with his nightstick, and shaking down tavern owners for graft, usually for the ward-heeling politician that

The Mann Act

One of the high-water marks of law enforcement during the Progressive Era came in 1910 when Congress passed the Mann Act, officially the White Slave Traffic Act. The purpose of the law was to end the sale and transportation of women as prostitutes across state lines. In practicality, it became an ugly political tool, used to humiliate celebrities and ordinary folks alike.

At the time, municipalities and states were cracking down on "red-light districts," bordellos, and the crime they created. The popular view of prostitutes was that they were only practicing their trade because they had been kidnapped, lured, drugged, and enslaved by pimps, and that no healthy young American girl would ever enter the trade voluntarily. In reality women became prostitutes for a variety of reasons: to flee abusive homes, to feed liquor or drug addictions, or to escape poverty. Nevertheless the Mann Act was the *coup de grâce* for the anti-prostitution efforts of the era. The act made it a federal offense to transport any woman or girl across state lines "for the purpose of prostitution or debauchery, or for any other immoral purpose." What defined an "immoral purpose" was vague, but when Congress took up the act, they debated prostitution and sexual commerce.

The Mann Act was quickly enforced, but not always for savory purposes. For example Jack Johnson, the famous black boxer, was living with a white woman, Belle Schreiber. He sent her $75 to travel from Pittsburgh to Chicago, where he would meet up with her. Johnson was charged with violating the Mann Act by doing so, convicted, and sentenced to a year in jail. The prosecutor claimed the verdict would "go around the world" as a warning against "miscegenation."

Between 1910 and 1915, more than 1,000 defendants were convicted for violating the Mann Act. Most of these defendants were men. The Mann Act returned to public scrutiny in 1944, when movie legend Charlie Chaplin was arrested for giving money to his lover, Joan Berry, to meet him in New York for the purpose of a romantic encounter. The trial was powered by Chaplin's great enemy, FBI Director J. Edgar Hoover, who considered Chaplin a Communist. Chaplin was already battling in court with Berry over a paternity suit. Chaplin was represented by celebrity lawyer Jerry Giesler, and gained an acquittal from the jury. But the press coverage was fierce, and Chaplin's reputation was scarred. It was further damaged when he lost the paternity suit.

The law hung on, though, used more often for personal revenge or against interracial sexual relationships, with the conviction rate dropping in the 1960s. In 1986 Congress finally rewrote the Mann Act. Dropped were the terms "white slavery," "debauchery," and "immoral purposes." The new Transportation for Illegal Sexual Activity and Related Crimes Act, written in a gender-neutral manner, made the act of transporting any "individual" with the "intent that such individual engage in prostitution, or in any sexual activity for which any person can be charged" a criminal offense.

had provided the cop with his job. Police work was described by the colorful Dutch-born New York City police detective Cornelius Van Willemse as "protecting decent people and treating crooks rough." This style of policing was beginning to prove inadequate to the demands of heavily-populated cities, with packed slums, often filled with poverty-stricken immigrants who either turned to crime, or became victimized by it.

As the 1890s began, so did organized crime in America. The street gangs of the earlier 19th century became larger, stronger, and grouped increasingly along ethnic lines. Among the new criminals finding a home in America in the 1890s were Italian, Sicilian, and Jewish gangsters. These groups began battling with each other and existing Irish-based mobs for control of new and lucrative rackets. Prostitution, gambling, and protection rackets had already existed in America, but the new gangs refined their operations, creating highly elaborate illegal gambling and prostitution dens. They also moved in on sweatshops, either as operators or by hounding owners with protection rackets.

With the rise of modern medicine, opiates, morphine, and cocaine became available for legitimate use. Persons who were administered these drugs for medical purposes often became addicted to them. Drug abuse and addiction was a new phenomenon in the 1890s. By the beginning of the 20th century, organized crime groups were running drug dens in the same style as their modern descendants. In New York opium dens were often controlled by Chinese-based "tongs." Visitors to New York sometimes were given guided tours of opium dens by anti-sin societies to raise awareness of the problem.

CHARLES PARKHURST AND THE ANTI-SIN MOVEMENT

One of the most powerful anti-sin efforts that would have a major impact on policing and crime was led by a slender, gray-bearded Massachusetts-born clergyman, Reverend Charles Parkhurst, pastor of the Madison Square Presbyterian Church in Manhattan. Parkhurst opened a February 1892 sermon by saying, "In its municipal life, our city is rotten. Every effort to make men respectable, honest, temperate, and sexually clean is a direct blow between the eyes of the mayor and his

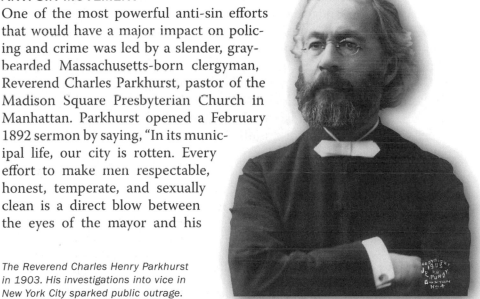

The Reverend Charles Henry Parkhurst in 1903. His investigations into vice in New York City sparked public outrage.

Police departments grew professionalized in the Progressive Age, and equipment, such as these 1920s handcuffs, was more uniform.

whole gang of drunken and lecherous subordinates." Parkhurst had just become president of New York's Society for the Prevention of Crime, which was made up of upper-crust businessmen, lawyers, and civic leaders. They were enraged by the spread of gambling dens, bordellos, and disorderly taverns in New York, the existence of which was tolerated by Tammany Hall politicians who depended upon them as a source of income through profit percentages or outright bribes.

Police officers of all ranks, themselves hired by Tammany whim, also benefited from looking the other way. One police superintendent admitted that despite a $3,500 annual salary, he had managed to sock away $300,000.

When Parkhurst hurled his broadside, it made all the papers and infuriated Mayor Hugh Grant and District Attorney DeLauncey Nicoll, who hauled the minister before a grand jury to ridicule him. Parkhurst had moral indignation, but no legal skill, and his anecdotal evidence did not meet legal standards of proof. Determined to get proof, Parkhurst hooked up with a private eye, Charles Gardner, who had once been a railroad detective. Gardner took Parkhurst on Saturday night guided tours of New York's seamier side, issuing the prim minister with a dirty shirt, checked trousers, sailor's jacket, and battered hat. They visited a waterfront saloon on Cherry Street where the owner fenced stolen goods; they fended off prostitutes in front of sailors' bars on Water Street; and they studied Chinatown opium dens where addicts lay amid prostitutes.

Gardner brought Parkhurst to a bordello on Third Street where the attractive young girls turned out to be men in drag, servicing a gay clientele. A furious Parkhurst bellowed, "I would not stay here for all the money in the world!" One of the final stops was Hattie Adams's bordello, near Parkhurst's church, where naked girls would perform a "dance of nature" for $3 each, which turned out to be the girls playing leapfrog by jumping over Gardner.

Armed with names, dates, addresses, and affidavits, Parkhurst summoned the press to his church on March 13 and told his story. The city was outraged:

the accused denounced Parkhurst as a "liar" and "poltroon," fellow clergy members expressed shock that a colleague would visit brothels, and civic leaders promised another grand jury. This one indicted four of the madams and said that the New York police were good at "preventing gross crimes" but "weak at suppressing disorderly houses, gambling places, and excise law breakers." Police Superintendent William Murray resigned, and his successor, Superintendent Thomas Byrnes, ordered a series of raids. Byrnes had a reputation as America's leading police detective, some of it well-deserved. Yet he also protected bordellos and gambling halls, and his officers worked to protect and support Wall Street financiers and their interests, treating arrested cutpurses with brutality. Byrnes created a "deadline" at Fulton Street, barring any known criminal from going south of the only street that crossed Manhattan from river to river, and amassed a $273,000 fortune doing so. Faced with Parkhurst's evidence and accusations, Byrnes acted with his usual flair. He shuffled precinct commanders, and hurled cops on show raids, reporting the closure of 444 houses of ill fame in his first seven months in office.

THE LEXOW COMMISSION

Two years after Parkhurst's investigation, U.S. Senator Thomas Platt pushed a joint committee to investigate the police, headed by State Senator Charles Lexow. He provided the rank, but the real power was Chief Counsel John W. Goff, a humorless Irish Catholic immigrant who hated Tammany Hall and later became a judge with a reputation for being tough on defendants and their lawyers. Goff slammed the cops, hauling Williams and one of his cohorts, Capt. "Big Bill" William Devery, into the witness stand. Williams and Devery proved arrogant and defiant. Williams attributed the funding of his 17-room house and yacht to real estate speculation in Japan during his seafaring days. The Japanese consul provided an affidavit that foreigners could not own property in Japan at the time, but Williams refused to retract that story.

But gamblers, madams, and saloonkeepers testified about police shakedowns and bribery. One madam said she had paid out more than $30,000 in protection over the years. Most importantly Capt. Max Schmittberger admitted not only his own sins—taking a $500 "New Year's gift" from a businessman—but incriminated many of his colleagues. Another, Capt. Timothy Creedon, a Civil War hero, admitted that he had purchased his captaincy from Tammany for $15,000. Byrnes proved a wily witness. He claimed his bankroll came from stock tips from Jay Gould, who was grateful for Byrnes's work in defusing a kidnapping threat. Byrnes further applauded the Lexow Commission for exposing so many bad actors in his force, and noted that whatever the outcome, as head of the Detective Bureau, his men had put away criminals for a cumulative 10,000 years.

The main result of the Lexow Commission was the dismissal of key cops, the exposure of many more, the jailing of others, and the election of a reform

The Leo Frank Case

The conflict of race, religion, law, and crime came to a bloody intersection in Atlanta in 1913, when a Brooklyn-born Jew stood trial for the murder of a young white girl. The case empowered two organizations that would stand in diametric opposition for the rest of the century—the Ku Klux Klan and the Anti-Defamation League of the B'nai Brith—and remains a shocking miscarriage of justice.

At 3 A.M. on Sunday, April 27, 1913, a night watchman at the National Pencil Company found the body of a young girl who had been raped. The body was soon identified as 13-year-old Mary Phagan, a factory worker, and the watchman, being black and on the scene, was the immediate first suspect. The police summoned factory co-owner and Superintendent Leo Frank, who claimed not to know her. On checking his personnel records, Frank found that Mary had actually been in his office, at noon on Saturday, to collect her $1.20 pay. After that, nobody had seen Phagan.

Leo Frank was granted a posthumous pardon on March 11, 1986.

The case was an immediate media sensation, as it linked two prime objects of southern white suspicion (blacks and Jews) with the murder of a young white girl. To make matters worse for Frank, he employed hundreds of southern whites and blacks, paying small wages for long hours—the very image of the northern "carpetbagger." On May 24 the Grand Jury took 10 minutes to indict Frank. The jury took only four hours to deliberate, returning a guilty verdict. The judge postponed sentencing for one day, and the jury approved death by hanging, on October 10, 1913. The appeal, with the key defense issue the jury's anti-Semitism, kept Frank and the case alive, as they were submitted in February 1914. In the meantime Chicago lawyer Sigmund Livingston reacted to the Frank trial by setting up the Anti-Defamation League of B'nai Brith in August 1913.

In July 1915 Frank was attacked by a fellow inmate and had his throat slashed. Quick work by prison doctors saved Frank's life, but just before midnight on August 16, 1915, a lynch mob of 25 armed men snatched Frank and drove him for seven hours to an oak grove outside of Marietta. There the lynch mob demanded that Frank confess to the Phagan murder. He denied any connection. The mob hung him and left him to die.

Exactly two months after the lynching, the "Knights of Mary Phagan" climbed the 1,780-foot Stone Mountain and burned a gigantic cross that was visible throughout Atlanta. The Ku Klux Klan, dormant since the 1880s, began a wave of terror and violence across the nation.

mayor, William J. Strong, in 1894. Members of the Lexow Commission also gained important positions. The Lexow Commission became a model for future probes of police misdeeds. Despite these incidents and investigations, police officers continued to fight crime. Officers were required to spend eight-hour shifts in "reserve," sleeping in poorly heated police stations and barracks between shifts. As now, they dealt with the horrible and the bizarre.

THEODORE ROOSEVELT

As the Progressive Era began in the 1890s, liberals, led by crusading reporter Jacob Riis, began the move to turn over some functions, such as providing shelter and food for the homeless, to charitable and welfare organizations, relieving cops of this burden. One such progressive to address police issues was Theodore Roosevelt, who became president of the New York Police Department's Board of Commissioners in 1895. Roosevelt wasted no time forcing Clubber Williams to retire. The press sneered that Williams would have more time to supervise his Japanese real estate holdings. Next Roosevelt planned to fire Byrnes. The superintendent resigned instead. Schmittberger, however, seen as a "reformed sinner," was brought back from patrolling the still-empty Bronx and given an Upper West Side precinct to command as an integrity test. It worked: when a bunch of gamblers tried to bribe Schmittberger, he beat them so badly, they landed in the hospital. Roosevelt was pleased.

Roosevelt set a good example, going out with Riis by night to see if the cops were doing their jobs, starting on June 7, 1895. Roosevelt and Riis prowled the East Side until 2 A.M., finding cops gossiping with citizens and another sleeping on a butter tub in the middle of the sidewalk. Roosevelt went to the neighborhood precinct at 4 A.M. and woke up the sergeant of reserves in order to locate three patrolmen who were "cooping." They turned out to be chatting with citizens in front of a 42nd St. saloon. The next morning Roosevelt had them report to his office at 300 Mulberry Street where they were all warned: one further infraction would lead to dismissal. Roosevelt's midnight tours pulled cops out of the bars and onto their posts, won him good press, and annoyed the old guard.

Roosevelt made the New York department more professional, a trend that would expand across the country. The cops he inherited were not well-educated men. Weapons and training were not uniform, and some cops had never fired a revolver at all. Roosevelt allowed applicants for New York City jobs to come from anywhere in the state, expanding the talent pool. He brought in an expert marksman to train cops on their new service weapon, a .32-caliber revolver. Two graduates put their training to work right off: Officers Patrick Reid and Daniel Ryan took fire from two burglars they surprised in the act. Ryan fired back and killed one of the suspects. The Detective Bureau was told to reduce the use of old methods of policing and to start using the new tools that were being developed, such as precise measurements, forensic autopsies by trained medical examiners, and a new idea that was demonstrated at the St. Louis World's Fair in 1904: fingerprinting.

PUNISHMENT

Also changing during the early 20th century were the mechanisms of trial and punishment. In many states, ancient jails that dated back to the Civil War were being replaced with the familiar stone-walled fortress, with stern, severe, but just treatment replacing more casual conditions and brutality. Southern states continued to rely on leasing out their criminals for public work projects and to private contractors. An 1893 report from Alabama's Chatham County showed 160 black males, 26 black women, and 11 whites, including two women, working from dawn to dark in muddy ditches, digging a canal. The prisoners included petty criminals. One white boy, on the gang for stealing a hat in a bar-room, tried to cut his throat after three days of this labor.

Capital punishment was only controversial in the early 20th century in how it was carried out. Public hangings, the standard throughout America, were increasingly seen as a remnant of the "dark ages," and the new electric chair was a "less barbarous manner," and a scientific solution.

Instead of being the center of a public fair, executions became midnight events in small prison rooms, with reporters in attendance instead of citizens. In 1890 William Kammler became the first man to be executed by the electric chair. Mrs. Martha Place, the first woman to do so, received 1,760 volts in 1899, still clutching her Bible when the doctors pronounced her dead. Juvenile justice was another issue addressed by the Progressive Era. In 1899 the Illinois legislature passed a law for Cook County (Chicago and its suburbs) that empowered judges to separate cases involving children who were "destitute or homeless or abandoned" or suffering from neglect, particularly any "child aged under 8 years who is found peddling or selling any article or singing or playing any musical instrument

Bloodhounds were trained to track escaped chain gang workers.

upon the street or giving any public entertainment." This began a process that moved the juvenile courts toward interventionism, rather than punishment.

FEDERAL LAW ENFORCEMENT

When the United States entered World War I, crime-fighting took on a new dimension, as police agencies across the nation had to address German espionage as well as ordinary crime. New York felt a touch of the war in 1916, when German spies blew up ammunition being readied for shipment to Britain from Jersey City. Across the nation, vigilantes and private groups either assumed or were given police powers, and used them to pursue perceived draft-dodgers, Socialists, and union activists.

The late 1890s and early 1900s saw other expansions of crime and punishment, many at the federal level. The "muckraking" journalists exposed the food, meat, and oil industries, which led to the Pure Food and Drug Act and new federal regulations against monopolies. That in turn required federal courts to act against violators of these offenses. To do so, the Bureau of Investigation, the forerunner of the Federal Bureau of Investigation, was created in 1908, with no arrest powers (special agents had to bring in local cops or federal marshals). It achieved more power during and after World War I, with the Palmer Raids and the Red Scare.

Federal regulation of food and drugs was copied by states. Louisiana passed a ban on adulterated milk in 1910, and a general food and drug law in 1914. Ohio created 49 criminal statutes on food, health, and workplace safety, among other areas. Cities passed their own ordinances, too. In 1907 New York arrested 6,000 people for violating health laws, steam boiler laws, pure food laws, and even arrested 35 people for violating New York's Game and Forest Law.

Another phase of law enforcement began in 1913 with the creation of the federal income tax and the Internal Revenue Service (IRS), which had power to prosecute tax evaders. By 1920, with the development of Prohibition, federal law enforcement had expanded dramatically from border patrol work, customs checks, and the Secret Service's war on counterfeiting, and would continue to do so.

DRUNK DRIVING AND OTHER CRIMES

Further developments impacted the ways laws were broken and enforced. The early 1900s also saw police departments, like the entire nation, becoming motorized. By 1910 states were requiring motorists to have licenses, and New York made drunken driving a misdemeanor on the first offense and a felony with prison time on the second offense. Cities established traffic and parking codes, which led to an endless flow of tickets and municipal revenue. Police departments in turn began to put their cops in police cars. Lacking the two-way radios and cell phones of later years, the first motorized cops had to use the same telephone call boxes as their brothers on foot.

Two New York City police detectives using a rogues' gallery of identification photographs in July 1909.

Liquor-licensing laws were enforced with increasing vigor during these decades. New York barred saloons from opening on Sunday, pleasing Sabbath-keeping churchmen, but infuriating hordes of workingmen and women, particularly Irish and Germans. Roosevelt ordered the law enforced. Police captains, fearing public and political retaliation, made just enough raids to appear to be obeying orders. The anti-saloon league would continue its efforts, though, and Prohibition would become the law of the land in 1919, effectively making America a nation of criminals.

Another line of crime that grew in the 1890s was the confidence game, often involving extremely elaborate operations. With limited federal oversight of banks, stock brokerage, and finance, swindlers could fleece unsuspecting victims with impunity. One such swindle was the "bucket shop," a stock brokerage house that would buy or sell stock against the orders of its clients, which was a form of insider trading. The term came from how these fake brokerages would buy stocks on one office floor, and sell stocks on the floor directly above or below, moving orders and information surreptitiously up and down elevator and fire shafts by bucket.

LYNCHINGS

As remunerative and evil as confidence games and "green goods swindles" were, the popular concern with crime was with the kind that left violence, destruction, and tragedy in its wake. Yet while gang killings and murder sprees dominated the headlines as atrocities, there was little outcry in the white-dominated media against a legally-tolerated form of violence that plagued America from 1890 to 1920—the lynching of blacks. By 1919 the National Association for the Advancement of Colored People (NAACP) reported that in the past three decades, 100 blacks per year, on average, had been lynched. There were 219 lynchings in the north, 2,834 in the south, and

156 in the west; 78.2 percent of the victims were African American. Some of the incidents were ghastly: Sam Holt, a black man accused of murdering a white man and raping his wife in Newman, Georgia, was tortured, mutilated, and burned at the stake before 2,000 people. Photographers would sell picture postcards of these events, and attendees often took souvenirs. Local police would not investigate, and coroner's juries would solemnly report that "parties unknown" were responsible.

Lynchings were warnings to African Americans not to step over the segregated south's innumerable social lines, mostly in their behavior toward white women. The ghastly specter of death by lynch mob was a major factor in black migration from the south to the north as the 20th century opened. Lynchings also show how reforms in the Progressive Era went only so far; many well-intentioned efforts did not extend to nonwhite people, or could make little progress in the face of entrenched attitudes. The professionalization of law enforcement during this time took place before a backdrop of widespread vigilantism and mass murder.

DAVID H. LIPPMAN

Further Readings

Asbury, Herbert. *The Gangs of New York. An Informal History of the Under world.* New York: Alfred A. Knopf, 1928.

Courtwright, David T. *Forces of Habit. Drugs and the Making of the Modern World.* Cambridge, MA: Harvard University Press, 2001.

Friedman, Lawrence M. *Crime and Punishment in American History.* New York: Basic Books, 1993.

Kessler, Ronald. *The Bureau.* New York: St. Martin's Press, 2002.

Lukas, J. Anthony. *Big Trouble.* New York: Simon & Schuster, 1997.

Lardner, Thomas and James Reppetto. *NYPD.* New York: Henry Holt, 2000.

McDonald, Brian. *My Father's Gun.* New York: Penguin, 1999.

Oney, Steve. *And the Dead Shall Rise: The Murder of Mary Phagan and the Lynching of Leo Frank.* New York: Vintage, 2004.

Rennert, Vincent Paul. *Western Outlaws.* New York: Crowell-Collier, 1967.

Reuter, Edward B. *The American Race Problem.* New York: Thomas Crowell, 1927.

Sloat, Warren. *A Battle for the Soul of New York: Tammany Hall, Police Corruption, Vice and Reverend Charles Parkhurst's Crusade Against Them, 1892–1895.* Lanham, MD: Cooper Square, 2002.

Van Willemse, Cornelius. *Behind the Green Lights.* New York: Knopf, 1931.

Wade, Wyn Craig. *The Fiery Cross: The Ku Klux Klan in America.* New York: Simon & Schuster, 1987.

Chapter 12

Labor and Employment

"It is wisely directed labor that has made
our country the greatest ever known."
— John Peter Altgeld

THE PERIOD BETWEEN 1890 and 1920 launched a dramatic shift in the American workplace and economy, as the frontier disappeared and the industrial boom expanded. While America's farmers fed increasingly large portions of the world, they in turn became increasingly dependent on a vast and developing industrial and service economy for everything from the barbed wire that hemmed in their cattle, to the railroads that hauled their produce to the cities. Behind every technological innovation was an army of middle-class workers—salesmen, clerks, secretaries, and accountants—whose often unglamorous work would lubricate the entire process.

The growth was massive, as American industries outpaced their European competitors. Assembly-line and mass-production methods, pioneered before the Civil War by Samuel Colt, reached grand scales in Henry Ford's factories, the steel mills of Pittsburgh, and the textile mills of Massachusetts. American industry demonstrated unparalleled efficiency in everything from steel production to potato-peeling. The efficiency in the workplace also created vast fortunes for the business operators of the time. Seemingly overnight John D. Rockefeller, J.P. Morgan, Andrew Carnegie, Henry Clay Frick, and E.H. Harriman became immensely wealthy, owning vast tracts of land, corporations, and huge chateau-like mansions on New York's Fifth Avenue.

However this immense economic growth was achieved on the strained backs of millions of American workers, many of whom were laboring under extremely unsafe conditions in factories, coal mines, and steel mills. Working between 10- and 12-hour days, including weekends, they were worse than underpaid. Coal miners in 1902 earned $560 a year, while loaders, dumpers, and other workers earned less. Often miners were paid in company scrip, which was only good at the company store, and were required to live in company-provided housing, the costs of which were deducted from their salaries. So were the costs for the gear and equipment miners had to use, the cost of sharpening their picks, and visits to the company doctor. The result was that workers found themselves in lifelong debt to their employers. At Pennsylvania's Markle Coal Company, 12-year-old Andrew Chippie's $.40 a day in 1902 was regularly credited against a debt left by his father, who had died in an 1898 mining accident. Another miner, James Gallagher, worked for his coal mine for 17 years without drawing a cent of cash pay, because of his debts to the company store.

Millions of American children worked from dawn to dusk. There was no alternative for the families who sent their children into grim sweatshops and textile mills. The average American family of 1910 needed to earn $800 per year to get along, but most unskilled laborers were paid less than $500 a year. With no pension plans, health insurance plans, unemployment compensation, Social Security, or other safety nets in place, additional family members meant more expenses. Thus kids had to work or starve.

A group portrait of the members of an African-American carpenters' union in Jacksonville, Florida, around 1900.

AFRICAN-AMERICAN LABOR

1890 saw the beginning of a vast wave of black migration from the south to the north. As King Cotton began to lose its grip on the southern farming economy, black sharecroppers found themselves in desperate straits. The solution was to answer advertisements placed by northern-based industries seeking cheap, unskilled labor. The trickle soon became a steady stream of African-Americans filling up neighborhoods in cities like Chicago and New York, taking often menial jobs, including janitorial work or as Pullman porters.

As large industry grew, workers found few organizations to represent them. Union-busting was perfectly legal, and owners practiced it. When miner Henry Coll tried to back his union, he was evicted from his company-owned home, along with his sick wife, four children, and 100-year-old mother. Companies kept and shared blacklists of former employees banned from working for union activism. The law was against unions, too. The 1890 Sherman Anti-Trust Act was designed to cut down on monopolies, but it prohibited "combinations in restraint of trade," and courts interpreted that to bar labor unions, as well.

LABOR UNIONS

Not that there were too many unions standing up. The Knights of Labor were in decline since the Haymarket fiasco of 1886. Rising to replace them, if only in the public mind, was the American Federation of Labor (AFL), founded that same year by London-born cigar maker Samuel Gompers. The AFL united craft unions of skilled workers across the nation. Often these craft unions were created by immigrant workers to protect not only their jobs, but their fellow countrymen. In New York the construction trades were divided by ethnicity: Italians ruled masonry, Englishmen and Irishmen did bricklaying, Germans put up trusses, and native-born Americans controlled plumbing. Ethnic lines helped dominate craft solidarity. These ethnic divisions would continue in American craft unions for the century to come. As late as 1978 craft unions in New York's newspaper printing plants were divided by the Irish county from which the members' great-grandfathers came.

The AFL owed its existence to three men: Adolph Strasser, Peter J. McGuire, and Gompers. Strasser, born in Germany, worked with Gompers to unionize cigar workers, creating the Cigar Workers Union, which became a model for other AFL unions, with its tight organization, firm leadership, and strong benefits package. Strasser and Gompers shuddered at radical ideas. Gompers himself was only arrested once in his life, for talking to a picket in 1879, and spent only one day in jail. Gompers's main concerns were higher wages, and safer working conditions for his constituency, and little more.

The hard edge of the AFL came from McGuire, the son of Irish immigrants, who grew up in New York and became a carpenter and a radical. He and Gompers were lifelong friends despite their opposition to each other's political views.

McGuire's opposition to the Knights of Labor and his energy in organizing the Carpenters Union made him a major leader in labor's struggles, and in 1890, he came up with a plan to regain the losses after the Haymarket fiasco of 1886. General strikes would not achieve gains, McGuire argued. One union should lead the way, and the others should follow.

The Carpenters took the lead, putting down tools on May 1, 1890. The bosses caved in quickly. In 36 cities, 23,000 carpenters won an eight-hour day, while 32,000 carpenters in 234 cities secured a nine-hour day. By 1891 building trade workers in New York, Chicago, St. Louis, Denver, Indianapolis, San Francisco, Brooklyn, and St. Paul all enjoyed the eight-hour day. Inspired by this success, a surviving union from the Knights of Labor, the United Mine Workers, went on strike on May 1, 1891, in the mines around Connellsville, Pennsylvania, demanding an eight-hour day. This strike failed. But it was only a minor precursor for the next big clash: the 1892 Homestead Steel strike.

Carnegie Steel Company, a forerunner of U.S. Steel, operated 12 steel and coke mills around Pittsburgh, darkening the city's sky while employing 13,000 workers. Carnegie Steel controlled the guts of America's steel production, and the 25,000-member Amalgamated Association of Iron and Steel Workers sought to represent the hard men (mostly Eastern European immigrants) who labored in the mills. Carnegie Steel's leadership was determined to eliminate the union. The showdown took place at Homestead, Pennsylvania, a town of 12,000 people, clustered around Carnegie Steel's mill. There, 3,800 workers produced boiler plates, beams, structural steel, and armor plate. The monthly payroll totaled $200,000; wages ranged from $.14 an hour for a common laborer to $280 a month for skilled workers. Most men earned about $200 a month.

In February 1892 negotiations began, and after three months of palaver, the company unilaterally announced a new scale of $23 a ton, which was a wage cut that ranged from 18 to 26 percent. Stunned workers hanged Frick and the mill superintendent in effigy. Company men turned a hose on the demonstrators, and shut down the mill on June 28, locking out the workers. Company men fortified the place, and local citizens called the mill Fort Frick. The 800 Homestead Carnegie workers, who were members of the Amalgamated, were joined by the 3,000 non-union men, who agreed to stand together and form an advisory council headed by Hugh O'Donnell.

On July 4 a force of 12 deputies showed up from Pittsburgh, but they were shipped back. A day later 300 armed members of the Pinkerton Detective Agency rode up the Monongehela River on barges towed behind a steamboat to the factory to break the strike. The detectives were greeted by angry townspeople, who warned the agents off. The Pinkertons shoved out a plank, and began to disembark. Someone fired a shot, and the detectives fired a volley into the crowd. As the women and children fled out of range, the townsmen found cover and returned fire. The Pinkertons returned to their barges, and

Ida Tarbell

"Muckraking" journalists like Ida Tarbell exposed the evils of meat-packing factories, impure food, and unfair trusts, leading to legislative reforms like the Pure Food and Drug Act, direct election of Senators, and "initiatives" and "referendums" to empower voters. Ida Tarbell grew up amid the oil derricks of the early Pennsylvania petroleum boom, and her town was economically battered by John D. Rockefeller's oil trusts. The plight of her family at the hands of the volatile oil industry may have energized her journalistic career. She graduated from Allegheny College in 1880 as the class's sole female member, spent two years teaching science, then gave it up to write. After writing in Paris, Tarbell became an editor for *McClure's* magazine. As part of the Progressive anti-trust politics of the time, *McClure's* was eager to play its part. Tarbell suggested a three-part series on the Rockefeller empire as a case study, and began to research Standard Oil's history. The three-part series became a 19-part series, and then the 1904 book *The History of the Standard Oil Company*, which was both powerful in its writing and meticulous in its evisceration of the Rockefellers, down to the old man's physical appearance. Tarbell condemned Rockefeller's rapaciousness and unethical behavior, while commending his brilliant operations and flawless corporate structure. In response, Rockefeller refused to comment or allow his family or employees to do so.

Tarbell's series would remain among the gold standards of American investigative journalism. While it was renowned for its blistering exposure of the corporation, it also revealed the rise of the influential middle-class economic world of newspapers and businesses that did not depend on physical labor (as in factories and mines) or vast amounts of wealth (as in banks and large corporations). The "service economy" was beginning in the early 1900s, and it spawned new fields of employment and training, such as secretaries, stenographers, accountants, and commercial artists. Because of their "respectable" working conditions (desks in new office buildings) and hours (9 A.M. to 5 P.M. on weekdays), single women from a variety of economic classes could find jobs in these fields.

Ida Tarbell's book on the Rockefellers was ranked among the top five works of 20th-century journalism in 1999.

Seven state troopers ready with riot guns in preparation for a strike in the steel industry in Farrell, Pennsylvania, in 1919.

found themselves trapped—the steamboat hired to bring them up had fled. The Pinkertons had no escape.

The Pinkertons and residents traded shots all afternoon, but it was a hopeless case. The Pinkertons ran up a white flag at 5 P.M. Three detectives and seven workers lay dead, and scores were wounded. The women roughed up the detectives and guards before shipping them back to Pittsburgh. After that, the townsmen repaired all damage done to the mill, and replaced the company watchmen with their own guards. Other steelworkers around Pittsburgh went out on strike in sympathy with the Homestead folks.

The state militia was called in next. The residents could not stand up to the blue-coated militia and their cannon, and the strike collapsed peacefully. The Homestead leaders faced six counts: three for murder, two for riot, and one for conspiracy. That fall 27 Homestead leaders stood trial for "treason against the state of Pennsylvania." The indictments and charges failed, but the union treasury was depleted, their power smashed. On November 17 the remaining union lodges voted to lift the ban against working for Carnegie Steel. Workers went back to earning $9.90 a week for a 12-hour day, with a 24-hour stretch every two weeks when day and night shifts were swapped out.

More strikes broke out: railroad switchmen in Buffalo, coal miners in Tennessee, and silver miners in Idaho's Coeur d'Alenes. The Idaho coal companies brought in scabs, but the striking miners surrounded the pits, demanding that the scabs be shipped out of state and the mines closed again. The coal companies complied, but only until they could pressure the state's governor to call forth the National Guard and federal troops to guard the strikebreakers and herd the union men into bullpens.

While these strikes were not successful or only led to modest gains, they spurred union activity. The Panic of 1893 pushed unionization further. The defeated miners of Idaho and Colorado formed the Western Federation of Miners, while Indiana's Eugene V. Debs quit the Brotherhood of Locomotive Firemen to form the American Railway Union, which soon scooped up whole lodges of railway carmen and switchmen, firemen, conductors, and engineers, as well as unrepresented section hands, engine wipers, and maintenance men. By the end of 1893 the ARU had 150,000 members. They showed their teeth in 1894, winning an 18-day strike against James J. Hill's powerful Great Northern Railway.

The next target was one of the most powerful railroad organizations in America, the Pullman Palace Car Company. George Pullman's company owned and operated one of the vast fleets of sleeping railroad cars that crisscrossed 125,000 mi. of American track. Pullman porters manned the cars, and Pullman workers built, maintained, and repaired them. Many Pullman employees lived in a model town built just south of Chicago, aptly named Pullman. Employees who lived there were required to pay an $18 monthly rent for five-room "pens with conveniences." One faucet supported five families. Those workers who moved out or lived in cheaper accommodations found themselves the first to be laid off. Pullman banned newspapers, public speech, town meetings, or open discussion in the community. His inspectors checked apartments for cleanliness, and tenants could be tossed out on 10 days' notice. A worker said, "We are born in a Pullman house, fed from the Pullman shop, catechized in the Pullman church, and when we die we shall be buried in the Pullman cemetery and go to the Pullman hell."

In 1893 the company paid out $36 million to stockholders and kept $25 million in undistributed profits. Workers, earning between $.04 and $.16 an hour, were hit with pay cuts that ranged from 25 to 50 percent. On May 11 some 3,000 Pullman workers downed their tools in the company's repair and construction shops, demanding reinstatement of the fired men and wage hikes, and mounted guards around the town.

The ARU held its first national convention on June 12 in Chicago, and the Pullman strike was the big issue. Debs was uncertain that his new union could handle a strike of such magnitude and called for negotiations and to submit the dispute to binding arbitration. Pullman refused. Debs and his leadership were caught between an intractable company and an angry rank-and-file that was calling for sympathy strikes across the nation. On June 21 the delegates voted unanimously to give Pullman four days to yield to mediation. If not, the ARU

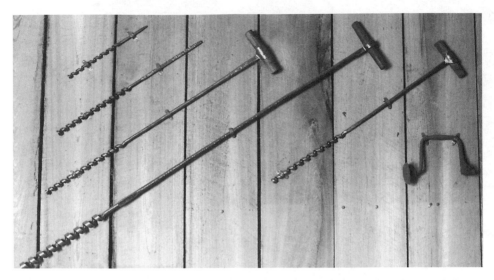

Craft workers, such as those who joined the AFL, would still have been skilled in using hand tools. These wood drilling augers continued to be used well into the 20th century.

workers would not handle trains with Pullman cars attached. Backed by the 24 railroads that used Pullman cars, the company stood firm. So did the ARU.

On June 24, 1894, the ARU launched one of the greatest nationwide strikes in American history. More than 125,000 ARU workers refused to handle Pullman cars. Twenty railroads were tied up. Attorney General Richard P. Olney, a former railroad corporation lawyer, appealed to President Grover Cleveland to send in federal troops to protect the mail and put down disturbances, over the objections of Illinois Governor John P. Altgeld, and Cleveland did so.

General Nelson Miles, who had avenged Little Bighorn by defeating the Native Americans, led thousands of blue-coated infantry and cavalrymen into Chicago to keep the Pullman cars moving and thus break the strike, setting up their tents on Lake Shore Drive. The troops escorted trains in and out of Chicago, driving off strikers and protesters with bayonets and cavalry charges. Violence broke out on July 7, and the troops opened fire, killing 30 people. Furious union men hurled incendiaries and wrecked rail cars, engines, and railroad buildings. Smoke hung over Chicago as troops and police officers fought strikers.

Debs appealed to the AFL for help, but Gompers, fearing that doing so would only drag the AFL down to defeat as well, refused. On July 7 Debs and other strike leaders were arrested for conspiracy and released on $10,000 bond. The strike continued. They were re-arrested for contempt of court on July 16, and the strike began to fizzle. On August 2 the ARU called off the boycott. The strikers at Pullman hung on until September before surrendering. Pullman required returning workers to sign "yellow dog" contracts that banned them from joining unions. Many workers found themselves blacklisted throughout the railroad industry. Debs, defended vigorously by Clarence Darrow, drew only a six-month sentence on the contempt of court charge—the conspiracy case was tossed—and spent his days in jail studying Marxism. The ARU also collapsed. Even so, a national commission investigating the strike determined that Pullman's rule of their town was a major factor in the strike. The rail company sold the community in 1898.

JOHN MITCHELL

That year the highly competitive midwestern bituminous coal industry reached an agreement with the United Mine Workers (UMW) that stabilized prices and granted recognition to the first such union. Leading the miners was a 28-year-old idealist, John Mitchell, who owed his permanent stoop to having started working in the mines at age 12. Within a few years, he had become a labor organizer, succeeding where the Molly Maguires of the 1880s had failed.

Shy, quiet, earnest, and dark-suited, Mitchell shrewdly reached out to the hordes of Immigrant Slavic, Hungarian, and Italian miners who were filling up the pits, accepting lower wages. He sent them organizers who spoke Italian or Hungarian. The immigrant miners quickly flocked to Mitchell's banner. By 1901 the UMW was the nation's biggest union. The following year Mitchell moved to unionize America's anthracite coal mines.

In March 1902 Mitchell demanded more pay, shorter hours, a uniform method of weighing coal, and union recognition. The coal operators, mostly railroad owners, refused. Mitchell took 150,000 anthracite coal miners out on strike on May 12. The strike dragged on all summer. When September came around, serious coal shortages took hold. Carloads soared in price from $5 to $20 a ton. Schools and plants across the country closed. Residents of Rochester, New York, cut down the city's telegraph poles for firewood. Even so, the strikers gained public and press sympathy for their grim working conditions, civil behavior, and earnest leader.

With the situation deadlocked and the weather turning cold, President Theodore Roosevelt intervened. But instead of sending in troops and marshals, he summoned Mitchell and the mine owners to meet him in Washington, D.C. There, Roosevelt appealed to their patriotism to end the strike. Mitchell asked Roosevelt to appoint a commission; he would go along with whatever it said. George Baer, president of the Philadelphia and Reading companies, refused to talk. A gloomy Roosevelt wrote that night, "Well, I've tried and failed."

The strike went on. In New York and Boston, residents clamored for fuel, and violence began. Strikers wrecked trains and blew up a bridge leading to a colliery. Roosevelt readied federal troops to take over the mines. But Secretary of War Elihu Root suggested to Roosevelt that the real problem was that the railroad owners were afraid to lose face by negotiating with Mitchell, but might be willing to deal with ordinary workers. With Roosevelt's blessing,

Lillian and Frank Gilbreth

Intellectual ability enabled talented women and minorities to succeed. Lillian Gilbreth, for example, worked with her husband as a motion-study engineer and industrial psychologist, gaining a doctorate in psychology in 1915 from Brown University. While Frank Gilbreth studied the physical movements of human beings to cut down physical tasks to their simplest essentials, Lillian studied the human aspects of the work place. She helped create job standardization, incentive wage-plans, and job simplification. She was among the first to recognize the effects of fatigue and stress on time management.

The two Gilbreths revolutionized the workplace. Working with the brand-new technology of movie cameras, they photographed industrial and service workers, and studied hand movements. Their studies resulted in the standardized processes by which soldiers would disassemble and re-assemble their rifles, and by which nurses and medics would line up surgical instruments on trays in operating rooms, among other things.

The Gilbreths had a rival at the time in Frederick Winslow Taylor, who pioneered the Progressive Era's Efficiency Movement, believing there was "one best way" to fix any problem. His "scientific management" of workplaces called for scientific study of tasks, employee training, and division between employees and managers such that employees performed the tasks while managers planned the work and made decisions. His processes standardized workplaces and increased efficiency and profitability, pointing American business in general, and Henry Ford in particular, toward the revolution in mass production.

Root met with banker J.P. Morgan on the latter's yacht. Morgan pressured his fellow money-men, and they agreed to an impartial commission appointed by Roosevelt. It would decide "all questions at issue between the respective companies and their own employees, whether they belonged to a union or not." That was what Mitchell wanted, but since the idea was publicly broached by Root and not a union man, the bosses could tolerate it.

In October the bosses agreed that the commission should consist of a businessman familiar with the coal industry, a mining engineer, an eastern Pennsylvania judge, a military officer, and "a man of prominence eminent as a sociologist." No union men. On October 15 the bosses and the White House haggled over this list, with the White House demanding a union man. Finally Roosevelt realized that the mine owners were not against a union leader on the commission, just against looking like they were yielding to one. Roosevelt appointed the Grand Chief of the Order of Railway Conductors as the "eminent sociologist"

and the commission went to work, ending the strike, and empowering feder-
ally-mediated collective bargaining as a labor-management concept.

Judge George Grey of Delaware presided over the commission, and the
United Mine Workers were represented by Clarence Darrow. The commission examined 558 witnesses and waded through 10,000 pages of evidence,
and issued its decision on March 21, 1903. It gave the contract miners a 10
percent increase in rates, eight-hour days, and the miners gained the right
to elect their own check weighmen and check docking bosses, which cut
down on abusive weighing and pay practices. Disputes would be submitted
to a six-man board of conciliation, with an umpire appointed by the courts to
break ties. However the UMW was not recognized, strikes and lockouts were
banned, and bosses could still fire workers for union activity. "Labor walked
into the House of Victory through the back door," snarled the fiery labor activist Mary "Mother" Jones. The agreement had a three-year lifespan.

Still, when George Baer finished his presentation for the operators to the
commission, Mitchell rose from his desk, crossed the floor, and shook the coal
boss's hand. Everybody wondered why, but the suspicion was that Mitchell
was seeking peace with honor. So did others: Gompers joined the National

*John Mitchell (right) with Andrew Carnegie, William Jennings Bryan, and James J. Hill at an
October 2, 1902, meeting at the White House called by Roosevelt.*

Civic Federation, a body of industrialists founded by Ohio Senator Mark Hanna, which brought labor's case directly to the wealthy. Mitchell himself joined it in 1908, and worked to settle more than 100 strikes.

But with strikes being settled without union recognition, and industrial workers still unorganized, labor-management tensions remained high. On June 27, 1905, Eugene V. Debs, the Western Federation of Miners' Bill Haywood, 75-year-old Mother Jones, and 200 equally angry and frustrated labor leaders convened in Cincinnati to form the Industrial Workers of the World (IWW), which would come to be known as the "Wobblies." With Haywood, head of 28,000 miners, holding the chair, the attendees drew up a charter that opened, "The working class and the employing class have nothing in common." Haywood would come under his heaviest fire and achieve one of his greatest triumphs in Idaho in 1907, when he stood trial for orchestrating the murder of former Governor Frank Steunenberg, and was acquitted.

WOMEN'S UNIONS

Meanwhile the war between blue-collar labor and capital continued to accelerate. In 1909 another AFL union took the tough road when the International Ladies' Garment Workers Union (ILGWU), then 10 years old, took on the thousands of unsafe New York sweatshops that were the backbone of America's clothing industry. Some 256,000 garment workers, mostly immigrant women and teenage girls, were turning out two-thirds of America's clothing, and they earned $5 for a 66-hour week, from which they had to pay for electricity, needles, thread, and sewing machine oil. Bosses docked pay further to workers who took breaks, talked, or even hummed on the job, and locked fire exits to prevent theft. Competition in this business was furious, so bosses had to take desperate measures to stay afloat, with frequent speed-ups.

In November 1909, 20,000 shirtwaist workers went on strike. Within five days 5,000 more went out. New York had never seen anything like it. Despite snow, cold, and public hostility, the women stood on their picket lines. The bosses hired thugs to attack the women, and they were followed by police officers, who arrested the strikers for "disorderly conduct." By December 1909 the ILGWU was nearly out of money, but they gained support from a new quarter, society women, usually daughters of millionaires, who supported the strikers and bailed them out of jail, co-opting their fight for decent wages into the fight for women's suffrage.

But by February the strike crumbled, defeated by lack of money and bitter cold. The bosses only gave minor concessions. However the women now knew how to strike. Three months later the cloak makers' union went out, doing so during warm spring weather, and with a strike fund. Sixty thousand workers joined the Great Revolt, and the industry was forced to the bargaining table, signing a Protocol of Peace that created an arbitration board, a 50-hour work week, and double pay for overtime.

These shirtwaist workers gathered indoors for a photograph during their strike in New York City in January 1910. Their strike would fail the next month.

These gains, important as they were, were overshadowed on Saturday, March 25, 1911, when fire broke out at the Triangle Shirtwaist Company on Manhattan's Washington Place, 15 minutes before quitting time. Some 500 workers, mostly teenage girls, were waiting to collect their pay, when a blaze started in a heap of discarded fabric. In seconds the fire turned the three-floor sweatshop into an inferno. Thirty-five responding fire engines could not reach the fire or the victims. More than 200 women were trapped amid searing heat and smoke. Workers climbed out the front windows, and plunged to their deaths.

Among the 146 dead were girls as young as 14 who had participated in the 1909 strike. The bodies were taken to a temporary morgue on the East River, where all but seven were identified. New Yorkers were enraged by the bloody toll. Tammany boss "Silent Charlie" Murphy, whose normal primary interest was maintaining the Tammany power base and not backing labor reform, recognized that Tammany's traditional politicking was obsolete in the mass industrial age, and hard-pressed to compete with the IWW's fiery speakers. His protégé, State Senate Majority Leader Alfred E. Smith, pushed out state laws between 1912 and 1914 that required factories to have enclosed staircases, fire

Textile workers in the mills of Lawrence, Massachusetts, went on strike in 1912. The crowds of strikers and their families included many children, seen here.

sprinklers, adequate lighting, ventilation, washrooms, and first aid. Women could not work more than 54 hours a week, and children were not allowed to work in factories at all. By 1914 New York had the most advanced factory laws in the United States. These became models for future union activism and the New Deal 20 years later.

Meanwhile the IWW heated up its campaigns for "one big union," but for all the IWW fire, they gained ink, but not members. The IWW's numbers never topped 250,000, but they showed that the industrial worker, despite lack of skills, could organize and fight. They would prove that by winning the Bread and Roses strike in Lawrence, Massachusetts. But the victory was illusory. The IWW had 14,000 members in Lawrence after the strike. By October 1913 the union was down to 700. As soon as the strike ended, the bosses imposed a speed-up in their mills, and flooded the mills with company spies, which weeded out union activists. A follow-up strike in Paterson, New Jersey, failed, and the IWW was in trouble.

STEEL AND COAL STRIKES
Steelworkers were in no better shape. Their 1909 strike against U.S. Steel's subsidiary, American Sheet and Tin Plate Company, failed in 1911, leaving U.S. Steel still an open shop. But George W. Perkins, U.S. Steel's Finance Committee chairman, saw that corporations had responsibilities to their employees, and

that labor trouble could be avoided if companies took care of their workers. He began modern corporate welfare for his workers, offering profit-sharing, pensions, safety programs, and ending seven-day work weeks. He also built model company towns that offered not only adequate homes, but also schools, playgrounds, and recreational facilities for workers and their families.

Another large corporation was forced into such behavior by a horrific battle with its workers. John D. Rockefeller Jr. controlled the Colorado Fuel and Iron Company (CF&I), the state's largest, but was apparently only partly aware or didn't care that the company's bosses were housing the 20,000 tenants of their company coal towns and camps in shabby conditions, controlling every aspect of their lives.

The situation erupted in September 1913 when the United Mine Workers of America chose to take on Colorado Fuel and Iron, seeing it as the worst offender of the many coal companies in the state. Some 9,000 miners and their families left the coal camps to set up tent colonies outside the coal fields. CF&I reacted by hiring strikebreakers and the Baldwin-Felts Detective Agency to guard the scabs and harass the strikers. The Baldwin-Felts crew were tough: they shined searchlights into the tent camps by night, randomly fired shots into them, and prowled the camp perimeters with an armored car built in the company's shops, called the Death Special.

Colorado Governor Elias Ammons sent in the state's National Guard to restore order. On April 20 militiamen showed up at the Ludlow striker camp to call for the release of one of their own who they claimed was being held against his will. A 12-hour gun battle resulted. The militia poured coal oil into the camp, and set the tents aflame. They also captured three strikers. Worse, four women and 11 children were hiding in a pit under a tent, and two of the women and all the children suffocated when the tent was set on fire. The bodies were left out in the ruined camp for three days, as a warning and example to other strikers.

The example backfired. Armed coal miners from across the state turned to guerrilla warfare. Anywhere from 50 to 200 people died in the Colorado Coalfield War, which lasted 10 days, at which time federal troops disarmed both sides. The strikers were replaced with non-union labor, and 400 strikers were arrested (all were ultimately acquitted), and the union forced to give in.

But the strike had huge impact. John D. Rockefeller Jr. was appalled by the violence, and hired former Canadian Labor Minister McKenzie King (a future Prime Minister of that nation) to investigate the whole disaster and recommend changes. A federal commission issued a 1,200-page report that called for granting most of the union demands, including a national eight-hour workday and ban on child labor.

Rockefeller and King developed the Rockefeller Industrial Representative Plan for CF&I, which called for a Joint Committee on Industrial Cooperation and Conciliation, consisting of company and employee representatives, as well as a slew of reforms in the company's operations and working conditions, including paved roads and a company union. The result was a model for industrial bargaining and company unions for the future, and Rockefeller avoiding strikes at its company's facilities for decades.

In 1914 labor won another victory when the Clayton Anti-Trust Act was passed as part of President Wilson's New Freedom legislation. This law exempted labor unions from anti-monopoly prosecution, which meant that strikes were no longer "illegal restraint of trade" and that businesses could sign collective agreements with labor unions.

LABOR AND WORLD WAR I

The United States did not enter World War I until April 1917, but American business found the sales of arms, ammunition, and other supplies to the Allied powers highly profitable, while American citizens debated their nation's neutrality and the question of "preparedness." The IWW opposed U.S. involvement in the war, seeing it as a battle between capitalists with workers for cannon fodder.

But when the United States entered the war in April 1917, the role of labor in the struggle became vital. President Woodrow Wilson set the tone in November 1917 when he made his first major public speech since declaring

Smoke surrounds the burning coal miner's camp at Forbes during skirmishes between the strikers and militia in Colorado.

war, doing so at the AFL convention in Buffalo. It was also the first time a U.S. president had addressed a labor convention. In his speech, Wilson called upon labor not to strike during the war, but promised that the federal government would support labor unions and labor issues in the postwar world.

This was recognition of organized labor as a legitimate organization in American society, and the AFL used that to great advantage, doubling its membership from two to four million by 1920. In 1918 the War Labor Board was established to mediate disputes. While it banned strikes and lockouts, it also recognized the right of workers to organize and negotiate collectively, to eight-hour days, and to an end to discriminatory firing of union members.

PURSUIT OF THE WOBBLIES

At the same time, the government pursued the Wobblies, which continued to pursue anti-war rhetoric. In June 1917, 150 top IWW leaders, including Eugene V. Debs, were jailed under wartime espionage laws. Federal and state harassment wrecked the IWW's organization. After the war many IWW leaders were tried in federal and state courts as part of the "Red-hunt" scandals of the time. Other union activists were deported to the new Soviet Union on the famous "Soviet Ark," the *SS Buford*. Among those fleeing the United States was Big Bill Haywood, the top IWW leader, who died in Russia in 1928, and had his ashes buried in the Kremlin wall.

When the war ended, unions, feeling toughened by their wartime gains, demanded their share of the new prosperity, and there were victories. Some 60,000 clothing workers won a 44-hour week; building and printing trade workers won strikes; and a textile strike in Lawrence, Massachusetts—scene of the Bread and Roses strike—won a 48-hour week and a 15 percent wage hike. Yet despite the gains made, particularly by the AFL, struggles and violence continued. Child labor remained legal, and vast numbers of industrial workers remained unorganized. After the war, labor unions were increasingly seen as agents of the Bolshevik revolution that had taken over Russia, and companies sought to reverse the clock.

Steel was the one industry untouched by the changes wrought by world war. William Z. Foster, who would later become the Communist Party's perennial presidential candidate, led the Chicago Federation of Labor's drive to unionize steel. He proposed to the AFL that it organize the various craft unions in steel into one union for a "hurricane drive" to unionize the industry. On August 1, 1918, the National Committee for Organizing Iron and Steel Workers was formed with the backing of 24 unions, and they went straight to work. By 1919 Foster was ready to move on Pittsburgh.

On September 22, 1919, 275,000 steelworkers went out on strike in nine states. In a month nearly 350,000 were on the picket lines. Company cops and state troopers attacked the picket lines, even charging into funeral processions and children going home from school. Civil rights were suppressed in steel towns, and steel companies imported black workers from the south as scab labor, adding a racial dimension to the bloody mess.

The strike collapsed on January 8, 1920. The workers sustained 20 dead and had lost nearly $120 million in wages, and U.S. Steel remained an open shop. So did many other industries—coal, shipping, and the new automobile industry. The open shop, the "yellow-dog contract," the company town, company scrip, child labor, all remained in place, seemingly as powerful as ever.

Yet massive changes had taken place in three decades of violence and strife. Factories and industries were not unionized, but unions were increasingly seen as a legitimate means by which workers could fight for their rights and welfare. Federal legislation had ended major barriers to union activities, and the public conscience had been stirred. Even corporate leaders had begun to recognize the importance of giving workers decent conditions and benefits. American unions and workers had a long way to go, but they had also come a long way, at enormous human price.

DAVID H. LIPPMAN

Further Readings

Arnesen, Eric, et al. *Labor Histories: Class, Politics, and the Working Class Experience.* Urbana, IL: University of Illinois Press, 1998.

Brooks, Thomas W. *Toil and Trouble.* New York: Dell, 1965.

Burns, Ric, and James Sanders. *New York.* New York: Random House, 1999.

Davis, Lance E., Jonathan R.T. Hughes, and Duncan M. McDougall. *American Economic History: The Development of a National Economy.* Homewood, IL: Richard D. Irwin, 1969.

eHistory at OSU. "Coal Mining in the Gilded Age and Progressive Era." Available online, URL: http://ehistory.osu.edu/osu/mmh/gildedage/default.cfm. Accessed January 2008.

Freese, Barbara. *Coal.* New York: Penguin, 2003.

Jacoby, Daniel. *Laboring for Freedom: A New Look at the History of Labor in America.* Armonk, NY: M.E. Sharpe, 1998.

Klein, Herbert S. *A Population History of the United States.* New York: Cambridge University Press, 2004.

Lord, Walter. *The Good Years.* New York: Longman, 1960.

Lukas, J. Anthony. *Big Trouble.* New York: Simon & Schuster, 1997.

Smith, Robert Michael. *From Blackjacks to Briefcases: A History of Commercialized Strikebreaking and Unionbusting in the United States.* Akron, OH: Ohio University Press, 2003.

Yellowitz, Irwin. *Industrialization and the American Labor Movement 1850–1900.* Port Washington, NY: Kennikat Press, 1977.

Chapter 13

Military and Wars

"Our object now ... is to vindicate the principles
of peace and justice in the life of the world
as against selfish and autocratic power."
— Woodrow Wilson

THE MILITARY STRENGTH of the United States grew in the aftermath of the Spanish-American War. The U.S. Navy was the particular beneficiary of this buildup, which was hardly surprising, as the defeat of the Spanish navy in the Philippines by Admiral George Dewey gave seeming vindication to the arguments of naval historian and theorist Alfred Thayer Mahan. Naval expenditures grew from $64 million in 1899 to $153 million in 1916. The number of naval personnel nearly quadrupled, while the number of battleships and cruisers doubled. The United States showed off its status as a rising naval power in 1907, when President Theodore Roosevelt sent the battleship fleet (the Great White Fleet) on a two-year cruise around the world at a time when tensions with Japan were on the rise. The size of the Marine Corps also tripled during this era.

As was typical of American military history up to this time, the Army was downsized after the Spanish-American War, but not for long. Although spending by the War Department dropped initially, it began to rise again within a few years and by 1916 had reached $183 million, not far below the 1899 expenditures of $229 million. The size of the Army decreased somewhat from 80,760 soldiers in 1899 to 70,837 in 1904, but by 1916 had risen again to 108,399. National Guard strength also grew, although not by a tremendous amount.

The peacetime growth of American military power was accompanied by technological change and organizational reform. The U.S. government wanted

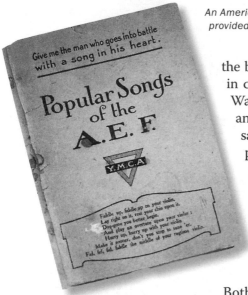

An American Expeditionary Force Songbook provided by the YMCA.

the best navy in the world, and succeeded in creating one that by the eve of World War I was outclassed only by Britain and Germany. While it was not necessary to maintain as large of a standing peacetime army as the major European powers, due to the fact that the United States had no need to fear a land invasion, the need for at least a somewhat larger regular army was recognized in the wake of the problems associated with mobilization for the Spanish-American conflict.

Both the maintenance of larger ground forces and the increase in naval strength were tied to the greater level of overseas involvement that the nation had undertaken. The United States was no longer concerned merely with securing its own borders and protecting its coasts, and the subjugation of Native Americans was complete. The recasting of the old idea of Manifest Destiny into an American version of the imperialism and colonialism popular among the Western powers and Japan had influenced the decisions to go to war with Spain and seize control of the Philippines, and would now lead to greater political, economic, and military involvement in the Caribbean, Latin America, and Asia. Greater involvement required a larger, stronger, and modernized military in order to fulfill the commitments and goals of the government.

THE PHILIPPINE REVOLUTION

Although the United States finally recognized Cuban independence following its victory over Spain, granting freedom to the Philippines proved to be another matter. Puerto Rico had become a U.S. possession as a result of the ongoing peace talks with Spain, and Hawaii was annexed earlier in the year. President William McKinley advocated continuing expansion of American power, a view supported by many politicians and by the imperialistic rhetoric emanating from much of the press. Businessmen also backed an expansive foreign policy, desiring to create new markets in the Caribbean, Latin America, the Pacific, and China. Many Protestants believed that the Catholic Filipinos were in need of "Christianization," which became yet another excuse for annexation. Caught up in the excitement of the moment and influenced by the views coming from much of the political, religious, and journalistic establishments, the American public firmly backed these ideas. Although Spain

An Age of
Technological Transition

The trend toward technological modernization in the U.S. armed services that had begun in the decades following the Civil War continued after the end of the conflict with Spain. One area that saw change was communications, of importance in not only linking army commanders with their governments and colleagues, but also in making sure that orders were quickly transmitted down the line to insure operational efficiency. By the early 1900s the telephone and the radio had joined the telegraph as a primary means of communication. However their usefulness was at this point limited on the battlefield.

Increased accuracy in firepower among both rifles and artillery continued with improvements in manufacture, making the life of an infantryman on the battlefield more difficult. Rapid-fire weapons continued to improve, as the Gatling guns of the Civil War era gave way to machine guns. The Army was slow to adopt the latter weapon, however, and the model that was initially chosen was not as efficient as its European counterparts.

Land transportation was also changing with the introduction of gasoline-powered vehicles. Trucks could transport materials and supplies from depots on properly laid-out roads much faster than horse-drawn vehicles. A number of factors, including the costs of fueling and maintaining vehicles and traditional opposition to change among the officer ranks, inhibited the adoption of motorized transport on a large scale until the eve of America's entry into World War I.

Technological change was also adopted by the Navy, although as in the Army conservative views inhibited the pace of development. Primitive submarines had been in use since the 19th century, but it was not until the early 20th century that they became more widely adopted. A variety of problems involving ventilation, hull strength, propulsion, and weaponry had to be solved first. After many years of experimentation, John Philip Holland developed a suitable submarine, which was purchased by the United States in 1900. By 1914 the Navy had 34 submarines.

Both the Army and the Navy showed interest in one new innovation, the airplane. The Army had created its first squadron in 1913, consisting of eight biplanes. The Navy also received funding for aircraft, experimenting with planes taking off from ships. Both branches of the service saw planes primarily as instruments of reconnaissance, or as spotters for gunners. The potential use of aircraft for bombers or fighter escorts still lay in the future. Thus by 1917 the armed services of the United States had reached a technological level more or less comparable to that of other major powers.

initially objected to the idea of U.S. annexation of the Philippines, it eventually agreed in exchange for a payment of $20 million.

The treaty was concluded in December 1898, but immediately ran into opposition in the U.S. Senate among members who objected to the direction in which the country was heading. The treaty was nevertheless ratified in February 1899. In the meantime, events reached a crisis in the Philippines. Emilio Aguinaldo y Famy, leader of the Filipino guerrilla movement against Spain, turned against the American occupation forces. The result was a brutal war that lasted for over three years. As is often the case in wars involving insurgencies, the line dividing combatants and non-combatants quickly became blurred, as it was often impossible to tell who the enemy was when the foe was part of the population and faded into the countryside following battles and raids. Neither the Americans nor the Filipinos were kind to prisoners, and mutual atrocities were committed.

Aguinaldo was captured by U.S. forces in March 1901. The fighting continued, with American troops suffering one of their worst defeats at Balangiga on the island of Samar in September. By this time, McKinley was dead, having been assassinated by an anarchist. The new president was Theodore Roosevelt. A long-time proponent of American naval expansion in the years before the Spanish-American War, Roosevelt had emerged as a popular hero in the latter conflict for the role he had played as lieutenant colonel of the 1st Regiment U.S. Volunteer Cavalry, the "Rough Riders." His rise to the presidency assured that U.S. expansionist policies would continue; in particular, Samar had to be pacified. Brigadier General Jacob Smith, the American commander assigned for the task, went far beyond Roosevelt's intent, enacting a brutal retaliation for Balangiga, giving verbal orders to kill everyone over the age of 10 (considered by Smith to be the youngest age group capable of bearing arms).

Two Muslim Filipino, or Moro, soldiers in the Philippines around 1900.

In the meantime another American commander formulated the strategy that brought an end to the conflict. General J. Franklin Bell established boundary lines around every center of population capable of supporting the guerrillas, forcing inhabitants in outlying areas to abandon their homes and move within the designated zones. The result was that the insurrectionists were severed from support within the population. The rebellion thus died out, and Roosevelt declared the conflict officially over in July of the following year. Some 7,000 Americans had been killed or wounded. Guerrilla deaths numbered around 20,000, while many thousands more among the civilian population died.

General J. Franklin Bell, who came up with a strategy that ended much of the guerrilla fighting in the Philippines.

The end of the revolution did not mean the end of violence in the Philippines. Muslim Filipinos on the Moro Islands staged their own resistance, unrelated to the nationalist rebellion. Fighting between the Moros and American troops, the latter assisted by Filipino forces organized to assist the occupiers, began in 1902 and lasted well into the next decade.

ASIA AND THE PACIFIC

While the United States was involved in suppressing the Filipino revolution, it participated in a conflict in China. Trade between the United States and China had steadily grown for decades, with the first treaty between the two nations dating to 1844. By the end of the 19th century, the United States espoused an Open Door policy, designed to insure that America had equal access to Chinese markets at a time when other major powers had established exclusive economic access to certain ports and territories. The most important of these nations was Britain, which had gained major concessions from China (including control of Hong Kong) in the Opium War of 1840–42. Other nations, including France, Russia, and the rising Asian power of Japan, followed. Increased access to Asian markets in order to promote American power was also a centerpiece of the theories of Mahan and like-minded individuals.

In the late 1890s a major nationalist movement arose in northern China. Called the Boxers because of the ritual exercises associated with the group,

These Boxer prisoners were held by the 6th U.S. Cavalry in Tientsin (Tianjin), China, in 1901.

the order espoused an anti-foreign and anti-missionary ideology buttressed by mystical ideas. By the end of the decade the Boxers received the tacit approval of the government of the Dowager Empress, which turned a deliberately blind eye to the group's activities in order to further its own goals of reviving Chinese strength and ending the foreign political and economic hold on the country. At the end of 1899 the Boxers began to kill foreign missionaries in the northern countryside. The violence gradually spread, and by June 1900 had reached the capital, Peking (Beijing). The foreign legations were besieged, defended by a handful of troops. Many foreigners and Chinese Christians were killed, while others found refuge in the legation buildings or other defended strong points. The Chinese government began to more openly support the Boxers, with Imperial troops joining them in some actions.

An expedition was organized to relieve the legations. It included American troops, some diverted from the fighting in the Philippines. Over 5,000 U.S. soldiers and 500 Marines were involved, besides troops from Britain, France, Germany, Russia, and Japan. U.S. naval vessels participated as part of the supporting fleet. On August 14, 1900, the allied forces broke into Peking and reached the legations. Afterward the Boxer movement went into decline, and negotiations began between the Chinese government and representatives of the victorious foreigners. A treaty was signed in September 1901, which included the imposition of indemnities from the Chinese to the foreign powers. The United States quickly reduced its military presence, with many of the troops heading to the Philippines as soon as was practicable. The United States left a small contingent of forces in China, however, to watch over America's interests there, although a long-term American military presence in Asia did not have strong congressional or public support.

Nevertheless Asia remained an area of concern among American leaders, and in particular naval strategists. One source of growing worry was Japan, which had undergone steady industrialization and military modernization over the last several decades. In 1904 and 1905 Japan defeated Russia in a war that demonstrated in particular the former nation's growing strength as a modernized naval power. Thereafter Japan pursued a program of increasing economic influence in China and ending Western colonialism in Asia. As a result, tensions arose between Japan and some of the Western powers active in Asia, as well as the United States, which was alarmed over the possible loss of access to Chinese markets. For a time there were concerns that war might break out between the two growing Pacific rivals. By 1911 strategists in the U.S. Naval Department had developed a strategic outline for a possible war with Japan. Known as the Orange Plan, it remained the basic American strategic plan for naval action in the Pacific until 1938.

During the negotiations at the end of the Boxer Rebellion in 1901, the 9th U.S. Infantry lined an approach to the Forbidden City in Beijing, China, to honor the German head of the joint troops.

The Panama Canal and American Military Strategy

From the age of exploration, finding a quick passage between the Atlantic and Pacific oceans was a major goal of both nations and individual mariners. The narrow Isthmus of Panama allowed goods to be transported by a combination of rivers and land carriage between the coasts, but there were still difficulties and time delays involved. During the colonial era the isthmus was part of the vast Spanish Empire. In 1821 it became part of the recently-created Granadan Federation, which had successfully revolted against Spain two years earlier. The federation separated in 1831 into the nations of Venezuela, Ecuador, and New Granada (Colombia). The isthmus was thereafter part of the latter country, although many of its people nursed nationalist aspirations of their own.

The United States became interested in the Isthmus of Panama in the mid-19th century, establishing a treaty with New Granada in 1848. According to its terms, the United States would defend the isthmus in exchange for free passage for U.S. citizens and goods. This marked the beginning of growing American influence in the region, including the construction of a railroad across the isthmus. Beginning in 1856 the United States began to project limited military power into the isthmus, dispatching several small naval expeditions to deal with labor unrest and other troubles.

Meanwhile in the latter part of the 19th century, many considered the possibility of building a canal across the isthmus, which would shorten the passage. The canal would have both economic and political benefits for whatever nation controlled it, as it would not only allow merchant vessels, but also warships to move between the oceans. Ferdinand de Lesseps, the Frenchman who had built the Suez Canal in Egypt, launched a construction project in 1882 to build a canal across the isthmus. The project bogged down, as Colombia became wracked by revolution. In 1885 the United States sent a major naval expedition to Panama in order to protect the railway and keep it running.

De Lesseps's project went bankrupt in 1889. The United States became more interested in establishing a canal under its own control. In 1899 a civil war broke out in Colombia that lasted until 1902. The United States again intervened in order to protect its economic interests in the isthmus. At the same time the government of President Theodore Roosevelt attempted to secure rights to construct a canal across the isthmus under American control. When things did not go as hoped, the United States cultivated contacts with Panamanian nationalists. The result was an American-backed revolution in 1903 that secured Panamanian independence. The United States acquired very favorable terms for the building of a canal under American control in return for its assistance, and the canal was built by the Army Corps of Engineers and opened in 1914.

LATIN AMERICA AND THE CARIBBEAN

Following the Spanish-American War, U.S. policy toward the Caribbean and Latin America crystallized. The region would become an American-dominated zone, free of foreign meddling and political instability. This view was institutionalized in what was known as the Roosevelt Corollary to the Monroe Doctrine, which was increasingly used to justify American intervention throughout the area in order to prevent the possibility of foreign intervention due to political and social unrest. The United States would also seek to build a canal across the isthmus of Panama, allowing quicker passage of ships between the Atlantic and Pacific oceans. The isthmus achieved independence from Colombia in 1903 in a revolution that had American support. The United States was granted concessions that led to the building of a canal under American control. It opened in 1914, following construction by a contingent from the Army Corps of Engineers.

Other regional interventions followed. A small force of Marines was sent to Nicaragua in 1910 to protect U.S. interests there during a civil war. In 1912 another revolution broke out, and U.S. forces were sent in to support the government. The Americans put down the rebellion and left token forces stationed in the country.

As the United States became increasingly active in Central America, it also kept an eye on the nations of the Dominican Republic and Haiti. Located on the island of Hispaniola, the two nations were frequently wracked by political instability. In 1915 growing violence in poverty-ridden Haiti led to a revolution. The administration of U.S. President Woodrow Wilson sent a small naval squadron and a contingent of Marines to restore order, with reinforcements following. Although the U.S. forces were able to suppress the violence, finding a political solution for Haiti's problems proved to be a more difficult matter. Nationalist resentment against the American occupation was high. In early 1916 a revolt against the occupiers broke out, with others following. In that same year, the United States also became militarily involved in the Dominican Republic, where another revolution was in progress. Once again, the Navy and the Marines acted as the instruments of U.S. policy. As in Haiti, the initial violence was suppressed, but further outbreaks followed, while the task of finding a stable government proved fruitless. The American occupation of the Dominican Republic ended in 1924, while the Haitian mission lasted another 10 years beyond that.

This campaign bugle was used in the abortive Pershing Expedition into Mexico in the effort to capture Pancho Villa.

In addition to the interventions in the Caribbean, the United States found itself taking action much closer to home. In 1910 a revolution broke out in Mexico that led to the dictatorship of Victoriano Huerta. Other revolutionaries fought the new regime. In a successful effort to undermine the Huerta regime, which had alarming ties to Germany, the administration of Woodrow Wilson sent troops to Veracruz in 1914. Infighting between the remaining revolutionaries continued, with Venustiano Carranza emerging to become Mexico's new president. The Carranza administration gained Wilson's support. In retaliation, Carranza's rival Francisco "Pancho" Villa struck across the border at Columbus, New Mexico, in March 1916. An expedition of 10,000 troops under Brigadier General John J. Pershing was sent into Mexico in pursuit, while additional soldiers and National Guardsmen guarded the border. Villa's forces were scattered, but he was not caught. By that time, tensions between the United States and Germany had assumed priority over matters in the Western Hemisphere.

WORLD WAR I

In 1914 a massive conflict erupted that eventually involved almost all of the major nations of Europe. The struggle committed Germany, Austria-Hungary, and Turkey against an alliance that included Britain, France, Russia, Italy, Serbia, and Japan. Initially the United States pursued an official policy of neutrality, although Woodrow Wilson's sympathy for Britain and its allies was not exactly a secret. Germany's use of submarine warfare against vessels trading with the Allies became a major point of contention with the United States, especially after over 100 Americans died when the British ocean liner *Lusitania* was sunk in May 1915.

Although Wilson would successfully campaign for reelection on a platform of having kept the nation out of the conflict, preparations were being made for the possibility of American involvement. A program of further naval modernization was introduced, while the Army and the National Guard underwent further expansion.

After a period of inactivity, Germany resumed unrestricted submarine warfare in 1917, determined to cripple the Allies' economic capacity to wage war. Shortly afterward Wilson made public the Zimmermann Telegram, passed along to the United States by British intelligence. The telegram was a message from the German foreign minister to his ambassador in Mexico, urging the formation of an alliance between the two nations that could lead to the latter country regaining territories lost in the Mexican War. It was ultimately the continued loss of American civilians on passenger ships sunk by submarines that led to the final breaking point, however. War was declared on Germany in April 1917.

World War I marked the first time that the United States experienced total war, a struggle in which all of a nation's resources were thrown into the war effort. A draft was introduced to bring the Army up to fighting strength, and the

Remaining Neutral in the World War

Woodrow Wilson was elected president in 1912 largely on a platform built around domestic issues. In the end, historians have largely defined his administration by its actions relating to World War I and the peace negotiations that followed the war. Wilson's August 19, 1914 message to the Senate, excerpted below, outlined his administration's intent to remain neutral and not to become involved in the conflict.

I suppose that every thoughtful man in America has asked himself, during these last troubled weeks, what influence the European war may exert upon the United States; and I take the liberty of addressing a few words to you in order to point out that it is entirely within our own choice what its effects upon us will be, and to urge very earnestly upon you the sort of speech and conduct which will best safeguard the nation against distress and disaster.

The effect of the war upon the United States will depend upon what American citizens say and do. Every man who really loves America will act and speak in the true spirit of neutrality, which is the spirit of impartiality and fairness and friendliness to all concerned. The spirit of the nation in this critical matter will be determined largely by what individuals and society and those gathered in public meetings do and say, upon what newspapers and magazines contain, upon what ministers utter in their pulpits and men proclaim as their opinions on the street....

I venture, therefore, my fellow countrymen, to speak a solemn word of warning to you against the deepest, most subtle, most essential breach of neutrality which may spring out of partisanship, out of passionately taking sides. The United States must be neutral in fact as well as in name during these days that are to try men's souls. We must be impartial in thought as well as in action, must put a curb upon our sentiments as well as upon every transaction that might be construed as a preference of one party to the struggle before another.

My thought is of America. I am speaking, I feel sure, the earnest wish and purpose of every thoughtful American that this great country of ours, which is, of course, the first in our thoughts and in our hearts, should show herself in this time of peculiar trial a nation fit beyond others to exhibit the fine poise of undisturbed judgment, the dignity of self-control, the efficiency of dispassionate action; a nation that neither sits in judgment upon others nor is disturbed in her own counsels and which keeps herself fit and free to do what is honest and disinterested and truly serviceable for the peace of the world.

Shall we not resolve to put upon ourselves the restraints which will bring to our people the happiness and the great and lasting influence for peace we covet for them?

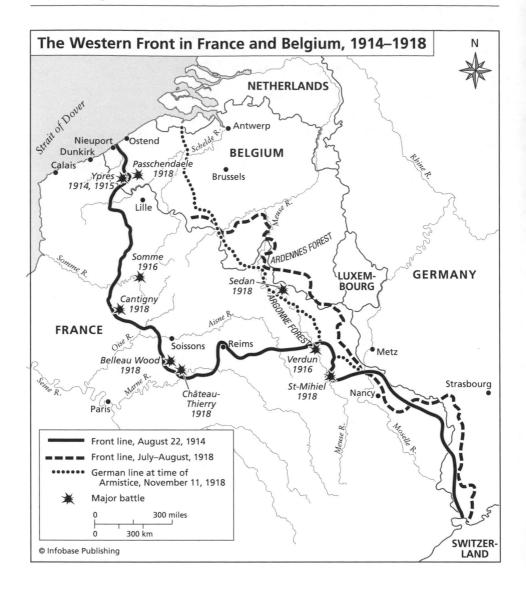

The Western Front in France and Belgium, 1914–1918

N

NETHERLANDS

Strait of Dover

Antwerp

Nieuport • Ostend
Dunkirk
Calais   Passchendaele   BELGIUM
Ypres   1918   Brussels
1914, 1915

Lille

Schelde R.

Rhine R.

Meuse R.

ARDENNES FOREST

Somme R.

Somme
1916

Sedan
1918

LUXEM-
BOURG

GERMANY

Cantigny
1918

ARGONNE FOREST

FRANCE

Aisne R.

Oise R.

Soissons   Reims

Metz

Belleau Wood
1918

Verdun
1916

Strasbourg

Marne R.

Château-
Thierry
1918

St-Mihiel
1918

Nancy

Seine R.

Paris

Meuse R.

Moselle R.

Front line, August 22, 1914
Front line, July–August, 1918
German line at time of
    Armistice, November 11, 1918
Major battle

0   300 miles
0   300 km

© Infobase Publishing

SWITZER-
LAND

National Guard was called up. The prices of food were fixed in order to encourage farmers to produce more for shipment overseas to the Allies, while American citizens were encouraged to save on food consumption. Propaganda was harnessed to motivate patriotic support for the war, while painting the enemy in the worst light possible (the latter a process which had actually begun well before America's entry into the conflict). Strikes by labor organizations were discouraged as unpatriotic and hurtful to the war effort. The Espionage Act of 1917 and Sedition Act of 1918 were used to dampen perceived dissent of any sort. Women played a major role in the war effort, moving into industry and other jobs vacated by men drafted into service.

American soldiers, National Guardsmen, and Marines were shipped to Western Europe as part of the American Expeditionary Force (AEF) under Pershing, now a major general. Once there, they would join the armies of Britain and France, where a long stalemate had ensued. Other Americans participated in the AEF Air Service; indeed, not a few Americans had already been serving in French or British air units as volunteers long before the American declaration of war. By this time air power was moving beyond the limited role of reconnaissance envisioned by many pre-war planners, with some planes acting as bombers, while others served as fighter escorts, the latter participating in "dogfights" with their opponents.

Once the land forces arrived, they went into training under Allied supervision before introduction to the trenches. Modern weaponry had quickly ended the traditional war of maneuver early in the conflict; machine guns, modern artillery, and poison gas made frontal assaults too costly. Both sides had adopted an elaborate system of entrenchments to defend their respective positions, protected by artillery and machine gun strong points. For the next three years, both sides struggled with trying to figure out how to break the stalemate, and the experimentation proved very costly to both sides. Gradually the Allies evolved tactics that involved making small breakthroughs for relatively small gains of territory, consolidating those gains and repulsing any counterattacks, and launching a fresh attack.

Due to growing manpower shortages caused by the attritional nature of the fighting, the Allied high command sought to break up the AEF and distribute its forces among their own depleted armies, something that Pershing fought hard to prevent. The earliest units to arrive went to the front under French supervision in late 1917. More units reached Europe in the next few months. In March 1918 the Germans launched the first of a series of major offensives designed to break the Allied position. Determination yielding to exigency, Pershing offered to send the available, fully-trained four American divisions at hand to the front as needed. The 1st Division of the AEF went into action under the French at Cantigny in May and made an impressive combat debut. As additional German assaults drove the French and British further back, the 2nd and 3rd Divisions went into action, the former counterattacking successfully at Belleau Wood in June.

In July the Allies began a series of counteroffensives, and the growing AEF played a major role. The largest American drive took place during the Meuse-Argonne offensive of September–November, which was still going on at the time when an armistice was agreed upon. Exhausted, Germany had had enough.

The Americans had over 50,000 killed and 200,000 wounded, while nearly 60,000 more died of disease—small by the standards of the European powers that had been involved in the conflict for a much longer period, but devastating enough for the nation.

In the aftermath Wilson sought to use the peace negotiations at Versailles to bring about major changes in the international status quo. Having proclaimed the struggle as an idealistic crusade in defense of democracy, Wilson had introduced his Fourteen Points to provide for a permanent international settlement. His goals were lofty indeed, involving not only such issues as national self-determination, democracy, and open diplomacy, but also disarmament and the destruction of imperialism. Predictably, the more pragmatic (and more cynical) heads of the other Allied nations rejected many of his goals, and Wilson had to compromise on many of his points in order to get a treaty that could be signed. In the end Wilson was unable to secure passage of the Versailles Treaty in Congress, as the nation retreated toward isolationism. America had fully emerged as a major power in World War I, but the role that it would play in the postwar world was uncertain.

MICHAEL W. COFFEY

Further Readings

Challener, Richard D. *Admirals, Generals, and American Foreign Policy 1898–1914*. Princeton, NJ: Princeton University Press, 1973.

Coffman, Edward M. *The Regulars: The American Army, 1898–1941*. Cambridge, MA: The Belknap Press of Harvard University Press, 2004.

———. *The War to End All Wars: The American Military Experience in World War I*. New York: Oxford University Press, 1968.

Cooling, Benjamin Franklin. *Gray Steel and Blue Water Navy: The Formative Years of America's Military-Industrial Complex, 1881–1917*. Hamden, CT: Archon Books, 1979.

Cooper, Jerry M. *The Rise of the National Guard: The Evolution of the American Militia, 1865–1920*. Lincoln, NE: University of Nebraska Press, 1997.

Merrion and Susie Harris, *The Last Days of Innocence: America At War, 1917–1918*. New York: Random House, 1997.

Millett, Allan R. and Peter Maslowski. *For the Common Defense: A Military History of the United States of America*. New York: The Free Press, 1984.

Musicant, Ivan. *The Banana Wars: A History of United States Military Intervention in Latin America*. New York: Macmillan Publishing Co., 1990.

O'Toole, G. J. A. *The Spanish War: An American Epic—1898*. New York: W.W. Norton and Company, 1984.

Preston, Diana. *The Boxer Rebellion: The Dramatic Story of China's War on Foreigners That Shook the World in 1900*. New York: Walker & Co., 2000.

Prior, Robin and Trevor Wilson. *The First World War*. The Smithsonian History of Warfare. Washington, D.C.: Smithsonian Books, 1999.

Strachan, Hew. *The First World War*. New York: Viking, 2004.

Chapter 14

Population Trends and Migration

*"All the people not actually needed to cultivate
the soil are being drawn into the towns."*
— Henry J. Fletcher

IN THE EARLY 1890s the U.S. Bureau of the Census announced that the American frontier had virtually disappeared. "This census," it said, "completes the history of a century; a century of progress and achievement unequaled in the world's history. A hundred years ago there were groups of feeble settlements sparsely covering an area of 239,935 square miles, and numbering less than 4,000,000. The century has witnessed our development into a great and powerful nation; it has witnessed the spread of settlement across the continent until not less than 1,947,280 square miles have been redeemed from the wilderness and brought into the service of man, while the population has increased and multiplied by its own increase and by additions from abroad until it numbers 62,622,250." There were just a few places on the map that remained sparsely populated, but there was no longer a definable line of settlement between the wilderness and the settled land.

The census takers of 1890 couldn't have imagined what kind of population changes they would see in the next 30 years. Immigration from Europe was going to change from a steady stream to a full-blown flood; Americans would begin the greatest internal migration in their history; a great foreign war would lead to an unprecedented military draft; and the country would suffer its share of history's worst epidemic. Cities would grow not just larger, but more racially and ethnically diverse. And at least two American cities would be almost entirely wiped from the map: Galveston, Texas, in a 1900 hurricane, and San Francisco, California, in a 1906 earthquake, both at the cost of many thousands of lives.

IMMIGRATION

Immigration reached historic levels during the 1880s, bringing 5.2 million new citizens to American shores during the decade. As the 1890s progressed, it seemed as if that might have been the peak, with 3.7 million new arrivals between 1891 and 1900, a reduction due largely to the worldwide economic depression that lasted for the better part of the decade.

Then, in 1902, immigration hit a one-year high of 648,743 and continued to climb for the next 12 years. In 1905 it crossed the one-million mark for the first time, and would cross that threshold another four times before 1914. The busiest year was 1907, when 1.28 million people disembarked in American ports. After World War I broke out in Europe in the summer of 1914, immigration essentially stalled, with just 110,618 emigres in 1918. Between 1901 and 1920 a grand total of 14,531,197 people joined the American scene.

This is not to say that they were particularly welcome, except perhaps by the steamship operators who sold steerage tickets for the Atlantic crossings and the land speculators eager to sell them plots of land on the Great Plains on "easy" credit terms. The immigrant wave of the early 20th century was very different from those that had come before it. For most of American history, the vast majority of immigrants had come from just a handful of countries in northern Europe: Ireland, Scotland, England, and Germany. But in the peak year of 1907, of the 1.28 million immigrants, 340,000 came from the Eastern European empire of Austria-Hungary, 285,000 came from Italy, and 260,000 came from Russia. These new citizens were dark-skinned Greeks, Turks, Slavs, Croats, Magyars, Poles, and Romanians. They were not just Catholic and Protestant, but Eastern Orthodox and Jewish. They spoke a babble of new languages. Workers in the textile mills of Lowell, Massachusetts—once the job of choice for the daughters of New England's farmers—spoke in any of 25 different languages by 1910.

While some of the new immigrants headed straight for the wide-open lands of the west, most ended up in the urban areas of the east, where they tended to settle in enclosed neighborhoods, creating networks of support and companionship in their often hostile new homes. Like all immigrants, these new Americans had to straddle the fine line between assimilation to their new culture and losing their old one. Through the creation of social clubs, newspapers, theater groups, churches, and unions, most managed to simultaneously

These Portuguese women worked in a textile mill in Lowell, Massachusetts, in the 1910s. They were part of a wave of immigrants from Portugal to fishing and mill towns in New England.

reach for the American Dream and honor the language, folklore, and culture of their former homes.

On the west coast there was a small but important migration from Asia. The Chinese, who had been living and working in the west since the Gold Rush, had become such a hated presence that their immigration had been halted by the Chinese Exclusion Act in the 1880s. The Japanese had picked up their immigration rate after a prohibition against them was lifted in 1894, but quickly found themselves targeted by opposition groups like the Asiatic Exclusion League and the press. Matters came to a head in San Francisco in October 1906. The school board decided to use the destruction of the city's schools in the April earthquake and fires to announce a plan to segregate Japanese schoolchildren in the "Oriental Public School for Chinese, Japanese and Koreans" in the decimated Chinatown neighborhood.

President Theodore Roosevelt opposed the plan and the message it sent to Japanese allies, with whom he had just successfully negotiated to end the Russo-Japanese War in 1905. For their part, the Japanese wanted to assure that their foreign nationals were not subjected to the humiliation of segregation. Over the fall and winter of 1907, Roosevelt brokered the "Gentleman's Agreement," an informal six-point diplomatic note in which the Americans agreed

A woman heads north on Nineteenth Street through a path cleared in the storm debris in the devastated city of Galveston, Texas, in September 1900.

The Galveston Hurricane of 1900

The Galveston Hurricane of 1900 came ashore at Galveston, Texas, on September 8, 1900. Researchers have estimated its winds at 135 mph (215 km/h) at the time of landfall. The hurricane severely impacted the population of the city, taking from between 6,000 and 12,000 lives and decimating the city's infrastructure. The dead were so numerous that survivors were required to build massive funeral fires to dispose of the bodies.

The surge of the hurricane brought over seven feet of seawater through the town, drowning unsuspecting victims, and leveling structures along the way. The Galveston hurricane of 1900 is arguably the largest natural disaster in U.S. history. The storm left behind a legacy that extends across the country. As families moved from the island, they carried with them the story of that night.

to keep Japanese immigrant children in the public schools, and the Japanese government agreed to stop issuing passports to citizens wanting to emigrate to the United States. The few exceptions were the wives, children, and parents of those Japanese already living in the United States. The Gentleman's Agreement stayed in effect until 1924.

Another group of west coast migrants were a small population of south Asians, or "Asian Indians," as they were then commonly called. Brought in from the subcontinent around 1900 as cheap labor for the timber industry, they proved even less popular than the Chinese and Japanese. On September 4, 1907, white rioters in Bellingham, Washington, broke into the homes of the 250 Indian workers and dragged them to the city jail. Most left on the next train. The Bellingham Riots were just the start in a wave of similar riots all over the Pacific northwest that year, stretching up into British Columbia.

OVERWHELMING NUMBERS

Asians were not the only ones to feel the sting of American nativism and xenophobia. Immigrants came in such great numbers that they quickly overwhelmed the native-born working population. Of the thousands of men who worked on the widening and modernization of New York's historic Erie Canal between 1908 and 1918, over half were Italians. In the anthracite coal fields of Pennsylvania, up to 60 percent of the workers were "Slavs"—a mix of Poles, Ukrainians, Czechs, Slovaks, Serbs, Croats, Lithuanians, and Hungarians from eastern Europe and Czarist Russia. The garment industry in New York City—long the domain of Germans—was taken over by Jewish immigrants.

This unleashed a tremendous amount of ill will against the new immigrants, which found a voice in a number of ways. The Ku Klux Klan, which had been dormant for decades, reinvigorated itself in 1915, targeting not just blacks, but Jews and Catholics as well. The American Protective Association claimed 2.5 million members in 1896, although these figures were clearly overblown. The Asiatic Exclusion League was popular up and down the west coast. Other groups funded radical anti-Catholic and anti-immigrant newspapers like the *Menace*. Populists raged against Jewish bankers. People accused foreign-born anarchists of plotting against the country. Scholars wrote books about the dangers of race-mixing and the mental and physical inferiority of the new immigrant groups. Even the government got into the act: in 1907 Congress launched the Dillingham Commission, which eventually produced 42 volumes of data on the economic and social impact of immigration. In the end the Commission confirmed the superiority of northern Europeans over southern and eastern Europeans and recommended the prohibition of both unskilled laborers and Asians.

Finally, the 65th Congress passed the Immigration Act of 1917, overriding President Wilson's veto to become law. The sweeping bill included some of the anti-immigration lobby's fondest wishes, including a controversial clause that excluded any immigrant over age 16 "physically capable of reading," who was not literate in at least one language and prohibiting "all idiots, imbeciles, feeble-minded persons, epileptics, insane persons; persons who have had one or more attacks of insanity at any time previously; persons of constitutional psychopathic inferiority; persons with chronic alcoholism; paupers; professional beggars; vagrants; persons afflicted with tuberculosis in any form or with a loathsome or dangerous contagious disease; persons not comprehended within any of the foregoing excluded classes who are found to be and are certified by the examining surgeon as being mentally or physically defective, such physical defect being of a nature which may affect the ability of such alien to earn a living; persons who have been convicted of or admit having committed a felony or other crime or misdemeanor involving moral turpitude; polygamists, or persons who practice polygamy or believe in or advocate the practice of polygamy; anarchists, or persons who believe in or advocate the overthrow by force or violence of the Government of the United States." The law also created the Asiatic Barred Zone, a huge swath of countries stretching from the Pacific Islands to the Middle East, from which no immigrants would be permitted. The bill went into effect in May 1917 and stayed in effect until an even more restrictive law was passed in 1924.

GREAT MIGRATION

Although they would grow much larger in the decades following World War I, the period between 1900 and 1920 saw the first stirrings of two huge waves of migration from the rural south to the urban north. This movement of nearly 25 million Americans in less than a century constitutes the biggest mass population shift in U.S. history.

The best-known of these two population flows is the Great Migration of African Americans out of the deep south, which began in earnest in 1916 and continued up through the 1960s. By the time it slowed down, somewhere between three and four million African Americans had left their homes in the south for the cities of the north. In 1900 about 90 percent of African Americans lived in rural areas below the Mason-Dixon Line; by 1980 about 90 percent lived in urban areas throughout the country. African-American culture became more closely tied to urban life.

Several factors came together to push African Americans out of the south on the eve of World War I. In 1892 a tiny black bug known as the boll weevil arrived in Brownsville, Texas, and began eating its way east at a rate of 40 to 160 mi. a year. The Central American pest was perfectly adapted to the climate of the south, able to survive the mild winters and burrow into a growing cotton boll in the spring, eating contentedly until the destroyed boll fell to the ground. A single boll weevil could produce two to 12 million offspring in a year. By 1922 boll weevils had infested 600,000 sq. mi. and were routinely decimating 50–60 percent of the annual cotton yield, at a

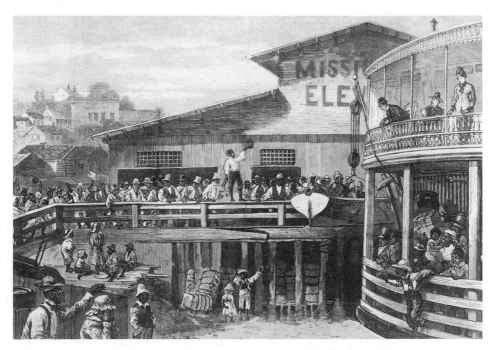

This engraving illustrates a scene from the beginning of the African-American exodus from the south, with migrants lining the wharves in Vicksburg, Mississippi, in 1879.

cost of millions of dollars a year in crop losses. Unable to come up with an effective strategy to eradicate the little bugs, many cotton producers simply gave up, switching to alternative crops such as peanuts. Over the long term, this forced diversification of crops benefited the southern economy as a whole, but in the short-term, it pushed poor African Americans and white sharecroppers to the brink of ruin.

Economic decline exacerbated racial tensions. African Americans found themselves disenfranchised by the widespread use of poll taxes, literacy tests, and grandfather clauses (allowing a black man to vote only if his grandfather had been able to, thus excluding the majority of black voters whose grandfathers had been born into slavery). The growing popularity of Jim Crow laws restricted access and movement in public spaces. Outright violence was also on the rise, with an estimated two to three lynchings a week throughout the period.

To some degree, these were the same types of conditions African Americans had lived with since Reconstruction. This time, however, there was a window of opportunity provided by World War I. Fighting in Europe stalled immigration, leading to a labor shortage in northern industrial centers just as industrial production shot up to fill orders from overseas. Finally, when America joined the fight, millions of young American workers were shipped to Europe. Economic need soon overcame racial prejudice, at least to some degree, and thousands of southern blacks headed north to seize this rare opportunity for economic advancement.

Between 1916 and 1918 about 400,000 African Americans left the south, a rate of about 16,000 per month. They would end up in many industrial cities, but most headed for the biggest urban centers. Between 1910 and 1920 the African-American population of Detroit grew by 611 percent. It grew 500 percent in Philadelphia. In Chicago it grew 148 percent, and in New York, 66 percent. Most migrants were young men looking for work, but they quickly brought their wives and children and extended families to join them. Letters home and the increasingly important black press helped convince others that a move north was a move toward a brighter future. Those who had gone on before them provided temporary shelter and help getting newcomers settled and employed.

For the majority of African Americans, the move north did not bring peace or prosperity. In many ways, they just switched one form of discrimination for another. Northern employers needed their labor, but that did not mean they liked or respected them. African-American wages were almost always lower than those of whites or immigrants. They were barred from meaningful promotions and advancements.

Nor were they particularly welcome on the home front. When African Americans moved into a neighborhood, whites and immigrants usually left, creating segregated communities in the least desirable parts of a city. These communities became horribly overcrowded, with population density in majority-black neighborhoods often twice what they were in nearby majority-white communities. African Americans also had trouble finding medical care: between the lack of black physicians and the unwillingness of many white doctors to treat black patients, they had no one to turn to when sick or injured. Given the high-risk jobs they were often forced to perform and the crowded conditions in their homes, illness and injury were common. As a result life expectancy was lower for African Americans than whites, and child mortality was significantly higher among black children than whites.

Tensions between communities soon boiled over into violence. In the so-called Red Summer of 1919, there were 26 race riots in cities across the nation. One of the most destructive took place in Chicago. Trying to escape a searing heat wave, a group of African-American children inadvertently paddled into the waters off a whites-only public beach. People began throwing stones from the shore, and one of the children drowned. This set off a chain reaction of events that led to riots across the predominantly black South Side, leaving 38 dead, 537 wounded, and more than 1,000 homeless.

Newly migrated African Americans quickly began to build community structures that helped them cope, and even enjoy, life in the city. Churches became an incredibly important part of community life. By 1926 New York

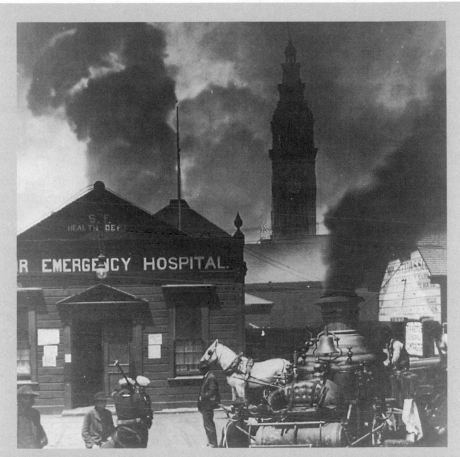

Firemen work a steam fire engine in front of the Harbor Emergency Hospital with the Union Ferry Building in the background, as San Francisco burns.

The San Francisco Earthquake of 1906

The San Francisco earthquake of 1906 hit San Francisco and the northern coastline of California on Wednesday, April 18, 1906. At almost precisely 5:12 A.M., local time, a foreshock occurred with sufficient force to be felt widely throughout the San Francisco Bay area. The great earthquake broke loose some 20 to 25 seconds later, with an epicenter near the city. Violent shocks punctuated the strong shaking, which lasted some 45 to 60 seconds. Researchers have estimated the magnitude was approximately 7.8. Many lives were lost during the earthquake, but by far the worst damage to the city came with the subsequent fires. As the city burned to the ground, authorities had to provide housing and relief for the thousands of residents who were displaced.

City's Harlem had 130 churches in 150 blocks, ranging from the established Baptist and African Methodist Episcopal (AME) denominations, to "storefront" churches for those attracted to a more charismatic congregation like Pentecostalism. African Americans developed their own newspapers, literary magazines, fraternal organizations, and social service centers. By the 1920s they had also created powerful political organizations like the National Association for the Advancement of Colored People (NAACP), founded in 1909, and the National Urban League, founded in 1911.

OUT OF THE HILLS

Less well-known but far larger in scope and size was the migration of southern whites out of the Appalachian Mountains. Over the course of 70 years, an estimated 20 million would leave the hills of Kentucky, West Virginia, Virginia, and North Carolina, headed toward the factories and fields of the midwest, driven as African Americans had been by the prospect of economic advancement.

Like African Americans, the young men were the first to go. Companies based in the Ohio Valley facing a labor shortage placed ads in newspapers across the Appalachians, calling for unskilled workers. They poured out of the hills to reach for these jobs with Goodyear, Champion Paper, Buckeye Steel, and dozens of others, jobs that were more lucrative and less dangerous than coal mining or the timber industry. Others joined the circuit of agricultural workers who moved from south to north with the harvests. As in all migrant communities, those who had established themselves provided a safety net for family and friends who wanted to join them.

While white southerners did not face racial discrimination, they did not transition seamlessly into urban life. Many found it hard to adjust to the noise and bustle of the big city after lives spent in isolated mountain towns and hollows. They faced discrimination and derision for their thick accents and "hillbilly" ways. Like other migrant groups, they tended to clump together in tight-knit communities, going to their own churches and joining in their own entertainments, rarely mixing with outsiders.

Perhaps because they were so uncomfortable with city life, there was a significant level of back-migration. Most African Americans who left the south never went back, no matter how rough life got in their new homes. White southerners were more likely to retreat to the mountains when or if they could. Some worked seasonally, going to the cities in the winters and returning home with the spring weather.

THE GREAT WAR

While increased industrial production due to World War I started spurring migration across the south as early as 1916, the United States did not actually enter the war until the spring of 1917, almost four years after the conflict began in 1914. Under the leadership of President Woodrow Wilson, the United States had followed a strong isolationist policy during those years. However the loss of at least seven merchant ships to German submarines and the intercept of the Zimmerman Telegram, which proposed a Mexican-German alliance against the United States, gave Wilson little choice but to urge Congress to declare war on April 6, 1917.

Despite its previous reticence, the United States mobilized with astonishing speed. As was common in peacetime, the Regular Army was fairly small, numbering around 125,000 officers and men. Yet over 19 months of war, the U.S. military enlisted a grand total of 4,743,991 soldiers and sent more than two million overseas. To assure a steady flow of troops, the government had turned to the military draft for the first time since the 1860s. Volunteerism alone wasn't going to fill the ranks: only around 300,000 men signed up for service in the first month after war was formally declared. President Wilson and Secretary of War Newton Baker quickly pushed the Selective Service Act of 1917 through Congress, requiring all men aged 21 to 30, later revised to between 18 and 45, to register for possible military service. Ten million men signed up on the first registration day, June 10, 1917, and some 24 million had registered by 1920.

Registration days were usually accompanied by patriotic parades and events. Schools and businesses closed for the day, and everyone turned out to

These men waited to register for the draft as required by the Selective Service Act of 1917 at a schoolhouse around 1918.

see the men go off to register, a not-so-subtle psychological pressure for those men who might be a bit unsure of their desire to fight the German "Huns." At the end of the registration process, each man was issued a light blue card signifying that they had done their patriotic duty. Then, their fate was in the hands of their local draft boards.

There were about 4,500 all-civilian draft boards established during the war, with the rule-of-thumb being at least one draft board per county, and additional boards per 30,000 population. Thus New York City had 200 boards operating during the war. The Civil War loophole of allowing the wealthy to hire a man to serve in one's place had been closed by the Selective Service Act, but draft boards had wide latitude when it came to issuing deferments from service. Financial hardship, mental or physical illness, and religious prohibitions were common reasons for deferment.

They could also reject men because of their race. While foreign nationals, Native Americans and even some Asian Americans fought alongside white troops during World War I, the 350,000 African Americans who made it past the draft boards served in segregated units, and were usually put to the most menial support tasks. While the majority of American troops fought as independent units, rather than being formally attached to foreign troops, several African-American units were sent to fight with the French. At least 170 of these soldiers were awarded the Legion of Honor for their bravery, and some African Americans found the French so much more hospitable than their own countrymen that they returned to Europe to live after the war was won.

American forces were a small part of a war effort that mobilized tens of millions of soldiers. Of the four million Americans under arms, about 2.2 million were sent to fight in France. By Armistice Day in November 1918, approximately 126,000 Americans had been killed and 234,000 had been wounded, a

A detail from a panoramic photograph of Romagne Cemetery in France in 1919, where more than 23,000 American soldiers had recently been buried.

casualty rate of about eight percent. By comparison, of the 42 million Allied troops who fought between 1914 and 1918, five million were killed and 13 million were wounded, for a casualty rate of 52 percent. At the end of the war 8.5 million men were dead, and 21 million had been wounded. America suffered fewer casualties than just about any other nation, but this did little to mitigate the pain and sorrow of thousands of American families who sent their young men off to fight, never to return.

THE INFLUENZA PANDEMIC
The war was still going on when America suffered one of the greatest blows to its population in U.S. history: the influenza pandemic of 1918. Called the Spanish Influenza at the time, many epidemiologists now believe that the 1918 flu originated in the United States, perhaps jumping from pigs to humans in the midwest in the spring of that year. In early March a young recruit at Fort Riley, Kansas, reported to the base hospital complaining of the typical flu symptoms of sore throat, fever, and aches. Within a week, at least 500 soldiers had come down with the flu, with about 50 dying. Such epidemics were common in military camps, and nobody thought much about it. Some of the soldiers were sent off to Europe after they recovered. Soon Allied troops all along the trench lines were coming down with flu. At some point between March and September the virus mutated into one of the most brutally efficient killers in world history.

By September 1918 it was back in the United States, as young soldiers began to die of a pneumonia-like illness at Fort Devens in Massachusetts. The first confirmed civilian casualties occurred in the nearby town of Quincy on September 11, when three people died of the same sudden illness. From there it picked up speed, passing from person to person as they went about their daily business in big cities and small towns all over the country.

The unusual nature of the 1918 flu cannot be overstated. Flu is most common in the winter; this one was at its worst in the spring and fall. Common flu leads to high fever, body aches, sore throat, and coughing; this one morphed into a form of pneumonia that clogged the victims' lungs with a frothy, bloody fluid. Flu usually kills the very old and the very young; this one killed the young and the healthy. In fact the death rate for men and women aged 15–34 was 20 times the norm. It moved with tremendous speed, sometimes killing within a couple of hours of the onset of a fever. A staggering one-quarter of Americans came down with the flu, and at least 2.5 percent of those afflicted died from the virus—far above the average flu mortality rate of 0.5 percent.

Public health officials at first downplayed the epidemic, then found they could do little to stop it. Doctors could only stand by and watch as patient after patient succumbed to the illness. Once a victim's lips had turned blue, one doctor said, "It was simply a struggle for air until they suffocate." The *American Journal of Public Health* warned health officials in areas not yet struck by

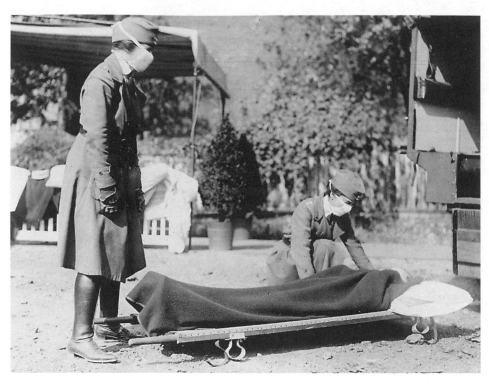

Two Red Cross workers demonstrate procedures for caring for a flu victim at the Red Cross Emergency Ambulance Station in Washington, D.C., during the influenza pandemic of 1918.

flu: "Hunt up your woodworkers and cabinet-makers and set them to making coffins. Then take your street laborers and send them to work digging graves. If you do this, you will not have your dead accumulating faster than you can dispose of them."

Philadelphia was one of the hardest-hit cities. On September 28 the city went ahead and held a planned war-bond drive, drawing a crowd of about 200,000. Thousands fell ill in the following days, and by the end of October, more than 11,000 Philadelphians were dead. Bodies piled up so fast that the city was forced to dig mass graves to hold them all.

October 1918 was the deadliest month. Nationwide there were 195,000 deaths attributed to the flu. On a single day in New York City, 851 people died. Society quickly went into retreat. Schools were closed. Some cities banned all public gatherings, including funerals. In Chicago crime dropped by 40 percent. People were afraid to go outdoors, and those who did were required to don white face masks that did almost nothing to protect them from the microscopic flu virus. Hospitals filled to overflowing, but with a large number of doctors and nurses serving with the armies overseas, there was not nearly enough medical staff. Many people fell back on folk remedies and brewed up home remedies. Wild stories began to circulate about the Germans having released the deadly flu as part of a last-ditch war effort.

Perhaps one of the strangest sights in American history was the Armistice Day celebration in San Francisco in November 1918, when 30,000 people took to the streets to sing and dance and celebrate the victory—with every single person wearing a white mask over their nose and mouth. Despite the precaution, by the end of November more than 5,000 had fallen ill.

By December the pandemic had peaked, although it would continue in some places until early 1920. In the final count 675,000 Americans had died of the flu—more fatalities than in all American wars combined. Thousands of children had been orphaned. Some insurance companies, forced to pay out claims for people who had been in the prime of life, went bankrupt. Life expectancy in the United States dropped by 12 years in 1918, and stayed depressed for the next decade. But the 1918 influenza was far more than an American tragedy; it was a global catastrophe. It struck virtually every community on the planet, with the exception of a few isolated islands. Estimates of the number of dead range from 50 to 100 million people in just two years, making it the deadliest epidemic in world history.

CONCLUSION

With the explosive growth of the U.S. population in the Progressive Era, migration trends became enormous events in the life of the nation. An increasingly concentrated urban population became even more vulnerable to natural disasters, as shown by the massive effects of the hurricane in Galveston, Texas, and the earthquake in San Francisco. The movement of African Americans out of the south, and poor whites out of the Appalachian Mountains, were long-term shifts that changed the populations of northern cities and the midwest. The Great Migration also set the stage for urban racial conflicts that would plague the country for generations. But immigration had the most immediate effect on the American psyche during the era, raising questions of how the nation would be defined, and whether any one group would belong more than another.

HEATHER K. MICHON

Further Readings

Grossman, James R. *Land of Hope: Chicago, Black Southerners, and the Great Migration*. Chicago, IL: University of Chicago Press, 1989.
Harkins, Anthony. *Hillbilly: A Cultural History of an American Icon*. New York: Oxford University Press, 2004.

Harrison, Alferdteen. *Black Exodus: The Great Migration from the American South*. Jackson, MS: University Press of Mississippi, 1991.

Irving, Katrina. *Immigrant Mothers: Narratives of Race and Maternity, 1890–1925*. Urbana, IL: University of Illinois Press, 2000.

Keegan, John. *The First World War*. New York: Vintage Books, 2000.

Kennedy, David M. *Over Here: The First World War and American Society*. New York: Oxford University Press, 1982.

Kolata, Gina Bari. *Flu: The Story of the Great Influenza Pandemic of 1918*. New York: Simon & Schuster, 2001.

Larson, Erik. *Isaac's Storm: A Man, a Time, and the Deadliest Hurricane in History*. New York: Vintage, 2000.

Lemann, Nicholas. *The Promised Land: The Great Black Migration and How It Changed America*. New York: Vintage Books, 1992.

Mead, Gary. *The Doughboys: America and the First World War*. New York: Overlook Press, 2002.

Obermiller, Phillip J., Thomas E. Wagner, and Edward Bruce Tucker. *Appalachian Odyssey: Historical Perspectives on the Great Migration*. Westport, CT: Greenwood Publishing Group, 2000.

Pacyga, Dominic A. *Polish Immigrants and Industrial Chicago: Workers on the South Side, 1880–1922*. Chicago, IL: University of Chicago Press, 2003.

Shenk, Gerald Shenk. *Work or Fight!: Race, Gender, and the Draft in World War One*. Hampshire, UK: Palgrave Macmillan, 2005.

Sterba, Christopher M. *Good Americans: Italian and Jewish Immigrants during the First World War*. New York: Oxford University Press, 2003.

Tuttle, William M. *Race Riot: Chicago in the Red Summer of 1919*. Urbana, IL: University of Illinois Press, 1996.

Weiner, Deborah R. *Coalfield Jews: An Appalachian History*. Urbana, IL: University of Illinois Press, 2006.

Chapter 15

Transportation

"Down the road of life we'll fly,
Automobubbling you and I."
— Vincent Bryan

THE PROGRESSIVE ERA lasted from approximately 1890 to 1920, although some historians date it to 1924, coinciding with the last gasp of the Progressive Party as a political movement. Others date it to 1917 and 1919 when a combination of events such as the advent of World War I followed by war weariness aggravated by the great Spanish Flu epidemic of 1918–19 exhausted crusading zeal. The Progressive Era began as a response to a number of factors. The so-called Panic of 1893 was actually a four-year depression in which millions of people suffered. The excesses associated with the Gilded Age resulted in a series of scandals that ushered in reforms. The desire for good government free from the influence of moneyed interest groups resulted in political reforms at all levels, such as the initiative, referendum, and recall at the state level, and city councils and city manager forms of government less vulnerable to patronage. Social ills, often attributed to alcoholism and loose morals, led to temperance and moral purity movements. Conservationism and consumer movements came to the fore. Utilities faced new types of price controls. Women's rights and children's rights were championed, as were the interests of workers. Social work appeared, as did prison reform, and treatment of the mentally ill.

There was an undercurrent to this period. Mostly supported by middle-class and upper class whites, the progressive movement was not particularly friendly to the rights of minorities. In response to the increasing prevalence of Jim Crow segregationist laws, African Americans formed the Urban League and the NAACP. Increasingly, there were movements for restrictions on immigrants (considered the purveyors of "un-American" ideals) starting with the Root-Takahira agreement, which limited Japanese immigration in 1906 and 1907. Native Americans and Latin Americans also faced discrimination—the former confined to reservations, and the latter often residing in ghettos or barrios in western cities. The heyday of the settlement house, which helped "Americanize" immigrants from overseas and migrants from the south, appeared to be a logical response in a nation that was majority urban by 1920.

The great perceived enemies of consumers, small farmers, small businessmen, and the average citizen were the corporations and the big city. Corpora-

A Lament on the Automobile

As the production of the automobile grew in the 20th century, most Americans enthusiastically embraced the new machine and the ever-increasing speeds it could attain. Frederick Dwight published an article in the *Independent* newspaper, "Automobiles: The Other Side of the Shield," lamenting the recklessness of car owners. Excerpts include:

Every new and popular device exercises more or less tyranny.... To begin with, although they [automobiles] are performing work in fields of usefulness, they have not as yet proved their necessity. That is, commercially, they are still in the experimental stage—too costly and unreliable to supplant horse-drawn vehicles widely. They are regarded doubtfully by emergency services, such as the fire and ambulance; and as an adjunct to armies have yet to demonstrate their value. The point I wish to make is obvious enough—that at the present time their conspicuous success has been achieved almost wholly as pleasure vehicles, so that their mention suggests to the average person only a new way of enjoying oneself....

I think the time when motor vehicles are desirable assets to society at large is yet to come, and that at present a certain excess must be charged to them in the debit column. They have engendered a reckless personal extravagance that must bring remorse and suffering to many some day. They have produced a new contempt for authority and an unusually lawless and irresponsible class. Finally, with little or no compensating advantage to the communities through which they hurry, they have caused the taxpayers heavy expense for roads, have almost driven the more leisurely from them, and have then proceeded to destroy the highways themselves. All of these things are doubtless curable and will be remedied in time. At present, however, they exist.

tions appeared or were portrayed to threaten the national self-image of *lais-sez-faire*, the just price, and fair competition through their combinations in monopolies and trusts. Similarly the big cities with their political patronage and political machines, which often gained support from vulnerable new immigrants and migrants with more collectivist ideals, were pictured as direct challenges to American individualism. Railroads appeared to be the enemies in both cases. As early as 1887, the Interstate Commerce Act had attempted to set up a commission to regulate interstate traffic mostly by railroads. The Credit Mobilier scandal of 1873, which involved kickbacks to politicians for a non-existent construction company for the Union Pacific, the Pullman Strike, and the protests of small farmers and small shippers, which had helped to form the agricultural protest organization the Grange in the midwest, had all revolved around railroads. In the big cities, the railroads that had come to dominate urban transit were accused of extracting exorbitant fees from passengers, and bribing city governments.

THE MUCKRAKERS

These abuses, especially those of railways, were highlighted by a group of novelists and journalists called "muckrakers"; writers who, in the words of Theodore Roosevelt, stirred up the muck underneath. In the case of railroads, the author Upton Sinclair included an exposé of railroads in his famous work, *The Jungle*, which exposed meatpacking practices and the treatment of immigrants. *The Jungle* helped to bring into existence the Pure Food and Drug and Meat Inspection Acts of 1905 and 1906.

Other works reinforced popular attitudes toward railroads as exemplified by President Theodore Roosevelt's philosophy of the Square Deal. It held that trusts and monopolies were not inherently evil if they were efficient and helped in the common good through the best prices. Therefore only when they indulged in price fixing and other unfair practices not in the public interest were they criminal and worthy of dissolution. Government had the power to regulate or even dissolve these trusts. With this rationale, a total of 44 combinations were dissolved in the next few years when there was an unreasonable restraint of trade. Railroads were particular targets as, by 1900, seven combinations—the Vanderbilt Group, the Pennsylvania Lines, the Morgan Group, the Gould interests, the Rock Island railroad, the Hill interests, and the Harriman interests—dominated many of the nation's railroads. Edward Harriman's attempt to dominate transportation west of Chicago by combining his railway interests (primarily the Union Pacific) with the Hill interests (primarily the Great Northern) through a holding company in which the great financier J.P. Morgan and the oil magnate John D. Rockefeller held prominent interests galvanized anti-trust action. Roosevelt asked his attorney general to bring suit against the trust in 1903. It was dissolved in 1904 through an application of the Sherman Anti-Trust Act of 1890.

Thereafter a whole series of legislative acts were aimed at reducing the power of railways over customers and clients. The Elkins Act of 1903 ended the practices of rebates to large shippers and free passes to VIPs; the Hepburn Act of 1906 strengthened the power of the Interstate Commerce Commission to set and enforce fair and reasonable rates; and the Mann-Elkins Act of 1910 eliminated rate discrimination against short haulers in favor of long haulers and strengthened the authority of the federal government over railroads. Other pieces of legislation strengthened the hand of railroad workers. States began to regulate child labor so that children under 14 (and later under 16) were forbidden from full-time work. At the same time attendance at school began to become mandatory. In 1908 the Supreme Court in *Muller v. Ogden* limited the labor of women to 10 hours per day. In 1916 workers could get workmen's compensation at least at the federal level. Finally in 1916 the Adamson Act gave railway workers an eight-hour day. This was a significant development, as by this time railway workers totaled over two million workers, over five percent of the national labor force.

In this period the location of cities, as well as of the general population and industries, was determined by man-made transportation as much as by natural phenomena. Usually cities with concomitant concentrations of people and varieties of employment were port cities with suitable anchorages or located strategically on lakes and rivers. Man-made forms of transportation such as railroads were built to connect these naturally formed cities. Cities located along the rail during this period began to take precedence even over natural location and topography during this time.

RAILROADS IN THE PROGRESSIVE ERA

Although the domination of railroads began to be challenged by vehicles that ran on oil and gas—cars for passenger traffic, trucks for freight delivery, and buses for interurban transit—as opposed to coal and water-powered steam and electric power, they still played prominent roles in transportation during this era. Investment in railroads peaked at $18 billion by 1917. Operating profit exceeded $4 billion by that year. Railway mileage also peaked at 254,000 mi. that year with World War I military mobilization.

Gilded Age luxury also continued during this period as Pullman Palace cars became prominent, especially along transcontinental routes. Sofas were placed in cars and widened into sleepers at night that would be enclosed by curtains for pri-

Railroad workers used lanterns like this for conducting and signaling.

A vast waiting room in Union Station in Washington, D.C., which was built in 1903 and was the largest train station in the world when it opened.

vacy. Dining cars also became common—at least for those willing to pay. In the more luxurious lines there were gourmet chefs and highly-trained waiters. In first-class Pullmans, compartments would be made available with attached porter service to bring newspapers and drinks, and even provide mail services.

This was the great age of the ornate train station. Architects built terminals in the classical style, especially in Washington, D.C., Philadelphia, Boston, Detroit, St. Louis, and New York City. The interiors of many of these stations soon had restaurants, shops, theatres, and hotels on different levels or concourses. The most impressive were Union Station in Washington, D.C., which was the largest station in the world and covered more ground than any building when it first opened, and Grand Central Station, built between 1913 and 1915. Grand Central was basically two stations—on the ground level adjacent to the tracks, waiting rooms served passengers who were traveling long distances, while an underground level with attached tracks, trains, and waiting rooms served passengers to and from suburbs. All told this split-level terminal could serve more than 30,000 people at one time quite comfortably.

The Pullman Railway Strike of 1894

One of the events that marked the end of the Gilded Age and the beginning of the Progressive Era was the Pullman Strike of 1894. It vividly illustrates the perception of a growing gap between "haves" and "have-nots" in the background of the economic depression of 1893.

George Montgomery Pullman, the founder of the Pullman Palace Car, had created a company town called Pullman City to house his employees. They had few rights. In 1893 at the start of the economic downtown, Pullman had arbitrarily reduced the wages of his employees by 20 percent without decreasing their rents. Moreover, if an employee in Pullman City fell behind in his rent or bills in a company store, the money was automatically deducted from his (now reduced) salary. As a result, 3,000 workers went on strike.

They were supported by the American Railroad Union (ARU) headed by Eugene V. Debs, the future socialist candidate for president. The strike soon deteriorated when the ARU and its members refused to allow trains with Pullman cars to move, except those carrying U.S. mail via railway cars. The General Managers Association then announced that any employee who refused to move a car would be fired. When 50,000 more employees quit in response, trains west of Chicago came to a standstill.

The railroads then appealed to the federal government to break the strike. President Grover Cleveland would only send in troops if the strike grew and violence occurred. The Managers Association then had newspapers portray the ARU as violent radicals and sent in non-union workers to work on the railroads. They secured the support of a local judge who supported employer rights. After a violent incident inside a railway yard, he issued an injunction and requested that President Cleveland send in troops. He adopted the position that the strike and its union supporters were acting in restraint of trade and therefore violated the Fourteenth Amendment.

President Cleveland sent troops in and bloodshed ensued. Debs and his associates were arrested, and he served six months. His union was destroyed, and the strike was crushed. Henceforth, employers would attack unions and get judges to issue injunctions claiming unions were illegal combinations that violated the equal protection of persons. As a result workers' rights and unions did not really recover for nearly a decade, until President Theodore Roosevelt recognized the right of the United Mineworkers Union to strike in 1901.

This 1913 Old Cabbage Head locomotive is named for its unusually shaped smokestack, which trapped embers from its wood-burning boiler.

URBAN TRANSPORTATION

During the Progressive Era trolleys, streetcars, and cable cars were gradually supplanted by interurbans and subways. Although the former ultimately gave way to the automobile and the developing highway system and the latter, although still operating as metro transit in some cities such as San Francisco (BART), Atlanta (MARTA), and New York, is a basically limited metropolitan phenomenon, they proved important in a period where suburbs and cities were becoming one socioeconomic unit. At this time conurbations were growing, such as those of Dallas–Fort Worth and San Francisco-Oakland. Interurbans were basically longer, larger, and more substantive than the trolleys and more comfortable than street cars. They were powered by electricity, but had 50 to 160 horsepower as opposed to trolleys and street cars, which had 40 to 50 horsepower in electric motors. They were like trains but were run by electricity rather than steam.

Introduced in 1891 between Minneapolis and St. Paul, interurbans were running into the countryside as well as between cities by 1900. In Ohio, for example, there was not one community over 10,000 that did not have interurban service. In greater Los Angeles, one system, the Pacific Electric, served 42 towns and cities. At their height between 1910 and 1920, all but 187 mi. between New York and Chicago were covered by interurban lines. Canada also made use of the interurban system, and trains routinely traveled between

Toronto and Buffalo. As was the case with the Pullman Palace cars, some of the units became quite luxurious. The neighboring Illinois Traction System between St. Louis, Missouri, and Peoria, Illinois, had cars with attached bedrooms with running water and toilets—not always so common in many residences at that time. As in the case of trains, there were dining cars with haute cuisine. Interurban operators emulated their trolley operator predecessors by offering trips to amusement parks. As was the case with trolleys, the interurban phenomenon facilitated the growth of suburbs.

More long-lasting than the interurban were subways. After an abortive attempt in 1870 in New York City, the first successful subway opened in Boston. In 1897 above-ground urban transportation had become so congested that city planners and engineers began to investigate underground transportation. By this period new types of building materials had been perfected so that watertight tunnels made of concrete and steel could be constructed underground. With improvements in air ventilation, the system soon spread, as different suburbs were connected as well as the central city. By 1900 subways had spread to Cleveland, Newark, and Philadelphia, and later to Chicago. Subways soon emulated their train counterparts with elaborate terminals with basic amenities and commercial facilities.

WATER TRANSPORTATION

Although canals were in decline, they still remained important as bulk carriers, especially as coal remained an important fuel. As late as 1918 the Erie Canal was expanded through a series of dams and locks to connect to internal lakes such as Lake Oswego and Lake Champlain. Others such as the Lehigh, Susquehanna, Chesapeake, and Delaware canals also continued to do bulk business. Internally the Bureau of Engineers began to construct dams and in some cases narrow the channels of rivers to improve traffic, especially on the Mississippi. This sometimes had disastrous effects when it came to flooding later in the century.

The increasing use of steam added to the continued dominance of schooners in coastal trade. Carrying coal, fish, lumber, tobacco, and building materials, these sail vessels dominated coastal trade until World War I. Ports along the eastern seaboard grew so crowded that a person could go from shipboard to shipboard for miles. In the pre-war period, some of these schooners even traveled all the way from Chile to Alaska on the west coast, the Caribbean to Maine on the Atlantic coast, and Brownsville, Texas, to Pensacola, Florida, on the Gulf coast. Great Lakes schooners were also active carrying Minnesota iron and Illinois farm products to factories and mills in both the midwest and northeast.

During this period, steam-driven transoceanic ships, especially transatlantic vessels, became the ocean liners that we know today. Until American ownership became prominent after World War I, foreign ownership,

DATE	TRAIN	FROM	TRACK	DUE TO ARRIVE	EXPECTED	TRAIN	FOR	TRACK	DUE TO LEAVE	REMARK
	7	NEW YORK		2:45 P.M.		8	NEW YORK		2:45 P.M.	
	25	VENICE		11:15 A.M.		26	VENICE		1:35 P.M.	
	75	NEW YORK		6:00 A.M		76	NEW YORK		10:30 P.M.	
	91	NEW YORK		3:40 P.M.		92	NEW YORK		11:00 A.M.	
	92	SARASOTA		10:30 A.M.		91	SARASOTA		4:05 P.M.	
	157	NEW YORK		1:20 P.M.		158	NEW YORK		11:35 A.M.	
	158	ST.PETERSBURG		11:25 A.M.		157	ST.PETERSBURG		1:30 P.M.	

A board showing railroad arrivals and departures such as those travelers across the country consulted before the age of interstate highways and air travel.

especially British and German, was most common. In addition to serving the millions of immigrants who came over mostly across the Atlantic, these ocean liners gradually came to play a new role by the 1920s. These ships came to be called liners because they sailed along certain lines. The Red Star ships went from Antwerp to U.S. ports, while the Cunard ships went from London to U.S. ports. By 1920 the Morgan and Mallory lines sailed between the east coast and Gulf coast, mostly carrying people who wished to winter in Florida.

These liners came to be seen as floating resorts, especially for first-class passengers, with dancing, music, gambling, and general entertainment, as well as lavish dinners, concerts, and balls. Other amenities might have included a library, clinic, beauty parlor, kennel for pets, post office, various shops, and night clubs. Adults could park their children at playrooms and theaters with adult supervision. Second-class and even third-class tourist cabins had some of the same amenities, if somewhat less commodious accommodations. Internal waterways such as the Great Lakes were also visited by luxury liners, which took passengers to resort areas such as Mackinac Island. Other ships carried cargo as well as passengers, such as the Grace Line between the United States and Latin America. Freighters continued to cross the Atlantic and Pacific oceans until they were replaced by modern cargo and super cargo ships. By 1920 oil tankers were also a common occurrence along the Gulf, Atlantic, and Pacific coasts, as well as on rivers as oil and gas began to replace coal as an energy source.

ROAD TRANSPORTATION

The seminal occurrence that turned Americans into a country of individual owners of transportation means and revolutionized American roads was the advent of automotive vehicles—the car, truck, and bus. These vehicles began to replace the railroad in carrying passengers, freight, and urban travelers, respectively. Two technological breakthroughs presaged this event—the development of pneumatic rubber tires, and the perfection of the internal combustion engine, which efficiently and cheaply converted oil and gas into sources of energy. Bicycle owners made use of the pneumatic tire by the early 1890s. When the French tire firm Michelin utilized the principle of the vulcanization of rubber discovered by Charles Goodyear to outfit cars, driving became safer. In the 1890s there was a debate as to whether steam or electric or gas driven vehicles were the future. However beginning with the Duryea brothers in 1893, the internal combustion gas engine began to dominate, supported by oil refiners.

At first considered a plaything of the wealthy, the automobile and its sister gas-powered vehicles gradually gained acceptance as innovations in production became common. As early as 1892 pioneer automaker Ransom Olds, founder of the Oldsmobile company, experimented with assembly-line techniques with workers in different pits working on different parts of the car until the total car was assembled. However it was Henry Ford with his Model T who pioneered the concept of the assembly line as the cornerstone of mass production. This process divided car production into various sectors, with each sector having an assembly line for a specific part in total car production. With this technique, automotive vehicles became much more affordable, as a car could be assembled in 93 minutes, thereby reducing labor costs.

A woman in a fur coat takes the wheel of an unenclosed Pierce Arrow automobile in winter 1906.

Within a few years the cost of cars beginning with the Model T had dropped to $350, and ultimately $240 by the mid-1920s. At the same time the invention of the electric starter made it possible to start a car without heavy cranking. Cars became both physically and

This 1902 curved dash Oldsmobile model made by Ransom Olds's company is preserved at the Antique Automobile Collector's Association Museum in Hershey, Pennsylvania.

fiscally accessible to the population, so that by the late 1920s one in five people had a car. The car had become a universal symbol of American society by 1920 as it embodied both mobility and freedom. The low price of gas and oil only served to increase its accessibility. Located in the midwest, especially Detroit and Flint, Michigan, the industry had access to the necessary ingredients of car-making—iron and steel, glass, chrome, rubber, machine tools, and petroleum.

Car consciousness soon permeated popular culture with such disparate institutions as Tin Pan Alley, children's books, and silent movies all featuring automobile themes. Clothing also changed in response to the motor phenomenon, as women wore shorter skirts and scarves to keep from being wind-blown, while men favored loose-fitting trousers for the same reasons. Both sexes began to wear long coats for protection from dust and dirt.

As the popularity of automobiles grew by leaps and bounds, so did bureaucracy. License plates, driver's licenses, and vehicle registration had become mandatory by 1918. The American Automobile Association (AAA), was formed in 1902 and by 1910 had over 25,000 members. It soon proved to be a powerful pressure group for the improvement of roads, including highways. As early as 1904, as a result of pressure from the AAA as well as from other auto enthusiasts plus the nascent carmakers, the U.S. Office of Public Roads was established. Its purpose was to distribute money to states for the paving of existing roads and the construction of new roads. It was

The Wright Brothers

Wilbur and Orville Wright were bicycle shop owners from Dayton who built their own wind tower in order to observe and measure empirically how to lift a flying machine into the sky. Their experiments, which they conducted from the mid-1880s, helped them to discover that a narrow and long wing shape was the ideal structure for flight. Further experiments helped them to move their vehicle across the land as well as up and down on a current of air. In addition the Wright brothers fashioned a pair of rudders to control sideways movements. Finally, they conducted wind tunnel experiments so as to perfect their flying instruments. These instruments included eight-ft. propellers that could turn in opposite directions. They developed their own machine when they could not locate a lightweight gas-powered engine. Initially, they created a 12-horsepower plane weighing 152 lbs.

The end result of this nearly two-decade research and experimentation effort was a gas-powered 1903 flyer, which was a rather skeletal structure the brothers constructed out of spruce, ash, and other woods. Ultimately, their machine had a wingspan of 40 ft. and weighed 600 lbs.

On December 17, 1903, Orville was at the controls when the brothers tested their plane at Kitty Hawk, North Carolina. The flight traveled 120 ft. and lasted 12 seconds. This brief flight changed the future of transportation and suggested what might be possible. This monumental achievement received little attention. The next day only four newspapers carried news of the flight, and some readers were under the impression that the flight was exaggerated and even semi-fictional.

The 1903 Wright Flyer, now on display at the Smithsonian Air and Space Museum, was made of spruce and ash covered with muslin fabric.

A man pumps gas into a 1917 Franklin from a suspended hose at an early gas station. Oil refiners had a hand in supporting the development and eventual dominance of the gas-powered automobile.

followed by the Federal Aid Road Act of 1916 that increased funding to states for the building of new roads and the resurfacing of existing roads. At the very end of this period in early 1921, a national highway system created a unified system with even number routes going east and west, and odd number routes going north and south.

Other motor vehicles rose to prominence in American life. Trucks had appeared as early as the 1890s. Like automobiles, early trucks often ran on steam or electricity and were called "power wagons." Gradually converting to gasoline in the early 1900s, they proved more efficient than horse-drawn carts, especially when applied to municipal services. Their breakthrough came in World War I when they proved invaluable to war mobilization efforts. By 1918 there were 600,000 trucks and 50,000 more were built for the war effort. By this date, the truck was recognized as the main purveyor of produce for long distances, as gas was cheap. The advent of the highway system soon after gave an impetus to the trucks to challenge railroads as bulk and freight carriers, just as cars were challenging railroads in the passenger area. At the other end of the spectrum, bus companies emerged to handle travel in cities and to and from cities and the suburbs. These vehicles could be considered trolleys and streetcars that ran on gas rather than steam and electricity, and served people who could not afford cars. By the end of the period, buses were used for travel and touring as families searched for relatively cheap vacations.

Overall these vehicles provided Americans with more leisure and access to spatial mobility denied to earlier generations. As such they were a symbol of increasing democratization in American culture and society.

NEW FORMS OF TRANSPORTATION

Even though motor vehicles were central to this era in terms of impact upon life in America and went on to become central to the economy after 1920, there were other developments in transportation and transit that were to have a profound impact on American life. The Wright brothers in December 1903 performed the first sustained air flight. Although ultimately airplanes were to dominate long-distance passenger flight, for over two decades their purpose was to deliver mail under federal contract. At this time they did not have engine technology capable of making sustained passenger flight profitable. They also could not fly high enough to negotiate mountains, making railroads the preferred means of long-distance transportation. The short journeys of commercial air carriers before 1925 were cold, noisy, and uncomfortable. Nevertheless planes used in World War I captured the public imagination so that after the war, barnstorming pilots (so called because they flew through barns) engaged in exhibition flights at public events such as county fairs.

The other form of transit that made an appearance in this period and became more important in the future was the oil pipeline. Pipelines were built linking newly opened oil and gas facilities in Louisiana, Texas, and California, and grew in number as oil and gas gradually replaced coal as the fuel of choice in the rapidly growing automobile and later airplane industries.

NORMAN C. ROTHMAN

Further Readings

Bell, G. *The Economics and Planning of Transportation*. New York: David & Charles, 1984.

Bourne, Russell. *Americans on the Move*. Golden, CO: Fulcrum, 1995.

Bowersox, D.J. *Introduction to Transportation*. New York: Macmillan, 1961.

Combs, Barry. *Westward to Promontory: Building the Union Pacific Across the Plains and Mountains*. New York: Crown, 1986.

Daniels, Rudolph. *Trains across the Continent*. Bloomington, IN: Indiana University Press, 2000.

Fischler, Stanley. *Moving Millions: An Inside Look at Mass Transit*. New York: Harper & Row, 1985.

Fitzsimmons, Bernard. *150 Years of North American Railroads*. Secaucus, NJ: Chartwell, 1982.

Husband, Joseph. *The Story of the Pullman Car*. Grand Rapids, MI: Black Letter, 1974.

Middleton, William D. *Time of the Trolley: The Street Railway from Horsecar to Light Rail*. San Marino, CA: Golden West Books, 1987.

North, Paul. *American Steam Locomotives*. New York: Bookman, 1988.

Porter, Jane. *American Railroad Stations*. New York: Preservation Press, 1996.

Sandler, Martin W. *On the Waters of the USA: Ships and Boats in American Life*. New York: Oxford University Press, 2003.

———. *Riding the Rails in the USA: Trains in American Life*. New York: Oxford University Press, 2003.

———. *Straphanging in the USA: Trolleys and Subways in American Life*. New York: Oxford University Press, 2003.

———. *Driving around the USA: Automobiles in American Life*. New York: Oxford University Press, 2003.

Whitman, Sylvia. *Get Up and Go: The History of American Road Travel*. Minneapolis, MN: Lerner Publishing, 1996.

Chapter 16

Public Health, Medicine, and Nutrition

"Important are the achievements in research that reveal ...
facts about diseases and provide the remedies."
— John D. Rockefeller

THE EARLY YEARS of the Progressive Era in the United States were characterized by limited knowledge of health, medicine, and nutrition. The turn of the
century ushered in a period of rapidly developing knowledge and technologies in these fields. Through inoculating Americans against known diseases
and preventing others through proper nutrition and sanitation, the population of the United States grew rapidly, expanding from 99 million in 1914 to
106.5 million in 1920. Life expectancy rose to 54.09 years. At the turn of the
20th century, the most common causes of death were influenza and pneumonia (11.8 percent), tuberculosis (11.3 percent), gastritis (8.3 percent), heart
disease (8.0 percent), vascular lesions (6.2 percent), chronic nephritis (4.7
percent), accidental injury (4.7 percent), cancers (3.7 percent), early infant
diseases (3.6 percent), and diphtheria (2.3 percent). The crude death rate of
Americans in 1900 was 17.2 per 1,000 persons.

The standard of living rose for many Americans in the Progressive Era.
Salaried employees received paid vacations, holidays, and sick leave. In January 1914 Henry Ford began a revolution in the workplace by announcing
that he would increase wages from $2.30 a day to an unprecedented $5.00
a day. On August 4 Britain declared war on Germany. Despite President

A doctor's drug folder and vials of medicine from the Progressive Era, now on display at the Robb House Medical Museum in Gainesville, Florida.

Woodrow Wilson's (1856–1924) determination to keep the United States out of the war in Europe, American manufacturers were called on to supply war materials to the warring nations. In October Congress elaborated on the Sixteenth Amendment that had been ratified the previous year by granting the federal government the authority to tax all annual incomes over $3,000. In summer 1916 Congress provided for relief for needy farmers by passing a federal loan program. In the fall Wilson signed a bill providing for eight-hour workdays on all interstate railroads. In 1917 the president backed away from neutrality and asked Congress to declare war. The American economy was transformed by the war, and taxes were further increased to fund the war effort.

DISEASE

Before the advent of the Progressive Age, reformers such as nursing pioneer Florence Nightingale (1820–1919) advanced the notion that noxious smells, rather than bacteria, produced outbreaks of infectious diseases. Progressive Era Americans benefited from the discovery that many diseases were caused by bacteria. As a result of vaccination drives, some diseases were eradicated in the early 20th century. Responding to advanced medical knowledge, governments at all levels entered the field of public health. New medical knowledge of nutrition led to healthier lifestyles and improved life expectancy. The result was that most deaths in America during the Progressive Era were a result of degenerative diseases and accidents. By 1915 the crude death rate had dropped to 13.2 per 1,000 persons.

Infants of the Progressive Era continued to be susceptible to certain diseases, and were more likely than adults to succumb to bacteria in contaminated milk and water. Although infant mortality had continued to decline, it was relatively high, at 16.2 deaths per 1,000 live births. In Massachusetts, for instance, it was estimated that 19 percent of all infants died before their first birthdays. Children of all ages frequently contracted common, potentially fatal diseases such as measles, scarlet fever, diphtheria, and whooping cough. Maternal mortality was also high. In 1917 the United States ranked 14th among the 16 most industrialized nations in maternal mortality. In 1921 Congress passed the Sheppard-Towner Maternity and Infancy Protection Act, appropriating grants for the establishment of child and maternal education and health.

Polio became a major issue in the United States for the first time during the Progressive Era. In 1894, 132 cases of polio were documented in Vermont. Other outbreaks followed. In 1907, 2,000 cases were reported in New York, 1,000 in Minnesota, and 800 in Massachusetts. A major epidemic in 1916 involved 27,000 cases in 26 states. More than 6,000 deaths resulted. Researchers learned that most poor children had developed immunity to polio because they had been exposed to a mild form in infancy. Polio epidemics continued until the discovery of a vaccine in the mid-20th century.

In 1906 a pellagra epidemic occurred at the Alabama Institute for Negroes, a mental hospital for African Americans. Of 88 people who contracted the disease, which is caused by Vitamin B-3 (niacin) and protein deficiency, 57 died. As a result of public outcry, physicians became more aware of the disease, and thousands of cases were subsequently identified, with most of them occurring in the south. A study of Macon County, Alabama, an area with an 82 percent black population, revealed that many families were living in shacks with dirt floors, no screens, outdoor privies, and uncovered wells. The typical diet consisted

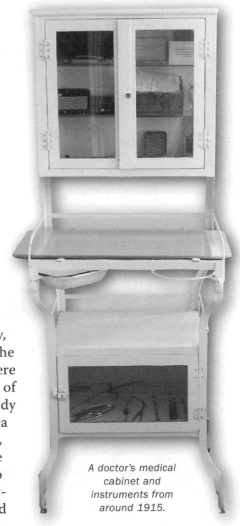

A doctor's medical cabinet and instruments from around 1915.

of salt pork, hominy grits, corn bread, and molasses. As a result, deficiency diseases such as pellagra were rampant. Over a third of the population was suffering from syphilis, which in many cases was congenital.

By 1899 American researchers began to suspect that typhoid fever could be spread by apparently healthy carriers. Within three years, these suspicions had been verified by Robert Koch (1843–1910) of Germany. Efforts to produce an adequate vaccine accelerated after the Spanish American War (1898) in which typhoid was responsible for more casualties than Spanish bullets. By 1913 when World War I broke out in Europe, a vaccination against typhoid was widely available. Within two decades antibiotics that could cure typhoid were marketed.

Wilbur Olin Atwater (1844–1907)

Earning the title of the Father of Nutrition, agricultural chemist Wilbur Olin Atwater responded to the reform movement of the Progressive Era by exhorting Americans to institute radical reforms in their diets. Expanding on the recently established science of nutrition, Atwater introduced the concept of the calorie as a means of determining how much energy was required to burn consumption of particular foods. Atwater's system was founded on the work of other scientists such as French chemist Antoine Laurent Lavoisier (1743–94), who had first identified calories, and Justus von Liebig (1803–73) of Germany, who had developed a means of breaking down foods into proteins, fats, carbohydrates, and minerals. In order to advance his own knowledge of nutrition, Atwater traveled to Europe where he extensively studied experimental food laboratories.

In addition to his duties as a professor at his alma mater, Wesleyan University, Atwater became the Director of the Connecticut Agricultural Experiment Station, the first of its kind in the United States. Atwater convinced Congress that it was a governmental responsibility to fund nutritional studies; and by May 1894 Congress had appropriated $10,000 for such studies. The success of these endeavors led Congress to appropriate $15,000 annually to each state to conduct additional nutritional studies. Today federal funding of nutritional studies and programs has grown to more than $200 million annually. Over the course of his career, Atwater became a special agent for the U.S. Department of Agriculture and oversaw more than 300 separate nutritional studies. His personal research centered on identifying the chemical composition of foods, determining the effects of cooking and processing on the nutritional value of food, and pinpointing the amount of caloric intake needed to balance calories burned each day. Atwater was particularly concerned with improving the lot of poor Americans through the science of nutrition.

Although Americans never experienced the affects of plague to the extent that occurred in Europe, incidences of plague periodically surfaced. At the turn of the 20th century, for instance, an epidemic occurred in San Francisco, California. Authorities responded by quarantining more than 20,000 Asian immigrants in Chinatown, even though no deaths had occurred. Strict trade and travel restrictions were subsequently imposed. The anti-plague vaccine developed by Russian Waldemar Haffkine (1860–1930) in 1897 was administered to the immigrants to prevent further spread of the disease, and a city-wide clean-up was launched to rid the city of the rats that spread the disease.

Many early Americans had developed immunity to yellow fever because it was so common. New immigrants, on the other hand, were more susceptible. As a result yellow fever became known as "stranger's disease." Despite widespread immunity, yellow fever continued to occur in New Orleans, known as the unhealthiest city in the country. As late as 1902 yellow fever was imported into the city by seamen arriving from South and Central America and the Caribbean. It was not until 1900 that the cause of yellow fever was discovered. This finding led to eradication of the disease.

DISEASE AND WAR

In 1898 American troops were dispatched to various camps along the Atlantic and Gulf coasts to drive the Spanish out of the New World. As a result of the climate, poor hygiene and nutrition, and overcrowded conditions, disease was rampant. Outbreaks of typhoid, malaria, and dengue fever were reported. In July a major yellow fever epidemic was reported in Louisiana, followed by an outbreak of what may have been dengue fever, and 6,000 cases were identified in Key West, Florida. As personnel were removed from the infected area, they spread the disease to other areas of the country. Researchers subsequently identified infected mosquitoes as the cause of both malaria and dengue fever.

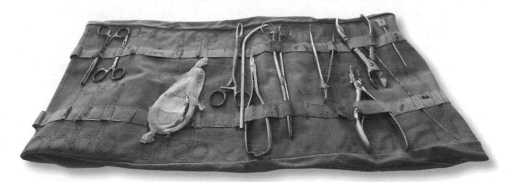

During World War I surgeons carried kits like this to treat battlefield wounds. This instrument set can be seen at the Robb House Medical Museum in Gainesville, Florida.

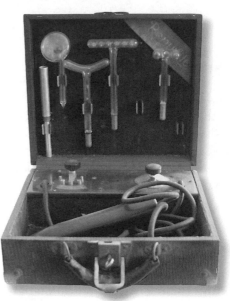

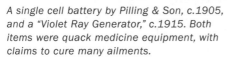

A single cell battery by Pilling & Son, c.1905, and a "Violet Ray Generator," c.1915. Both items were quack medicine equipment, with claims to cure many ailments.

Influenza and its complications were the leading causes of death in the United States during the World War I period. It has been estimated that one fourth of all casualties in the U.S. Army were due to influenza and that one in 24 victims also contracted pneumonia. Before it was over, the influenza epidemic had reached 46 states.

Unlike participants in earlier wars, those involved in World War I had the benefit of advanced medical and nutritional knowledge. In 1909 French bacteriologist Charles Nicolle (1866–1936) had discovered that body lice were responsible for spreading typhus. In 1916 Brazilian physician and infectologist Henrique da Rocha Lima (1879–1956) succeeded in isolating the organism that caused the disease. This discovery was followed by improvements in hygiene and the use of DDT to eradicate disease-causing lice. Consequently milder forms of typhus, such as Rocky Mountain spotted fever, Brill's Disease, and Trench Fever commonly replaced the virulent form of typhus. Brill's disease was concentrated among New York Jews. During World War I Trench Fever was prevalent among both Allied and German troops. On the other hand, the more virulent form of typhus was absent from the Western front, but was rampant among the Serbs and Russians. Between 1917 and 1921, around 20 million cases of typhus were reported in the European area of Russia. Estimates of typhus-related deaths in this area ranged as high as three million. Within two decades, however, vaccines virtually eradicated the disease in the developed world.

OCCUPATIONAL DISEASE

After the end of the Civil War, the pace of industrialization accelerated in the United States. Between 1870 and 1910 the number of Americans employed in mining and manufacturing rose from 2.9 to 11.6 million. This industrialization was accompanied by a rise in occupational diseases as Americans were exposed to large amounts of pollutants. Accidents were also responsible for large numbers of deaths in the workplace. At the turn of the century 57,513 Americans died from work-related accidents, and accidental death was the seventh overall leading cause of death. Some 7,865 deaths and 50,320 injuries were reported among railroad workers. In 1913 there were 25,000 accidents in the workplace that led to death, as well as 300 serious injuries and two million minor injuries. Accidents were most common in mines, steel plants, and packing houses.

Overall as many as one tenth of all workers were exposed to harmful substances on the job, including metallic, mineral, and organic dust, lead, mercury, and arsenic. The first researchers to insist that dust particles were responsible for respiratory and pulmonary diseases among miners were

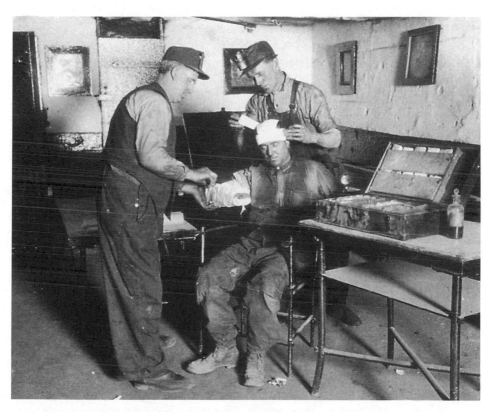

In an emergency clinic for workers in an anthracite coal mine in Pennsylvania, two men tend to an injured miner in the early 1900s.

ridiculed by capitalists seeking to increase their profits, even though as early as the late 19th century medical researchers had maintained that the dust released in mines was responsible for a plethora of health problems. By the turn of the 20th century researchers had identified anthracosis, known familiarly as "miner's asthma," as a leading cause of death and ill health among miners. This disease, now known as black lung disease, was caused by exposure to dust inside poorly ventilated mine shafts. Due to a series of reports published in the late 19th century, scientists of the Progressive Era were more successful in calling public attention to the lead poisoning contracted by workers in various industries.

In the south textiles were the major industry, and many mill workers developed tuberculosis as a result of exposure to cloth fibers. Researchers and physicians were initially baffled by deaths among mill workers following the appearance of dermatitis and dementia. It was discovered that the condition was likely caused by a niacin deficiency common among populations in which corn meal formed the bulk of the diet. The new technologies that led to the removal of essential nutrients in refined grains made many Americans, particularly the poor, more likely to suffer from vitamin and mineral deficiencies. Workers in packinghouses, hat makers, and wallpaper and paint manufacturers frequently suffered work-related conditions.

By the first decade of the 20th century, medical schools were offering specializations in occupational health, and workers' compensation laws were common. 1910 was a significant year in the history of occupational health. The first National Conference on Industrial Diseases was held, and the Bureau of Mines was created. The first clinic devoted to occupational diseases was established at Cornell Medical College in New York. John B. Andrew published his landmark studies detailing phosphorous poisoning in the American match industry, and Alice Hamilton (1869–1970), a Harvard expert in occupational medicine and sanitation, brought attention to industrial lead poisoning and miners' consumption. As a result of the research on industrial pollutants, the U.S. Department of Labor published a list of common industrial poisons. The Board of Sanitary Control of Cloak, Suit, and Skirt Industry of Greater New York launched an extensive study of health conditions in the garment industry. The U.S. Public Health Service began developing a program designed to reduce health hazards in the workplace. By 1914 a division of Industrial Hygiene and Sanitation was established, sponsoring a study on the health of garment workers in New York City who were contracting tuberculosis in greater numbers than in the general population.

MEDICINE
During the latter years of the 19th century physicians had often lacked knowledge to treat and cure specific diseases. This lack of knowledge led some physicians to treat symptoms rather than diseases, prescribing highly addictive

Deaths and Death Rates for 1908

The U.S. Census Bureau tracked death causes and rates in the United States during the Progressive Era. An excerpt of its 1908 report reads:

"The total number of deaths returned for the year 1908 from the entire registration area was 691,574, and the death rate was 15.4 per 1,000 of estimated population. For the preceding year the number of deaths was 687,034, or only 4,540 less than the number returned for 1908, although the registration area for the latter year was increased by the addition of the two new registration states, Washington and Wisconsin. The year 1908 was a year of remarkably low mortality throughout the United States, so far as can be determined from the available registration records, and was marked by a general absence of severe epidemics and of unusual mortality from other causes. In a few exceptions, where the rates are somewhat higher, deaths of nonresidents or deaths in institutions may affect the local rates.

"Females contributed a slightly larger proportion of the deaths in 1908 than they did in 1907, and the actual number of deaths of males registered for 1908 was less than for 1907. The figures for age show a somewhat increased percent of deaths of infants under 1 year for 1908, but the ratios for each of the individual years from 1 to 4 are identical for 1907 and 1908. A close agreement appears in the subsequent quinquennial periods, although the distribution is slightly more favorable for 1908 for the ages 15 to 49 years.

"Nearly one-fifth of all of the deaths that occurred were those of infants. There were more than one-eighth of a million (136,432) deaths of babies under 1 year of age in about one-half of the total population of the United States in 1908, and nearly 200,000 (with allowance for defective returns) deaths of little children under 5 years of age in the same aggregate of population."

medicines to make patients more comfortable. Before the availability of antibiotics in the early 20th century, surgery was risky and likely to prove fatal. Despite increased medical knowledge, infant mortality continued to be high, and it was estimated that one out of every 10 infants would not survive their first year. Pregnancy and childbirth complications were major contributors to the death rate, and the nonwhite population was particularly vulnerable. In 1915 the maternal death rate for whites was 60.1 per 100,000 births. For nonwhites, the death rate was 105.6 per 100,000 births.

In addition to improved sanitation and increased knowledge of proper nutrition, improved health among Americans was a result of significant advances in the medical profession. Medical schools began offering post-graduate courses,

"Typhoid Mary"

In the United States the most famous case of an apparently healthy typhoid carrier involved Mary Mallon (1869–1938), who became known as "Typhoid Mary." During the first decade of the 20th century, Mallon was employed as a cook for several families in the New York area. Her employment was invariably followed by outbreaks of typhoid fever. For instance, she was believed to be the cause of an epidemic in Ithaca, New York, that resulted in 1,400 cases of typhoid. In 1906 Mallon was hired as a cook at the Oyster Bay summer home of banker Charles Henry Warren. After consuming homemade peach ice cream, six of 11 members of the household became ill, experiencing headache, fever, nausea, abdominal pain, diarrhea, and vomiting. Subsequent investigations were conducted by sanitary engineer Dr. George Soper who identified Mallon as the typhoid carrier. She had immediately become a suspect because she had vanished as soon as the outbreak began.

After refusing to voluntarily cooperate with health inspectors, Mallon was forcibly isolated and tested. She was later convicted of intentionally spreading typhoid and sentenced to a three-year prison term. Soper's investigations had revealed that Mallon's poor hygiene was chiefly responsible for spreading the disease. For instance, she never washed her hands after using the restroom. Mallon was ordered to remain in touch with local health officials after her release, and she was banned from seeking further employment as a cook. Nevertheless she managed to disappear and continued to work as a cook. In 1915 Mary Mallon was again located and returned to isolation at a New York hospital on North Brother Island, where she remained until her death 23 years later. "Typhoid Mary" had directly infected at least 47 people during her years as a cook, and three of those victims died from the disease. Over 1,000 others had been indirectly infected by Mallon.

and some physicians opted to specialize in particular areas, rather than serving as general practitioners who were expected to know a little about all fields of medicine. The availability of sulfur, penicillin, and broad-spectrum antibiotics meant that many patients were able to survive the diseases that had proved fatal in the past. Although communicable disease continued to be a factor in the Progressive Era, major progress had been made in preventing and treating these diseases. The last cholera epidemic in American history occurred in 1892, and smallpox was controlled through the use of mandatory vaccinations.

At the turn of the century, tuberculosis was the second leading cause of death in the United States and was a major cause of death among infants and adults aged 25 to 44 and 65 to 84. However research on tuberculosis continued, building on Robert Koch's (1843–1910) identification of mycobacterium tuberculosis. Sanitariums established for TB patients helped to build up immune systems and checked the spread of the disease. The introduction of artificial lungs and surgical procedures designed to reduce lung volume further advanced understanding of the disease. In 1895 German physicist Wilhelm Conrad Röntgen (1845–1923) discovered X-rays and provided a major tool for the fight against tuberculosis.

In 1896 Swiss chemist Svante Arrhenius (1859–1927) identified the greenhouse effect that would continue to be controversial into the 21st century. In 1900 American surgeon Walter Reed (1851–1902) posited that yellow fever was spread by infected mosquitoes. That same year three biologists working individually reaffirmed the pioneering work of Austrian Gregor Mendel (1822–84), the "father of modern genetics." Two years later American pathologist Eugene Opie (1873–1971) discovered that diabetes was caused by destruction of pancreatic tissue. In 1905 German-born Albert Einhorn (1856–1917) synthesized Novocain, which was thereafter widely used as a dental anesthetic. Five years later French physicist Marie Curie (1867–1934) isolated pure radium, revolutionizing cancer treatments.

In 1913 Americans Elmer McCollumn (1879–1967) and Marguerite Davis (1887–1967) identified Vitamin A. That same year Bela Schick (1877–1967),

A c.1910 family bathroom with running water and porcelain fixtures at the Florida Heritage Museum in Largo, Florida.

a Hungarian-American pediatrician, perfected a test for determining susceptibility to diphtheria. Other significant medical contributions of the era included those in general physiology by Jacques Loeb (1859–1924), in neurophysiology by Joseph Erlanger (1874–1965) and Herbert Gasser (1888–1963), and in digestive and regulatory physiology by Walter Cannon (1871–1945). The establishment of laboratories such as the University of Pennsylvania's Institute of Hygiene and Chicago's Institute for Infectious Diseases played an essential role in medical advances of the period.

PUBLIC HEALTH AND SANITATION

The increased urbanization of the Progressive Era precipitated a host of health problems and resulted in a controversial campaign for health insurance. Overcrowding and poor sanitation led to the easy spread of germs and diseases. The lack of ventilation inside tenements made it even easier for contamination to spread. Public baths were made available to urban residents who would not have otherwise had access to such facilities. However disease and germs could also be spread in these baths. Wells were often built close to privies, resulting in gastrointestinal diseases that included chronic diarrhea, typhoid fever, and cholera.

Sanitarians emphasized the need for clean water and streets. By 1909 most states had established their own boards of health to supervise local boards that carried out public health duties. Local agencies were responsible for inspecting properties and initiating changes such as moving privies away from wells, and supervising smallpox vaccinations for schoolchildren and new immigrants.

In 1894 Boston health officials were responsible for stemming an outbreak of diphtheria by conducting health inspections in schools. These inspections helped Boston to combat malnutrition, measles, scarlet fever, and skin and eye diseases in the children of the city. Within three years Philadelphia, Chicago, and New York City had instituted similar inspections. During the Progressive Era New York City continued to set an example for improving the health of city residents through wide-scale vaccination campaigns. In 1893 the Health Board vaccinated 26,994 individuals against smallpox for

Outhouses were still in use in rural areas, as not everyone enjoyed indoor plumbing, even in the Progressive Era.

the first time and revaccinated 171,197 individuals. Over the following two years, only 10 New Yorkers died from smallpox.

Local health boards were particularly important in large cities and in the south where mild winters failed to rid areas of disease-carrying parasites. Despite this need, few southern states allotted adequate funding for essential activities. Philanthropic agencies such as the Rockefeller Sanitary Foundation stepped into the breach. At the national level, the American Public Health Association continued to bring public health practitioners together, and the organization began publishing its own journal in 1895, highlighting major issues of concern including cholera and yellow fever epidemics.

Sanitary reforms led to state laws that made it a punishable misdemeanor to ignore orders issued by county public health officials. New laws were also passed that prohibited children who had not been vaccinated against smallpox and typhoid fever from attending school. Businesses became involved in promoting public health, and some banks added restrictions to loans, requiring that homeowners seeking loans show proof that all privies were in compliance with local regulations and that all family members were free of hookworm and had been vaccinated against typhoid fever. By 1915 most Americans living in cities with populations over 5,000 were able to connect home plumbing to city water mains.

REFORMERS AND HEALTH

Reformers of the Progressive Era were determined to establish the link between poverty and ill health. Rickets, for instance, which was associated with poor nutrition, was common in urban areas, particularly in slums and among black and Italian families. Caused by a deficiency of Vitamin D, calcium, or phosphate, rickets led to softening and weakening of the bones and could cause infertility among females. Children often died from complications such as pneumonia and convulsions. In 1904 a study of New York children led to the finding that between 60,000 and 70,000 children went to school hungry each day. Five years later British physician William Hunter (1861–1937) established a link between conditions such as anemia, gastritis, chronic rheumatic infections, and kidney disease and dental problems.

In 1906 Upton Sinclair (1878–1968) published *The Jungle*, which sent a shockwave throughout the United States. A staunch socialist, Sinclair's purpose in writing the book was to call attention to ill-treatment of workers in Chicago's stockyards. Instead he succeeded in awakening Americans to the horrors of the meatpacking industry. While describing the deplorable conditions that caused accidents, ill health, and even death among workers, Sinclair detailed the practice of using condemned meat in products sold to the public. In response to public outcry, President Theodore Roosevelt (1859–1919) appointed an investigatory committee. In 1906 Congress passed the Pure Food and Drug Act, establishing the Food and Drug Administration and charging it with oversight of foods and drugs sold in the United States. Many drugs were thereafter available only by prescription, and labels were required to identify habit-forming drugs.

In 1906 the publication of *The Bitter Cry of Children* by British immigrant John Spargo (1876–1966) launched a campaign to improve the lives and health of urban children suffering from malnutrition and a host of work-related diseases and conditions. A socialist and a union organizer, Spargo worked as a granite cutter in Britain while receiving an education through extension courses at Oxford and Cambridge. In *The Bitter Cry of Children*, he described the lives of children working in the coal mines of Virginia and Pennsylvania. He wrote that young boys were required to sit for hours crouched over chutes in order to separate slate and refuse from coal. As a result their bones became deformed and their shoulders were rounded, giving the boys the appearance of old men. At best, the hard coal cut the boys' hands. At worst, their hands were broken or crushed. At times a young boy would be caught by the machinery and smothered to death. In addition to physical deformities, children who worked in the coal mines developed asthma and miners' consumption.

These children, who were aged 10 to 12, labored 10 hours a day, earning a wage of $.50 or $.60 per day. They rarely saw the sun. Their hearing was adversely affected by the roar of the mining machinery. They were generally illiterate, although the most ambitious of the group attended night school after working 10-hour days. As they grew, the boys were transferred to other mining jobs such as door tenders, switch boys, and mule drivers. At 14, the boys were considered full grown and given jobs as miners. Even those parents who understood that mining was detrimental to their children's health were helpless, because the boys' wages helped their families to survive.

Philanthropic organizations were an essential element in the reform and sanitary movements of the Progressive Era. The Rockefeller Sanitary Commission was the best known of these groups. From 1909 to 1914 the commission worked with county boards of health to educate the public about public health issues and teach them about preventive measures. In 1915 the work of the Rockefeller Sanitation Commission was taken over by the International Health Board, which continued in operation until 1930. This philanthropic work was particularly important in deprived areas of the south where state and local public health funding was low. In such cases, philanthropies provided funding for hiring full-time county health officials. Florida was an exception in the south, financing public health through property taxes. The eradication of hookworm became a major focus of the Rockefeller Sanitation Commission's activities, and the commission worked with local officials to provide supplementary school programs on health-related issues. Schools were also encouraged to add health to their regular curricula. The Rosenwald Fund and the Russell Sage Foundation, which operated from 1909 to 1930, were also involved in promoting public health issues. The focus of these agencies was more restricted, promoting the public education of southern blacks and economically disadvantaged whites in Appalachia.

NUTRITION

The Progressive Era was marked by great advances in the understanding of the connection between diet and health. While wealthy Americans dined on French cuisine, entrepreneurs were quick to seize on opportunities for meeting middle-class consumer demands. A wide variety of canned foods were available, and by 1910, prices per can dropped drastically with the introduction of the double-crimped can that allowed manufacturers to produce as many as 35,000 cans a day. In 1914 the two largest canning companies were the Alaskan Packing Company, which canned salmon, and the California Fruit Canners Association, which subsequently became Del Monte. As the United States was transformed into an industrialized nation, canned foods became an essential part of family meal plans. Moving away from the traditional tomatoes, corn, peas, and beans, canning companies responded to popular demand and began offering such products as condensed milk, asparagus, okra, succotash, green corn, pumpkin, baked beans, French mushrooms, black beans, apples, applesauce, pears, peaches, plums, cherries, quince, grapes, pineapple, strawberries, raspberries, blueberries, gooseberries, oysters, lobster, salmon, corned beef, roast beef, salmon, veal, lamb, mutton, turkey, chicken goose, lamb's tongue, pig's feet, tripe, sausage meat, shrimp, clams, deviled crab, and mackerel. In addition to this wide range of choice, canned foods were available even in isolated areas, and drastically reduced food preparation time. Commercial canning did not totally replace home canning, and many families continued to preserve their own products, particularly fruits and pickles.

Health and nutrition advice was often a mixture of good sense and superstition during the Progressive Era. With the introduction of condensed milk and infant formulas, many mothers had given up breastfeeding. This practice was considered either "evil" or "lazy" by some writers. Mothers were advised not to give their children milk that had been "tainted" by a thunderstorm, or ever to enter an infectious sick room on an empty stomach. Some writers urged mothers to give their children plenty of fresh air and exercise, while others advised that activities such as jumping rope could cause damage to the brain and spine. Standing on the head was assumed to cause nerve and circulation damage.

Canned food became more common after 1910, when manufacturers started to produce up to 35,000 cans a day.

Red flannel was to be worn winter and summer to prevent colds, which could be caused by haircuts. To prevent this occurrence, mothers were told to wet their children's heads after a haircut. One columnist warned mothers that all candy was poisonous because it contained lead, mercy, copper, and arsenic. On the other hand, homemakers were advised to use lye to clean greasy dishes.

Home cures for various ailments varied from onion poultices for the croup, to greasing the navel to cure constipation, to using the hand of a dead man to cure warts. One writer believed that by the age of 50, old age was inevitable, leading to a loss of appetite, fading complexion, a furred tongue that accompanied any physical or mental effort, flabby muscles, weak joints, drooping spirits, and restless sleep. By the age of 80, symptoms of aging also included blunted nerves, failing senses, rigid muscles, failing memory, ossified brains, buried affections, and a loss of hope. If anyone lived to the age of 100, they were likely to die simply because they were unable to live.

During World War I women's groups and Prohibitionists succeeded in lobbying Congress to propose a Prohibition amendment. On January 29, 1919, Nebraska's ratification of the Eighteenth Amendment cleared the way for a ban on the "manufacture, sale, or transportation of intoxicating liquors" within the United States and banned the import and export of such products. Taking effect on January 16, 1920, the amendment led to the appearance of speakeasies in many areas, and allowed organized crime to flourish. The amendment was repealed in 1933 with the passage of the Twenty-first Amendment.

Other Progressive Era reforms and advances related to public health had more success. The significant advances made in medicine during the period, such as the identification of bacterial causes of disease, were put to great use through vaccination campaigns and improved sanitation. The urgent needs of a population now at work in increasingly fast-paced and mechanized industries were beginning to be tended to by professionals in the growing field of occupational health. Food safety and nutrition had improved through the work of muckraking journalists, new boards of health, and others. In spite of all this effort, no one could have been prepared for the onslaught of the flu pandemic of 1918, when the nation and the world were hit by one of the most extraordinary epidemics in world history.

ELIZABETH R. PURDY

Further Readings

Bennett, James T. and Thomas J. DiLorenzo. *From Pathology to Politics: Public Health in America*. New Brunswick, NJ: Transaction, 2000.

Bray, R.S. *Armies of Pestilence: The Effects of Pandemics on History*. Cambridge, UK: Lutterworth Press, 1988.

Bullough, Bonnie and George Rosen. *Preventive Medicine in the United States 1900–1990: Trends and Interpretations*. Canton, MA: Science History Publications, 1992.

Cartwright, Frederick F. *Disease and History*. New York: Thomas Y. Crowell, 1972.

Cassedy, James H. *Medicine in America: A Short History*. Baltimore, MD: Johns Hopkins University Press, 1991.

Derickson, Alan. *Black Lung: Anatomy of a Public Health Disaster*. Ithaca, NY: Cornell University Press, 1998.

Foy, Jessica H. and Thomas J. Schlereth, eds. *American Home Life, 1880–1930: A Social History of Spaces and Services*. Knoxville, TN: University of Tennessee Press, 1992.

Gramm, Barbara Fairchild. *...And You Think You've Got It Bad: Turn-of-the-Century Life and Housekeeping*. St. Cloud, MN: North Star Press of St. Cloud, 1987.

Grob, Gerald N. *The Deadly Truth: A History of Disease in America*. Cambridge, MA: Harvard University Press, 2002.

Husband, Julie and Jim O'Laughlin. *Daily Life in the Industrial United States, 1870–1900*. Westport, CT: Greenwood, 2004.

Kiple, Kenneth F. *Plague, Pox, and Pestilence*. London, England: Weidenfeld and Nicolson, 1997.

Kyvig, David E. *Daily Life in The United States, 1920–1939: Decades of Promise and Pain*. Westport, CT: Greenwood, 2002.

Levenstein, Harvey A. *Revolution at the Table: The Transformation of the American Diet*. New York: Oxford, 1988.

Parachin, Victor M. "Typhoid Mary: 'The Most Dangerous Woman in America.'" *American History* (v.40/16, 2006).

Pillsbury, Richard. *No Foreign Food: The American Diet in Time and Place*. Boulder, CO: Westview, 1998.

Rosen, George. *Preventive Medicine in the United States 1900–1975: Trends and Interpretations*. New York: Science History Publications, 1975.

Ross, Gregory. *Modern America 1914 to 1945*. New York: Facts on File, 1995.

Schifflett, Crandall. *Victorian America 1876 to 1913*. New York: Facts On File, 1996.

Sealander, Judith. *Private Wealth and Public Life: Foundation Philanthropy and the Social Reshaping of American Social Policy from the Progressive Era to the New Deal*. Baltimore, MD: Johns Hopkins, 1997.

Sinclair, Upton. *The Jungle*. Urbana, IL: University of Illinois Press, 1988.

Stacey, Michelle. *Consumed: Why Americans Love, Hate, and Fear Food.* New York: Simon and Schuster, 1994.

Williams, Susan. *Savory Suppers and Fashionable Feasts: Dining in Victorian America.* New York: Pantheon Books, 1985.

organized crime 157, 159
police work/law enforcement 157–159, *159, 160,* 165
street gangs 159
trial and punishment 164, *164,* 165
"crowd poison" 129
Cuba 188
cubist style 41
Cunard 225
Curie, Marie 138, 243
Curie, Pierre 138
Custer, George A. 142
Czolgosz, Leon 144

D
Daimler, Gottlieb 131
Darrow, Clarence 179
Darwin, Charles 3, 15, 57
Darwinism 5
da Vinci, Leonardo 137
Davis, Marguerite 243
Davis, Sammy, Jr. 149
Dawes Act 3, 55, 94
Daytona Normal and Industrial School for Negro Girls 122
DDT 238
Debs, Eugene V. 175–176, 177, 180, 185, 222
de Lesseps, Ferdinand 194
Del Monte 247
dengue fever 237
Denslow, William 6
Department of Church and Country Life 89
department stores 38, *38*
Depression 2
Detroit 39, 67, 93, 132
DeVere's High Rollers Burlesque Company *147*
Devery, William "Big Bill" 161
Dewey, George 187
Dewey, Harriet 114
Dewey, John 61, 111, 114
Dewey, Melvil 9
Dewey Decimal System 9

Y

yellow fever 237, 243, 245
Young Men's Christian Association (YMCA) 85, 107, 150
Young Women's Christian Association (YWCA) 64, *64*

Z

Zeppelin, Ferdinand Graf von 137
"Zimmermann Telegram" 196, 211

Produced by GOLSON MEDIA
President and Editor   J. Geoffrey Golson
Layout Editors   Oona Patrick, Mary Jo Scibetta
Managing Editor   Susan Moskowitz
Copyeditor   Ben Johnson
Proofreader   Mary Le Rouge
Indexer   J S Editorial